Peacekeeping and the Protection of Civilians

This book critically examines the evolution of protection practices in UN peace operations over the past two decades.

Protecting civilians has become central to the work of contemporary UN peace operations, yet the ability of peacekeepers to offer meaningful levels of protection to vulnerable civilians in conflict zones remains highly circumscribed. Focusing on the implementation of protection of civilians (PoC) mandates across three high-profile UN missions – UNMISS in South Sudan, MONUSCO in the Democratic Republic of the Congo and MINUSCA in the Central African Republic – this study asks who precisely UN peacekeepers protect and how they go about protecting them. Drawing on the key distinction between coercive and non-coercive protection strategies, this book examines how peacekeepers have struggled to translate ambitious and far-reaching protection mandates into effective protection practices in some of the world's most dangerous and difficult conflict contexts.

This book will be of much interest to students of peacekeeping, civilian protection, African politics, war studies and security studies.

Timothy Donais is a Professor in the Department of Global Studies at Wilfrid Laurier University and at the Balsillie School of International Affairs, both in Canada. He is author of *Peacebuilding and Local Ownership: Post-Conflict Consensus-Building* (2012) and *The Political Economy of Peacebuilding in Post-Dayton Bosnia* (2005).

Cass Series on Peacekeeping
General Editor: Michael Pugh

This series examines all aspects of peacekeeping, from the political, operational and legal dimensions to the developmental and humanitarian issues that must be dealt with by all those involved with peacekeeping in the world today.

Cooperative Peacekeeping in Africa
Exploring regime complexity
Malte Brosig

Evaluating Peacekeeping Missions
A typology of success and failure in international interventions
Sarah-Myriam Martin-Brûlé

UN Peace Operations
Lessons from Haiti, 1994–2016
Eirin Mobekk

Peacekeeping and the African Union
Building Negative Peace
Jude Cocodia

Gender Equality in UN Peacekeeping
Fact or Fiction?
Sally Anne Corcoran

Peacekeeping and the Protection of Civilians
From Moral Imperative to Effective Practice
Timothy Donais

Peacekeeping and the Protection of Civilians

From Moral Imperative to Effective Practice

Timothy Donais

Routledge
Taylor & Francis Group
LONDON AND NEW YORK

First published 2025
by Routledge
4 Park Square, Milton Park, Abingdon, Oxon OX14 4RN

and by Routledge
605 Third Avenue, New York, NY 10158

Routledge is an imprint of the Taylor & Francis Group, an informa business

British Library Cataloguing-in-Publication Data
A catalogue record for this book is available from the British Library

ISBN: 9781032270500 (hbk)
ISBN: 9781032270517 (pbk)
ISBN: 9781003291114 (ebk)

DOI: 10.4324/9781003291114

Typeset in Times New Roman
by codeMantra

Contents

	Preface	*vii*
	List of Acronyms	*xi*
1	Introduction: Situating Protection in Peacekeeping Contexts	1
2	Robust Protection Debates	23
3	Non-coercive Protection: Protection by Peaceful Means?	46
4	All Necessary Means, with an Asterisk: How UNMISS Has Operationalised Its PoC Mandate	67
5	MONUSCO: Innovation without Transformation?	89
6	Protecting Civilians and Expanding State Authority in the Central African Republic	112
7	Conclusion: PoC's Uneven Past and Uncertain Future	131
	Index	*143*

Preface

Writing some 30 years ago – in the aftermath of the Rwandan genocide and months before the Srebrenica massacre of July 1995 – the American moral philosopher Michael Walzer issued an impassioned *cri de coeur* in support of assertive intervention "whenever cruelty and suffering are extreme and no local forces seem capable of putting an end to them." Walzer's article – entitled *The Politics of Rescue* – acknowledged the very real moral, practical and political quandaries surrounding the use of force in other people's countries, but insisted that in the face of unfolding human disaster, the consequences of doing nothing were unacceptably high; the risks of intervention, consequently, 'must be accepted.'

Three decades on, the dilemmas with which Walzer was struggling in the mid-1990s remain very much alive and well. From Haiti to Sudan to Gaza, debates surrounding the responsibilities of the so-called international community *vis-à-vis* civilians trapped in conflict zones are no less fraught, and no less divisive, despite the emergence of a Responsibility to Protect (R2P) doctrine in the early years of this century. While R2P has generated more spirited polemic than principled humanitarian action – especially after it was implicated in, and compromised by, NATO's controversial 2011 intervention in Libya – it is almost certainly the case that investing UN peacekeepers with protection of civilian (PoC) mandates has been the more consequential development in the search for ways to connect the moral imperative of protecting civilians with more effective practice. R2P's fatal flaws were, and remain, the absence of a reliable vehicle for delivering on its ambitious principles and the persistence of strong pushback, especially from the Global South, on questions of state sovereignty. By contrast, peacekeeping – however imperfect the fit with civilian protection imperatives – has at least provided a legitimate and capable presence within some of the world's most insecure environments which could be harnessed for protection purposes.

This book examines how that experiment in explicitly tasking contemporary UN peace operations with protecting civilians has worked out over the past quarter century. As someone whose generation came of age during the early 1990s, the collision between the heady promise of the early post-cold war era and the hard realities of genocide and ethnic cleansing was deeply formative for me, and has shaped my own thinking, and research, about international politics ever since. Researching the implementation of PoC mandates in UN peacekeeping operations has therefore provided an opportunity to gauge the extent to which peacekeeping has been able to find some measure of redemption for past protection failures. It has also allowed me to examine long-standing questions around the paradox of using force in the name of peace and, conversely, around the merits of the argument that protection, as with peace, is best pursued through peaceful means. Throughout, the focus has been on what peacekeepers actually do in the name of protection, and the dilemmas and compromises they must navigate along the way, rather than on what penholders in the Security Council say they should do.

Given the reality that contemporary peacekeepers operate in distinctly unpeaceful environments, protecting civilians in conflict-affected contexts remains, in the phrasing of one early study, the impossible mandate. Even those missions with the best of intentions, robust mandates and capable, well-trained forces cannot hope, as Paul Williams once noted, to address more than the tip of the iceberg of civilian suffering in war zones. And despite considerable innovation and experimentation over the years, existing peace operations with PoC mandates have struggled to keep up both with the evolving nature of conflict and with shifting geopolitical trends that augur poorly for the future of intervention, peacebuilding and sustainable conflict resolution. Still, in both qualitative and quantitative terms it is undeniable that peacekeepers do protect civilians, within the limits of their capacities, and that in their absence the situation for civilians would, in most cases, be immeasurably worse.

Over the course of this project I have interviewed many dozens of individuals, including civilian and uniformed personnel from UN missions, diplomats and Secretariat staff at UN Headquarters in New York, local civil society activists and members of the diplomatic and humanitarian communities in national capitals of mission-hosting states. I almost always left these interviews humbled by the commitment and thoughtfulness of my interlocutors, and by their patient willingness to educate an outsider on the complexities of conflict contexts, the nuances of UN mandates and the struggles to make a constructive difference in very difficult circumstances. I remain enormously grateful for those who took the time to help me try to make sense of it all. While I cannot name them all here, I would like to acknowledge a few individuals, without whose assistance this would have been a much different project. Evan Cinq-Mars – now with the PoC team at the UN Department of Peace Operations – has been an invaluable source of guidance, and contacts, since the start of this project, and his commitment to the cause of protection remains an inspiration. Line Andersen opened doors and facilitated logistics during her tenure at UNMISS and was instrumental in helping me get out of Juba and see the UN's protection work through my own eyes. Ayiko Solomon has also been both an inspiration and guide, and an indispensable source of support in helping me find my way to and around South Sudan. Daniel Levine-Spound, formerly of the Center for Civilians in Conflict, provided sage advice on the situation in the eastern DRC, and I've leaned heavily on the reports that he and his CIVIC colleagues have produced over the years to help understand the evolution of MONUSCO's protection practice. At the Balsillie School of International Affairs, Eric Tanguay helped frame the project from its early days, including through two co-authored articles, while Sarah Murray helped me work through some of the gendered elements of the broader PoC agenda, also through a co-authored article. Finally, none of the fieldwork for this project would have been possible without the financial support of the Social Sciences and Humanities Research Council of Canada (Grant # 435-2019-0742).

Timothy Donais
Guelph, Ontario

Acronyms

3R	*Retour, reclamation et rehabilitation* (CAR)
ADF	Allied Democratic Forces (DRC)
AMISOM	African Union Mission to Somalia
APPR	Agreement for Peace and Reconciliation in the Central African Republic
AU	African Union
A4P	Action for Peacekeeping
BRICS	Brazil, Russia, India, China, South Africa – Forum of Developing Countries
CAN	Community Alert Network
CAR	Central African Republic
CIVIC	Center for Civilians in Conflict
CLA	Community Liaison Assistant
CNDP	*Congrès National pour la Défense du Peuple* (DRC)
CODECO	*Coopérative pour le développement du Congo* (DRC)
CPAS	Comprehensive Planning and Performance Assessment System
CPC	Coalition of Patriots for Change (CAR)
DDR	Disarmament, Demobilization, and Reintegration
DPO	Department of Peace Operations
DPKO	Department of Peacekeeping Operations
DPPA	Department of Political and Peacebuilding Affairs
DRC	Democratic Republic of the Congo
EPON	Effectiveness of Peace Operations Network
EUTM	European Union Training Mission (CAR)
EWRR	Early Warning/Rapid Response
FACA	*Forces armées centrafricaines*
FARDC	*Forces armées de la République démocratique du Congo*
FIB	Force Intervention Brigade (MONUSCO)
FCC	Finance-contributing country
FDLR	*Forces démocratiques de libération du Rwanda* (DRC)
FPRC	*Le Front populaire pour la renaissance de la Centrafrique* (CAR)
HIPPO	High-Level Independent Panel on Peace Operations

HRDDP	Human Rights Due Diligence Policy
HRL	Human Rights Law
IASC	Inter-Agency Standing Committee
ICC	International Criminal Court
ICISS	International Commission on Intervention and State Sovereignty
IDP	Internally displaced person
IGAD	Intergovernmental Authority on Development
IHL	International Humanitarian Law
LPC	Local Peace Committee
M23	*Mouvement du 23 mars* (DRC)
MINUSCA	United Nations Multidimensional Integrated Stabilization Mission in the Central African Republic
MINUSMA	United Nations Multidimensional Integrated Stabilization Mission in Mali
MINUSTAH	United Nations Stabilization Mission in Haiti
MONUC	United Nations Organization Mission in the Democratic Republic of the Congo
MONUSCO	United Nations Organization Stabilization Mission in the Democratic Republic of the Congo
MSS	Multinational Security Support Mission (Haiti)
NATO	North Atlantic Treaty Organization
NGO	Non-governmental organization
OCHA	United Nations Office for the Coordination of Humanitarian Affairs
OHCHR	United Nations Office of the High Commissioner for Human Rights
PSCF	Peace, Security and Cooperation Framework (DRC)
PoC	Protection of Civilians
QRF	Quick Reaction Force
R2P	Responsibility to Protect
R-ARCSS	Revitalised Agreement on the Resolution of the Conflict in South Sudan
RCD	*Rassemblement congolais pour la démocratie* (DRC)
SDGs	Sustainable Development Goals
SEA	Sexual exploitation and abuse
SOFA	Status of Forces Agreement
SPLA	Sudan People's Liberation Army
SPLA-IO	Sudan People's Liberation Army-in-Opposition
SPLM	Sudan People's Liberation Movement
SPLM-IO	Sudan People's Liberation Movement-In-Opposition
SPM	Special Political Mission
SRSG	Special Representative of the Secretary General
SSPDF	South Sudan People's Defence Forces
SSR	Security Sector Reform
TCC	Troop-contributing country

UCP	Unarmed civilian peacekeeping
UNAMA	United Nations Assistance Mission in Afghanistan
UNAMID	United Nations-African Union Mission in Darfur
UNMISS	United Nations Mission in South Sudan
UNITAMS	United Nations Integrated Transition Assistance Mission in Sudan
UNPROFOR	United Nations Protection Force (Bosnia-Herzegovina/Croatia)
UPC	*Unité pour la paix en Centrafrique* (CAR)

1 Introduction

Situating Protection in Peacekeeping Contexts

Introduction

In March 2021, the UN Mission in South Sudan (UNMISS) formally re-designated its protection of civilians (PoC) site in the northern town of Bentiu as an internally displaced persons camp, in the process formally transferring authority over the site and its 100,000 inhabitants to South Sudanese authorities. The move was part of a longer-term effort to unwind the UN's most ambitious and sustained experiment in protecting civilians, an experiment which began in late 2013 with the mission's decision to shelter terrified civilians fleeing a brutal wave of violence that accompanied the collapse of South Sudan's nascent post-independence transition process. What began as a short-term expediency – an undeniably life-saving gesture from an organisation badly damaged by high-profile protection failures in the mid-1990s – stretched into an open-ended, multi-site operation as South Sudan descended deeper into civil war. At the height of the operation, close to a quarter of a million civilians were living in the so-called PoC sites. UN soldiers provided perimeter security, UN police patrolled within the sites and a phalanx of humanitarian organisations supported everything from primary health care to clean water to basic education.

Despite being an unplanned and ad hoc instrument for protecting civilians, the PoC sites quickly became not only the focal point of the UNMISS peacekeeping effort in South Sudan but also a magnet for controversy. While no one's idea of Club Med – the Bentiu site is especially grim, a grid of white tents ringed with berms and barbed wire in a remote, open field, which turns almost impassably muddy during the rainy season – the sites collectively provided a degree of both security and services unavailable outside the wire. Because they also absorbed the lion's share of the mission's resources and energies (Berdal and Shearer 2021), protecting those within the sites seriously compromised UNMISS' abilities to provide protection to the vastly greater number of vulnerable South Sudanese living outside them. As time passed and the conflict evolved, there were also growing concerns that the reluctance of the sites' residents to return to their homes had more to do with services than with insecurity, with the implication that the sites had themselves become an impediment to a return to 'normalcy.'[1] Moreover, the PoC sites were also a long-standing sore spot in relations between UNMISS and

DOI: 10.4324/9781003291114-1

the South Sudanese government, with the latter consistently accusing the former of harbouring armed opposition fighters within them. When an interim power-sharing agreement collapsed in 2016, PoC sites briefly became frontlines, and when dozens of residents were killed in the ensuing violence, the UN was forced to defend itself against charges that it had abandoned those it had promised to protect.

For a host of reasons, then, UNMISS was eager to unburden itself of responsibility for the PoC sites, with then-Head of Mission David Shearer announcing in September 2020 an accelerated timetable for the transition. By late 2021, only the Malakal site, with some 34,000 residents, remained under UN control (as it remained through 2024). Shearer, and the mission more generally, cited an improved security situation and the formation of a transitional government – a key component of the Revitalised Agreement on the Resolution of the Conflict in South Sudan (R-ARCSS) – as justification for transferring the PoC sites to government control. As Joshua Craze and Naomi Pendle (2020) pointed out at the time, however, not even the UN fully bought into the narrative that transitioning the PoC sites was warranted on the basis of progress in peace implementation. While the ceasefire between the conflict's two main factions has largely held, the UN's Commission on Human Rights in South Sudan chronicled intensified intercommunal violence throughout 2020, a product not only of long-standing interethnic grievances but also of overt manipulation on the part of national-level actors and ongoing political dysfunction which contributed to a wider 'governance and security vacuum' across large swaths of the country (HRC 2021: 3). For many camp residents themselves, ongoing political volatility and a marked absence in progress towards reforming South Sudan's security sector – including the national police force – have generated profound unease about the transition, and genuine fear that responsibility for their security is now in the hands of those from whom they fled in terror not so long ago. As Sam Mednick (2021) reported, "most camp residents distrust the government and fear a breakdown in the peace process could leave them exposed to new atrocities."

While the South Sudanese case is in many ways *sui generis*, especially since the UNMISS experience with managing and maintaining formal PoC sites has not been replicated in other mission contexts, the dilemmas that it raises are hardly unique. Since the turn of the millennium, UN peace operations have regularly been mandated to protect civilians in contexts where the gaps between protection capacities and protection needs are enormous. Missions, including UNMISS and MONUSCO in the neighbouring Democratic Republic of the Congo (DRC), have engaged in considerable experimentation and innovation in their mix of protection practices in an effort to close this gap, but failures in peace implementation and downward pressure on peacekeeping budgets have made this a decidedly uphill struggle. At the same time, the challenge of protecting civilians in active conflict zones has pushed to the forefront long-standing questions of both the legitimacy and the efficacy of the use of force on the part of peacekeeping missions. Despite bold initiatives such as the introduction of the so-called Force Intervention Brigade (FIB) in the DRC, which was mandated to 'neutralise' particular armed factions, thereby addressing threats to civilians at their source, there remains a wide divergence of opinion within the UN Secretariat and among UN member states on the extent to which peacekeepers should use 'all necessary means,' up to and including deadly force, in the name of saving civilian lives. Lost in much of the policy debate, unsurprisingly, has been any serious consideration of the agency of civilian populations themselves. For the most part, civilians caught up in conflict are assumed to be not only vulnerable but also helpless, and thus completely reliant on the agency of armed international actors for their survival. This has slowly begun to change in recent years, both through growing attention to the complex nuances of community self-protection mechanisms and through careful reconsideration of the deeply gendered assumptions underpinning contemporary protection practices. Still, the implications of moving beyond simplistic 'white knight' protection narratives have not yet been fully taken on board at the operational level.

It is precisely these kinds of issues, which exist at the interface of 'protector' and 'protected,' that are at the heart of this book. While much has been written about the evolution of the PoC debate in recent years, especially concerning its legal and normative dimensions, I focus more narrowly on *protection practices*, with a particular emphasis on who the UN protects, how it protects them and – in contexts where the UN cannot hope to protect all vulnerable civilians from all possible violent threats – what constitutes 'good enough' protection. This book explores these questions, in part through examining three of the most prominent protection-centric UN peace operations of the 21st century, not only to better understand how protection practices have evolved over the past two decades, but also how they might be improved in years to come. More concerningly, it also asks what the implications might be if – as seems increasingly likely – PoC recedes as a moral and operational imperative for both current and future peace operations.

In exploring these questions, this book's central framing revolves around the ongoing – and unresolved – tension between coercive and non-coercive protection strategies. While these are better understood as poles of a continuum rather than as a choice between clear, self-contained alternatives (given the considerable grey area in the middle, and the complex interactions between the two at the operational level), framing the debate across the coercive/non-coercive distinction serves two important functions. First, it acknowledges the important ways in which the debate around PoC intersects with the much older debate on the use of force in peacekeeping contexts. Given the reality that deploying 'all necessary means' – including deadly force – to protect vulnerable populations remains controversial, especially among troop-contributing countries, understanding the evolution of PoC practice also requires analysis of how use of force debates have evolved within the UN system. Second, while the non-coercive dimensions of the PoC project – most prominently dialogue, engagement and presence – fit more comfortably with traditional peacekeeping principles, not only around the use of force but also around impartiality and consent of the parties, it is also the case that both the potential and the limits of non-coercive protection strategies remain imperfectly understood and inadequately explored in specific peacekeeping contexts. As Richard Jackson (2019: 218) has argued, the marginalisation of pacifist thought within international relations scholarship and policy means that coercive counter-violence is regularly considered the *only* practical response to serious threats to human security (a presumption reinforced in peacekeeping contexts by the reality that most peacekeepers are still soldiers). Consequently, the question of whether 'protection by peaceful means' represents a viable alternative still lacks a clear and compelling answer, despite the 2015 HIPPO Report's insistence that unarmed strategies "must be at the forefront of UN efforts to protect civilians" (UN 2015). This book's central contribution to the literature on contemporary peacekeeping, then, lies in its close empirical examination of the *malleability* of the limitations on the ability of UN peacekeepers to protect civilians through force of arms, the *potential* of non-coercive protection strategies in offsetting these limitations and the *linkages* between these two broad forms of protection.

The Argument in Brief

As of early 2025 – when this chapter was finalised – ongoing and seemingly intractable conflicts in both Ukraine and Gaza provided grim daily reminders of the limits of international norms, and of both international criminal and international humanitarian law (IHL), in protecting civilian populations from the scourge of war. The intervention of the International Criminal Court in both conflicts – most dramatically through the indictments of Russian President Vladimir Putin and Israeli Prime Minister Benjamin Netanyahu – has to date had little discernible impact on the rate at which civilians are being killed in either conflict. Similarly, the Responsibility to Protect (R2P) doctrine, one of the few other instruments available in a rather spartan international toolkit of civilian protection strategies, seems increasingly like a spent force, both a casualty of the overreach of Western powers in Libya and an artefact of an era in which liberal internationalism was still ascendant. For all its well-publicised flaws and limitations, then, the institution of peacekeeping remains one of the very few vehicles through which international agency has been and continues to be actively mobilised in support of the idea that civilians caught in the midst of conflict are entitled not only to humanitarian assistance, but to life-saving physical protection. While this instrument has been wielded imperfectly, inconsistently and often tentatively – with well-publicised protection failures and 'own goals,' such as sexual exploitation and abuse (SEA) perpetrated by peacekeepers themselves, overshadowing successes – the notion that peace operations have a more narrowly construed responsibility to protect when it is in their capacity to do so has now become part of the contemporary common sense of peace operations. In the context of the long-standing project to regulate and restrain the conduct of war, this development is almost certainly as consequential – not least for those on the receiving end of unregulated and unrestrained war – as the parallel project of attempting to hold accountable those guilty of the most egregious of war crimes, all the while deterring those who would commit such crimes in the future.

The three peace operations that comprise the central empirical focus of this volume – UNMISS in South Sudan, MINUSCA in the Central African Republic and MONUSCO in the DRC – offer a geographically contiguous yet diverse set of cases illustrating the myriad challenges of translating PoC principles into practice. For while PoC language – emphasising the use of 'all necessary means' to 'ensure effective, timely, and dynamic protection of civilians under threat of physical violence,' as the 2024 mandate extension of UNMISS puts it – has now become so commonplace in Security Council Resolutions as to be almost banal, the PoC devil is most certainly in the details. Indeed, dilemmas around who precisely to protect and how precisely to protect them have become inseparable from many of the core – and hitherto unresolved – debates around the very nature and purpose of peacekeeping. These include debates around the utility and limits of 'robust' peacekeeping, around the relationship between peace operations and sovereign host states (still presumed to possess ultimate responsibility for the security and safety of their own populations), around the relationship between short-term protection efforts and longer-term peacebuilding processes and around the metrics used to evaluate success and failure in peacekeeping contexts. At the operational level, individual peace operations remain decidedly imperfect vehicles for protecting vulnerable civilians: the UN has long struggled to bridge both the disciplinary divides (especially military/civilian) and the cultural cleavages that are the inevitable reality of any multinational deployment, and to shed its reputation for bureaucratic sclerosis in environments demanding agility, flexibility and creativity. Individual missions have also been hampered by a perennial shortage of resources relative to the degree of difficulty of their operating environments, and by severe limitations on their ability to gather and process the field-level intelligence necessary to anticipate and head off potential protection threats. It remains simultaneously the case, therefore, that PoC remains both an 'impossible mandate' (Holt and Berkman 2006) – no mission can protect all the vulnerable all the time, and some have struggled to protect even their own personnel – and that the presence and the actions of peacekeepers have made a marked and measurable difference in the reduction of civilian loss of life in contexts of ongoing conflict. Just about any mission with a PoC mandate can be judged as both a partial success and a partial failure, and disagreements between qualitatively and quantitatively inclined scholars over which half of the glass to emphasise have been one of the more notable features of the peacekeeping debate in recent years. All this considered, then, a central argument to be developed in the pages that follow is that UN peace operations are in fact uniquely configured by virtue of their hybrid nature – and by their sheer ability to be present in the most difficult of conflict-affected environments – as agents of protection. While missions have not always been able to effectively combine the range of coercive and non-coercive protection tools at their disposal – or to manage tensions and contradictions among them – I argue that effective PoC should ultimately not be understood as a choice between coercive and non-coercive, or defensive and offensive, but rather as a creative and intelligent blend of the two. For the purposes of this analysis, the crucial question is not whether peacekeepers protect *some* civilians – any multilateral operation with significant military assets, a budget in the hundreds of millions of dollars and a specific mandate to protect civilians should be able to offer vulnerable civilians some measure of protection – but whether they reduce civilian insecurity as much as is realistically possible given the mandate and asset mix available to them, and whether protection practices can and do evolve. In other words, is there a process of 'learning by doing' happening that promises to deliver better results over time?

One of the ironies of the present moment is that just as sufficient ground-level experience exists that should enable lessons learned to be translated into sustained improvements in protection practice, virtually all of the strategic levers available to peace operations appear to be weakening. With no new missions authorised since 2014, UN peacekeeping has, for a range of practical and geostrategic factors, ceased to be the go-to international response to crises in fragile and conflict-affected contexts, and the peacekeeping story for the better part of the past decade has been one of shrinking budgets and exit strategies, with the Mali mission being the latest (as of end-2023) to be shuttered. Surviving missions are increasingly asked to do more with less, with marked impacts on performance; in the case of MONUSCO, belt-tightening prompted a shift from a strategy of protection through presence to one of protection through projection, even while the mission's ability to project itself into crisis situations was also diminished. Of equal concern in each of the three mission contexts at the heart of this study, the UN's political and diplomatic heft – and its ability to make use of 'good offices' to affect broader conflict trajectories and advance peace processes – has also been much reduced in recent years, to the extent that Special Representatives of the UN Secretary General (SRSGs) have become increasingly marginal presences in the conflict resolution processes that peace operations exist, ultimately, to support. Across all three cases, therefore, a deepening disconnect between protection and peacebuilding is both a recurrent theme and an ongoing concern.

The Interplay of Norm and Practice

Geopolitical factors – including the ability of an increasingly divided and fractious Security Council to authorise missions and the willingness of UN member states to provide them with both resources and personnel – obviously matter a great deal in terms of the larger context in which PoC practice has developed and the degree to which it has a future. Nevertheless, it is also a key premise of this study that the specific manner in which PoC has developed in the context of peace operations is very much a function of field-level practices. This has much to do with both the amorphous and expansive nature of protection as an emerging norm and with the character of the UN Security Council as the architect of the mandates that both enable and constrain peace operations. In the first place, PoC, and the humanitarian discourse into which it has inserted itself in recent decades, remains what Jon Harald Sande Lie (2012) has termed a 'knowledge battlefield,' marked by ongoing contestation over how protection should be both conceptualised and operationalised, with humanitarian, human rights and security interpretations all vying for pre-eminence and priority. At the same time, as Richard Gowan (2019: 7) has noted, the Security Council remains a political body rather than a managerial one, dominated by international diplomats, riven by ideological divisions, and ill-configured to deliver more than general, reactive and often opaque statements about the imperatives of

PoC in peacekeeping contexts. While opacity has its uses in enabling consensus and papering over divisions, in an era of deepening dissensus it also means that the Council is unlikely to evolve towards greater precision and specificity in its articulation of protection mandates. In a very real sense, then, it is not "the ruminations of diplomats in Manhattan" (Gowan 2019: 10), but rather the actions of peacekeepers and other international forces on the ground – and their struggles to reconcile ambitious mandates with scarce resources, to balance impartiality with non-indifference and to reckon with the paradoxes of using violence to restrain violence (Slim 2007) – that have shaped the evolution of PoC practice over the past quarter-century.

It is for this reason, then, that the primary focus here will be on the specific practices of PoC as they have emerged and continue to evolve on the ground in particular conflict contexts. In doing so, I draw theoretical inspiration from the so-called 'practice turn' in international relations theory, which emphasises the role of 'socially meaningful patterns of action' – in other words the exercise of agency in organised social contexts – in the making of international politics (Adler and Pouliot 2011: 4). As Jeremie Cornut (2017: 5) has noted, the study of practices begins from the basic intuition that social realities are constituted by what human actors 'do' both in and on the world: in his words, the social world is brought into being "by the flesh and blood of people doing things." In most professional environments, the things that people do are mostly routine, regularised and predictable, and rely on settled and often unconscious background knowledge about what it means to be a nurse, a diplomat or a peacekeeper and what it means to perform these particular roles competently. A focus on practice is also a useful corrective to more static considerations of the normative underpinnings of specific domains such as peacekeeping or humanitarianism; by emphasising how norms are translated (or not) into concrete action, the practice turn enables the weaving together of the discursive/ideational and material worlds. Practice, in other words, is where the normative rubber hits the road, and should, in principle at least, allow us to develop better understandings of the chains of thought and action that connect New York-based ruminations and policy deliberations with those field-level activities thousands of miles away that carry life-and-death consequences not only for vulnerable civilians but also for those entrusted with protection mandates.

For my purposes, two additional and related insights of practice theory are particularly relevant to making sense of PoC in peace operation contexts. First, despite the emphasis on background knowledge and repetitive, routinised action, practice theory is also attuned to the ways in which practice is also a motor of change. As Cornut suggests (2017: 8), "an analysis of practice enables us to develop a deeper understanding of the causal structures that tilt the field of policy practice in particular ways." This supports insights from comparative public policy on the relationship between principles and agents, and the importance of avoiding simplistic assumptions about causal arrows flowing unproblematically downwards from those who make decisions and set policy to those tasked with policy implementation. Particularly in emerging, contested and ambiguous fields of practice, therefore, we need to be open to the possibility that practices produce policy just as much if not more than policy generates practice (Mosse, cited in Sande Lie 2012: 155). Second, just as policy is given shape and form by the way it is enacted in practice, so too does practice play a critical function in adding detail, nuance and specificity to particular norms; in this case, too, as practices or standard operating procedures become unsettled and shift in response to changing environmental conditions, so too does the substantive content of the norm. In her examination of shifts in the ways in which the impartiality norm has been understood and rationalised in the context of peace operations, Marion Laurence demonstrates precisely this dynamic. Following the critical constructivist insight that far from being stable and settled, norms are better understood as malleable 'works in progress,' subject to ongoing contestation, her work shows how the field-level struggles of peacekeepers to reconcile growing normative ambiguity in the face of seemingly contradictory imperatives – supporting the extension of state authority, for example, while continuing to insist that peace operations do not take sides in ongoing conflicts – has led the UN to exchange a passive conception of impartiality for an active, assertive version emphasising the defence of the mandate. While the impartiality norm remains central to the very identity of peacekeepers, and indeed offers a sort of 'rhetorical security blanket' that helps stabilise that identity, it is also malleable in that its meaning is defined, and redefined over time, "in and through the day-to-day practices of mission personnel" (Laurence 2019: 259).

For a variety of reasons, then, it makes sense to examine PoC in peacekeeping contexts through the lens of practice. For all their diversity, peace operations and the personnel who staff them comprise a relatively coherent community of practice, bound together through the joint enterprise of supporting peace, stability and security in conflict-affected societies. The work of peacekeepers – whether military, police or civilian – is also marked by a well-established and long-standing repertoire of standard operating procedures, from patrolling to human rights monitoring to engagement with armed factions, civil society leaders and political elites. The persistence of such practices, along with the strong attachment of many of the most important troop-contributing countries to peacekeeping's foundational principles, has also coexisted since the turn of the millennium with a strong sense that not only is the 'standard treatment' for civil wars – negotiated settlements followed by peacekeeper-facilitated peace implementation processes (Gowan and Stedman 2018) – no longer working, but that the legitimacy of peace operations rests increasingly on their ability to protect civilians. This has led to a persistent and hitherto unresolved tension between continuity and change, which has been manifest most prominently by a form of 'normative layering,' with the mandates of peace operations becoming broader, more ambitious and more potentially contradictory. Nowhere is this more evident than in the case of PoC, where strong commitments to peacekeeping's foundational pillars – among both Security Council members and troop contributors – coexist awkwardly with forceful language about the imperative of using 'all necessary means' (up to and including lethal force) in order to protect vulnerable and threatened civilians. It is not entirely fair to suggest that field-level staff have been left to their own devices to manage the normative and operational ambiguity inherent in this new peacekeeping environment, as the

UN Secretariat has provided (and has regularly updated) detailed guidance on PoC implementation in an effort to enable missions to better interpret mandate language, notably by detailing a three-tier structure for PoC activities, emphasising dialogue and engagement, physical protection and the establishment of a protective environment (UN DPO 2023). It *is* fair to suggest, however, that as official PoC policy at most articulates a repertoire of protection practices, without insisting on any inherent hierarchy or sequencing among them, the most important decisions around the how and the who of PoC continue to be in the hands of field-level decision-makers, from SRSGs and contingent commanders down. This includes not only the kinds of life-and-death decisions that come to mind most immediately in PoC contexts, such as whether and how to intervene in the fog and confusion of ongoing violence, but also more strategic decisions that require a careful balancing of mandate imperatives that are difficult to reconcile, such as responding to civilian abuses of government forces without jeopardising the cordial relations with the government that are crucial to ensuring the mission's continued presence on the ground. In a very real sense, then, the innovations, the compromises and the quotidian decisions (or non-decisions) made at the operational level in missions with PoC mandates have over the past two decades defined what it means to say that peacekeepers have a responsibility to protect civilians, and have at least laid down some important markers for distinguishing between competent and incompetent practice in this emerging field.

In preparing the groundwork for the subsequent discussion of both practices and cases, the balance of this introductory chapter offers a brief historical overview of the evolution of PoC within the UN peacekeeping ecosystem, followed by an analysis of each of PoC's component elements, since neither 'protection' nor 'civilian' are unproblematic, uncontested concepts. Indeed, it is the unsettled nature of these constituent elements – and by extension the unstable nature of PoC as a composite concept – that underpins much of the ongoing controversy around what precisely the UN's obligations to civilian populations in peacekeeping contexts are, and how precisely these obligations should be honoured (Russo and Cinq-Mars 2019: 2).

The Evolution of PoC within the UN System

The logical starting point for any history of PoC within the UN system is the surge of post-cold war peacekeeping of the early 1990s, which simultaneously saw the UN both empowered to intervene and overwhelmed by the scope, scale and complexity of the conflicts into which peacekeepers were inserted. While peacekeeping became operational as never before in this era, the taken-for-granteds of first-generation peacekeeping that served the UN well in contexts such as Cyprus – and in which PoC did not feature – quickly proved to be ill-suited to the challenges of conflict zones as diverse and chaotic as Rwanda, Bosnia and Cambodia. While missions struggled to become not only multidimensional but also flexible enough to function in conditions where there was precious little peace to keep, the UN came under growing pressure to intervene proactively in the face of atrocities against civilians. An important Rubicon was crossed by the UNPROFOR mission in Bosnia in early

1993, when the French General Philippe Morillon announced to the residents of the besieged town of Srebrenica that they would henceforth be "under the protection of the UN forces," (cited in Burns 1993) with the UN Security Council ultimately moving to declare six so-called 'safe areas' across Bosnia. The experiment, of course, ended catastrophically when Bosnian Serb forces called the UN's bluff and overran Srebrenica in July 1995, before proceeding to systemically massacre upwards of 8,000 men and boys. In combination with the shameful retreat from Rwanda the year prior as that country's genocide gathered force, the Srebrenica episode shook the UN, and institution of peacekeeping more specifically, to its very foundations.

The latter part of the 1990s witnessed a discernible ebb in UN peacekeeping, as an obviously traumatised organisation ceded ground to more robust NATO interventions, most notably in Bosnia and, shortly thereafter, in Kosovo. It was also a period of serious and much-needed introspection, culminating in late 1999 in "an extraordinarily candid, self-critical report" on the Srebrenica disaster by Kofi Annan, who was the head of UN peacekeeping in the mid-1990s before serving two terms as Secretary General (Smyth 1999). Coincidentally or not, the Annan mea culpa on Srebrenica arrived just as UN peacekeeping was again in the ascendency, with 1999 witnessing the launch of ambitious new protectorates in Kosovo and East Timor. The same year also marked an important turning point in the institutionalisation of PoC within the UN Security Council, with a dedicated thematic resolution (1265) on PoC and, weeks later, a subsequent resolution (1270) – on the establishment of the UNAMSIL mission in Sierra Leone – which for the first time formally mandated peacekeepers to protect civilians "under imminent threat of physical violence."

While hardly a golden era, the subsequent period – roughly bracketed by the 2000 Brahimi Report and the 2015 HIPPO Report, both of which sought to update peacekeeping doctrine for the realities of the 21st century – saw rapid growth in both the size and the ambition of peace operations, as well as a decided shift towards Africa as peacekeeping's new centre of gravity. By early 2015, some 108,000 uniformed personnel served under the UN flag, and unlike previous eras a significant majority of peacekeepers now came from the developing world, with just four countries – Ethiopia, Bangladesh, India and Pakistan – contributing fully 30 per cent of all peacekeepers (Gao 2016). By this point as well, the so-called big four peace operations on the African continent – UNMISS in South Sudan, MONUSCO in the DRC, MINUSMA in Mali and MINUSCA in the Central African Republic – had come to dominate peacekeeping debates, overshadowing long-standing (and relatively stable) legacy missions in places like Cyprus and Western Sahara. Each of the big four operations has struggled mightily to impose itself on fluid and volatile security environments, where the transition from war-fighting to peacekeeping to peacebuilding has been anything but linear, and in each the protection of civilians has emerged as a priority component of the mission mandate.

Much like in the mid-1990s, however – but mercifully without the large-scale disasters of Srebrenica or Rwanda – recent years have seen something of a retrenchment. No new missions have been established since 2014, while five have been wound down over this same period. The UN peacekeeping budget has been similarly pared back, while existing missions – notably MONUSCO – have seen significant material and personnel cuts, and growing pressure to develop clear exit strategies, despite ongoing volatility. Overall numbers of uniformed peacekeepers have now dropped below 60,000, with nearly three-quarters of these forces distributed across the big three African missions (down from four with the closure of MINUSMA) (UN DPO 2025). While myriad factors have contributed to this downsizing – among them growing tensions among the Security Council's permanent five members, a deepening budget crisis across the UN system, a decidedly unsympathetic US administration (especially during the first Trump administration) and a gradual shift towards partnership peacekeeping, notably in Africa – there is also a growing malaise, in New York as elsewhere, concerning the efficacy of peacekeeping. While the SEA scandals of recent years have taken a reputational toll, equally damaging has been a growing sense that peace support operations – even those with robust mandates – lack the critical weight necessary to decisively shift conflict trajectories in the direction of sustainable peace. As Richard Gowan (2015: 32) has observed, the sense that the UN's largest and highest-profile missions "are trapped in quagmires of endemic violence and dysfunctional politics" has begun to raise questions as to whether the continued presence of peacekeepers in such contexts is doing more harm than good. Along the same lines, a sense that recent years have witnessed peacekeeping overstretch – with missions not only saddled with so-called Christmas tree mandates but beginning to lose sight of core principles, especially around the non-use of force – has generated something of a back-to-basics movement. This sentiment is nicely captured by Arthur Boutellis and Alexandra Novosseloff's (2017: 3) observation that "the age of large, unwieldy, multidimensional missions might be gone," presumably to be replaced by a new era of smaller, cheaper and less intrusive missions (already visible in the recent trend towards special political missions).

Alongside the ebbs and flows of peacekeeping over the past several decades, of course, there have simultaneously been profound changes to the nature of contemporary conflict, as well as the unhappy constant of civilian suffering. From Mary Kaldor's 'new wars' to Barbara Walter's 'new new wars' (Kaldor 2012; Walter 2017), scholars have spent much of the post-cold war period trying to discern clear patterns in the shifting trajectories of contemporary armed conflicts. Where Kaldor focused on the increasing prevalence of intra-state conflicts fought by irregular forces through irregular means, and for reasons of identity rather than ideology, Walter's focus was the post-2003 shift of conflict to Muslim-majority countries and the injection of radical Islamist – and largely transnational – ideas and aims into many recent conflicts, from Mali to Syria to Yemen, with the wider Sahel region emerging more recently as ground zero for such conflicts. Equally important, and certainly more widespread, has been the accompanying fragmentation of fighting forces in civil war contexts, which has immeasurably complicated the challenges of both peacekeeping and conflict resolution. At one point in the Syrian conflict, for example, the US Defence Intelligence Agency estimated that there were 1,200 distinct rebel groups fighting the Assad government (cited in

Lund 2013: 23), while in the DRC some 120 separate armed groups operate in the Kivus alone (Stearns 2022). Such numbers, and the fluidity through which armed groups morph, combine and shift allegiances, threaten to make a mockery of the traditional peacekeeping principle of 'consent of the parties,' and present interveners with near-overwhelming challenges in terms of keeping track of the relevant actors, let alone engaging effectively with them.

The 'irregularisation' of both fighting forces and fighting modalities (with population control in particular emerging as a key strategy) might suggest that the deliberate targeting of civilians in conflict is part of what differentiates new wars from old. Statistical data – such as the claim made by the UN Development Programme, in its 1998 *Human Development Report* (UNDP 1998: 35), that civilian fatalities as a proportion of all war-related deaths have risen over the past century from 5 per cent to more than 90 per cent – would seem to support such a conclusion, although as Adam Roberts (2010) has noted, such ratios need to be taken with a large grain of salt given the serious methodological obstacles involved in counting war-related civilian deaths. It would also be a serious oversimplification to equate violence against civilians with the emergence of untrained and undisciplined militias. From the massive levels of civilian suffering inflicted via aerial bombardment during World War II to the slaughter at Srebrenica to the destruction visited on civilians in Gaza by the Israeli Defence Force throughout 2024, professional, hierarchically structured armies over the past century have demonstrated themselves to be fully capable of setting aside polite distinctions between civilian and combatant when it served their interests. Indeed, as Hugo Slim (2007: 5) has observed, over the sweep of history perhaps the only firm conclusion one can draw from the evidence is that "civilian suffering is to war what rain is to a thunderstorm." While massive violence against civilian populations is clearly a key feature of contemporary conflicts (as is the reality of war's equally devastating *indirect* impacts on civilians), it is a feature that is not particularly novel, nor especially modern. As Slim suggests (2007: 3), few warring parties see civilians as humanitarian agencies might like them to; rather, throughout history fighting forces have refused to consider civilians as 'merely' innocent bystanders, and this ambiguity has rationalised the killing of them in large numbers when it was considered expedient or necessary to do so. Indeed, it is precisely the weakness of normative prohibitions against abusing civilians in times of war that has generated – slowly, imperfectly – parallel efforts to more actively protect civilians caught up in the chaos of war.

The Many Meanings of Protection

If civilian suffering in conflict contexts can be seen as a constant – albeit with important variations across time and space – there have been significant changes, accelerating over the past two decades, concerning the practice of both responding to and/or preventing such suffering. Long-standing debates around the legitimate limits to be placed on the conduct of war, prominent for example in the Christian just war tradition, have more recently come to be codified in IHL, and more specifically in the idea that it is possible to *not only* distinguish clearly between combatant and civilian (or non-combatant), but *also* spare the latter from the brutality of armed conflict. The absence of concrete enforcement mechanisms leaves the operationalisation of such provisions in the hands of fighting forces themselves, who – as the ongoing conflicts in both Ukraine and Gaza have forcefully reminded us – have not always proven themselves to be enthusiastic IHL adherents. While the International Criminal Court has come into existence precisely as a vehicle for meting out *post facto* retributive justice against those suspected of the most egregious crimes against humanity, while at the same time deterring future perpetrators, this experiment remains very much in its infancy (and perilously fraught from a political standpoint). In parallel, an entire tradition (and industry) of humanitarian protection has emerged, constituted by a complex array of organisational actors with a strong commitment to treating the downstream consequences of war-induced human suffering, but with almost zero ability to address its upstream causes.

At this point, then, it is helpful to distinguish 'PoC' as it has evolved in recent decades not only from the more long-standing humanitarian understandings of protection, but also from the notion of the 'responsibility to protect' which emerged more or less concurrently with PoC. From the humanitarian perspective, understandings of protection are both broader and more indirect than those that have emerged in specific peacekeeping contexts. The Inter-Agency Standing Committee (IASC), which is the UN system's high-level humanitarian coordination forum, defines protection as including "all activities aimed at obtaining full respect for the rights of the individual in accordance with the letter and spirit of relevant bodies of law" (cited in Captier 2003: 16). Operationally, the Global Protection Cluster, an umbrella network of non-governmental organizations and UN agencies mandated by the IASC, engages in protection work in humanitarian crises across four broad areas of responsibility: child protection, gender-based violence, housing, land and property and mine action. While the humanitarian enterprise has always been driven by the imperative of providing aid and alleviating suffering in crisis contexts, whether natural or man-made, as Victoria Metcalfe-Hough (2022: 14) has argued, the idea of humanitarian protection emerged from the growing recognition that "provision of life-saving assistance and services is not on its own enough to spare civilians from the worst effects of armed conflict." This was precisely the paradox faced by UN peacekeepers in Bosnia in the early 1990s: providing food and water to conflict-affected individuals today only to watch them be killed by militias tomorrow, a dynamic which prompted cynical Bosnians to describe themselves, not inaccurately, as lambs being fattened for slaughter (Woodward 1995: 320).

Since humanitarian organisations are by definition even less capable than peace operations of providing actual physical protection to threatened civilians, in a humanitarian context protection has come to be understood primarily in terms of advocacy. In other words, as Captier (2003: 18) has argued, humanitarian protection in practice means "identifying and denouncing failures of protection and highlighting the proper responsibilities of states, warring parties, mandated international organizations or new non-state actors, like multinational corporations and private security firms." The extent to which all humanitarian actors active in a conflict zone have a responsibility to take on such advocacy roles – rather than just specialised agencies such as the International Committee of the Red Cross, which plays a unique role in educating conflict parties about their obligations under IHL – has been a matter of some controversy within the humanitarian community. Just as peacekeepers have struggled with the obligations and limits of the impartiality imperative in conflict contexts, so too have many humanitarian agencies worried about the extent to which protection advocacy crosses the line into political activity, thus compromising the neutral humanitarian space that relief agencies rely on, ironically, for their own protection. While some agencies, notably *Médecins sans frontières*, have made names for themselves by refusing to stay silent as their field staff are overwhelmed by atrocity, others continue to adhere to a more rigid understanding of what impartiality entails, in part out of fear of the consequences of crossing some invisible line. As a consequence, there is a growing sense – underlined by a recent report by the Humanitarian Policy Group (Metcalfe-Hough 2022) – that while there are clear structural limits to humanitarian influence in active conflict zones, relevant agencies could still be doing far more to leverage the limited influence that they do enjoy over the behaviour of armed groups.

Contemporary protection debates have also been influenced – and often unhelpfully muddied – by the near-simultaneous emergence of both PoC and R2P as 'close cousins' (Paddon Rhoads and Welsh 2019). As Thierry Tardy (2012: 429) has noted, both concepts started from the same process of critical self-reflection triggered by the tragedies of Srebrenica and Rwanda, and both shared the same normative foundation: the imperative of "providing protection to populations that are threatened by armed groups or governments in violation of international humanitarian, human rights and refugee law provisions." Despite their conceptual proximity, however, writing over a decade ago Tardy elaborated what remains a convincing rationale for keeping the two concepts distinct. Beyond the fact that the two norms emerged from different procedural dynamics – PoC from within the established institutional structures of UN peacekeeping and R2P, at least initially, as an externally driven policy exercise embodied by the International Commission on Intervention and State Sovereignty (ICISS) – the coercive elements of R2P were always conceptualised as an exceptional response to a narrow set of circumstances, namely mass atrocities in the form of genocide, war crimes, ethnic cleansing and/or crimes against humanity. By contrast, the protection remits of peacekeepers functioning under PoC mandates are much broader, given the myriad sources of peril faced by civilian populations in the kinds of conflict-affected environments in which peacekeepers typically find themselves. Questions of consent, too, look different from an R2P lens than from a PoC lens. Coercive, R2P-inspired interventions – with the 2011 NATO intervention in Libya being the most prominent case in point – almost necessarily unfold without the consent of, and likely in the face of opposition from, the affected state, and in this sense bear a closer resemblance to peace enforcement than to peacekeeping. Conversely, while the emergence of more robust peacekeeping practices has necessitated – as with impartiality – shifts in how 'consent' is understood in contemporary peace operations, it remains the case that *strategic* consent on the part of the host state remains a *sine qua non* of peacekeeper presence. At the *tactical* level, however, consent is no longer deemed necessary; a mission is assumed to have the necessary authorisation to act, in other words, to protect civilians by whatever means necessary against any armed threat. While in principle this latter category includes threats emanating from government forces, in practice the political sensitivities and trade-offs involved have limited the degree of coercion contemplated, keeping it well below the levels that might be considered necessary in an enforcement context (Tardy 2012; Williams 2016).

Despite such nuances, for much of their respective histories debates around both R2P and PoC have remained mutually entangled, especially when it comes to the fraught questions around when and how coercive force should be deployed in the name of protecting civilians. Conflationist and segregationist arguments have also played out within the UN system itself, with the Secretary General and the Department of Peacekeeping Operations (DPKO) at times finding themselves on opposite sides of the argument. In the aftermath of the Libya episode, however, with NATO widely viewed – by Russia, China and a significant cross-section of states from the Global South – as having overplayed its hand by extending a protection mandate to incorporate regime change, the segregationist camp appears to have prevailed. The not-inconsiderable fallout from Libya, combined with a resurgence in recent years of powerful 'pluralist' norms, among them sovereign equality, state primacy, national ownership and non-interference (Paddon Rhoads and Welsh 2019: 614), appears to have decisively relegated R2P to the back-burner of international security politics, and rendered the term itself increasingly toxic, with unpleasant associations to increasingly discredited neocolonial aspirations on the part of certain Western states. Thus, while there may be sound conceptual reasons to avoid conflating PoC and R2P, in the end the clear separation between the two concepts may be primarily a function of trying to prevent the former from being contaminated by too close an association with the latter.

The Nature of 'Civilians'

In 2025, the world will observe not only the 30th anniversary of the 1995 Srebrenica massacre, but also the 25th anniversary of Security Council Resolution 1325, which marked the arrival of the Women, Peace and Security agenda at the world's apex international security forum (Kirby and Shepherd 2016: 252). If 1325 marked the beginning of a concerted, and ongoing, effort to elevate women's protection and women's empowerment in the context of international security, the Srebrenica disaster also revealed, albeit in a different way, the fundamentally gendered nature of both conflict and conflict management. As Charli Carpenter has demonstrated (2006: 1), the deaths of nearly 8,000 civilians – overwhelmingly men and boys – in the Srebrenica enclave near the end of the Bosnian conflict were products not only of the ruthlessness of the Bosnian Serb Army, but also of the particular nature of the international regime protecting war-affected civilians. Gendered notions embedded in the principle of civilian immunity enabled the women, children, the elderly and the sick in the enclave to be rescued and/or spared, while any male civilian old enough to carry a weapon was left to his fate. Curiously, while a shamed and chastened UN began to rethink civilian protection in peacekeeping contexts just as the momentum towards SCR 1325 was beginning to build, and while the PoC and WPS agendas have evolved in parallel in recent decades, neither agenda has fully engaged with the other, despite the fact that both are concerned with the protection of vulnerable populations (Taylor and Baldwin 2019).

A key reason for this disconnect can be found in the fact that since its inception, the PoC agenda within UN peacekeeping has emphasised the *how* more than the *who* of protection. Given the overwhelming geography of insecurity in contemporary conflict-affected contexts, UN missions have been hard-pressed to offer even a modicum of protection to civilian populations, and to bridge yawning gulfs between ambitious mandates and limited resources. At the same time, with the specific exception of sexual and gender-based violence, both the language and the practice of PoC have been pitched largely in gender-neutral terms (Hultman and Sellstrom 2019), albeit with ritual acknowledgement of the needs of particularly vulnerable groups such as women and girls. In this context, there has been considerably less attention paid within PoC debates to the specific nature of the civilian populations that peacekeepers are increasingly mandated to protect, or to the challenges of distinguishing civilians from combatants for the purposes of protection; for the most part, the question of who precisely constitutes 'the protected' has been taken as a matter of settled international law. Nevertheless, the nature and character of civilian populations in need of protection matters a great deal in the context of how concrete protection strategies are designed and implemented. In particular, approaching civilian protection issues with gendered lenses can shed light on critical tensions between protection and empowerment – issues at the heart of the WPS agenda – particularly as they apply to the agency (or perceived lack thereof) of vulnerable populations.

Unlike its R2P cousin, which privileges the protection of *populations* from genocide and other crimes against humanity, the PoC agenda relies on a fundamental distinction between combatants and *civilians*. As a key tenet of IHL, the principle of distinction insists, as a means of placing moral limits on what is and is not permissible in war, on the existence of a bright, clear boundary between those who take up arms and those who do not; the former may be legitimately targeted and killed, the latter may not. As Hugo Slim suggests (2016: 17), in the context of the suffering endured by non-combatant populations during the two world wars – and particularly in the aftermath of the 'total war' of World War II – "civilians rightly became central moral subjects in the ethics and practice of war." Both R2P and PoC represent logical extensions of this moral concern.

As Slim (2016: 17) also notes, however, both world wars, as well as the myriad conflicts – both civil and international – which followed also revealed the more complex reality that non-combatants "did not simply suffer in war and inhabit some politically neutral space." The line separating combatant from civilian in conflict contexts, in other words, has never been as stable nor as solid as international legal scholars might portray it to be. From World War II's Rosie the Riveter to contemporary African farmers helping to feed 'their' side (willingly or otherwise) amidst ethnic conflict, civilians experience war not only as victims but also as agents, with individual motivations running the gamut from simply trying to survive to actively and self-consciously contributing to the war effort. Conversely, the signal atrocities committed against civilians over the past century, from Hiroshima to My Lai to Srebrenica, have been at least in part a product of the discomfort on the part of military decision-makers with the principle of distinction, as well as the difficulty in sorting out the guilty from the innocent.

It is here, in fact, where gender enters the equation as a key strategy for stabilising the distinction between combatant and civilian and, more particularly, for finding a way to separate – by means of visible physical markers – the *harmless* from the potentially *harmful*. In her discussion of the negotiations around the 1949 Fourth Geneva Convention, Helen Kinsella notes the significance of this latter distinction, citing an ICRC Commentary from the time worrying about the difference between the wounded and prisoners of war "who have become harmless" and the civilian population more generally, who "have not in most cases been rendered harmless" (cited in Kinsella 2005: 265). The imperative of differentiating the harmless from the non-harmless led, ultimately, to the practical emergence of a distinct set of categories of 'harmless' civilians – specifically children, women, old people, the wounded and the sick – who, *by definition*, take no part in the fighting (Kinsella 2005: 266).

While demonstrably false – even a cursory glance at ongoing debates around child soldiers and women in combat reveals that some women and children are active, if not always enthusiastic, participants in contemporary war-fighting – this categorisation of 'civilian' into identifiable groupings of the harmless has stuck and, as the Srebrenica massacre revealed, continues to inform live-and-death decisions around who is worthy of being spared and/or protected. Ideas around gender, as Kinsella notes, play an especially important role in distinguishing combatant from civilian; unlike children, the elderly, or the incapacitated, the assumed vulnerabilities of women are fixed/permanent rather than transitory/temporal, and as a result women in particular have come to function as a synecdoche for civilian (2016: 268–269). It is this, perhaps, which best explains why gender appears to be both everywhere and nowhere in contemporary PoC discourse. Hidden beneath the superficially gender-neutral language of 'civilians' is considerable historical baggage – accumulated since Hugo Grotius was laying the foundations for the laws of war in the 17th century and graphically reproduced in fairy tales of white knights and damsels in distress – that underpins a fundamentally gendered understanding of the principle of distinction: men are the protectors, women the protected.

One further aspect of the struggle to clarify the combatant/civilian distinction is of particular relevance for the purposes of thinking about the character of 'the protected' in peacekeeping contexts, and as well as about the relationship between protector and protected. To the extent that the imperative of navigating ethically slippery distinctions between those who bear arms, those who support those who bear arms and those who are genuinely outside the conflict requires, increasingly, that civilians be seen not just as non-combatants but as *harmless*, then those civilians deemed to be in need of protection are also at risk of being seen as lacking agency.

Their very vulnerability, in other words, undermines their ability to be *perceived* as agents, rather than objects, by those mandated to protect them. The paradox is that the perception of weakness and vulnerability among civilian populations may lead those on the other side of the combatant/civilian divide (including uniformed peacekeepers) to view civilians as 'nothing': weak, old, female and thus undeserving of respect (Forsyth, cited in Kinsella 2016; 268); the connection between such perceptions and the scourge of peacekeeper-related SEA that the UN has spent the better part of the last two decades trying to stamp out is at least suggestive. Similarly, the image of civilians as helpless, harmless and stripped of agency sits awkwardly alongside the idea, prominent in debates surrounding the recent 'local turn' in peacebuilding, that the agency of these same civilians as drivers of peacebuilding is both underestimated and underemployed, as well as the argument that PoC mandates "should be recalibrated to help build resilient local communities and empower civilian populations to have a greater say in their national governance structures" (Williams 2013: 287). In practice, this dissonance has generated at least the perception of an incompatibility between protection and empowerment. With respect to women's protection needs in particular, it has led to the now common lament that women in conflict contexts tend to be treated first and foremost as *victims* of (primarily sexual) violence, rather than as agents of protection in their own right (Puechguirbal 2010: 177; Taylor and Baldwin 2019).

Such considerations matter to any wider consideration of protection practices, especially given the tendency of the PoC debate, at least to date, to place overwhelming emphasis on peacekeeping personnel, and especially those who carry guns, as the only relevant actors on the PoC stage. Yet as Andrew Bonwick (2006: 274) has noted, it remains a rarely spoken truth about protection "that the main players in the protection of civilians in conflict are the civilians themselves." This reality, as noted above, has slowly begun to assert itself in the academic literature, if not necessarily in practice, especially in the context of community self-protection strategies that unfold in situations where a peacekeeping contingent is too slow or too distant to respond. Indeed, Baines and Paddon (2012: 232) write that the marked contrast in the efficacy of top-down and bottom-up approaches to protection lends considerable credibility to the argument that "civilian self-protection strategies should be the starting point for all attempts to design protection strategies on the ground." Daniel Levine (2013) has similarly championed a 'protection-with' rather than a 'protection-from' model of PoC, suggesting that the practice of PoC – like the practice of peacebuilding before it – may be ripe for its own local turn, one which takes seriously the positionality, the agency and the perspectives of the individuals and communities that peacekeepers are mandated to protect. Such themes have indeed found their way into official UN documents in recent years, in the form of language around 'people-centred' peacekeeping and 'inclusive, community-level engagement,' with the former head of UN peacekeeping going so far as to suggest that the broader goal of peace operations should not be in fact to protect civilians, but rather to empower them (cited in Williams 2013: 295). Still, protection and empowerment remain uneasy bedfellows, and have proven difficult to reconcile in light of the gendered tropes that remain prevalent in contemporary protection contexts. As subsequent chapters will elaborate, the tensions between treating civilians in conflict contexts as active agents in their own protection or harmless, agentless victims in need of rescue play out at the intersection of the debate between coercive and non-coercive protection strategies.[2]

Conclusion

This chapter has laid out a broad framework for understanding the range of issues that are relevant in trying to come to terms with the evolution of PoC practice in peacekeeping contexts. It has traced the key developments in the field over the past three decades, identified key points of contention and conveyed a sense of why both 'protection' and 'civilian' remain contested concepts, even as broad normative agreement exists around the principle that civilians should be spared from being direct targets of conflict, and protected when they are targeted. But while it may be "hard to quibble with saving lives in a crisis" (Gowan 2016: 72), consensus around what exactly to do in specific circumstances has proven to be far more elusive. And while notable progress has been made since PoC emerged as both norm and mandated task around the turn of the millennium, the unavoidable reality is that the bodies of civilian war-dead have, over the past 25 years, kept piling up, with the UN Secretary General (UN 2024: 1) recently describing the global state of the protection of civilians as 'resoundingly grim.' Given current conflict and geopolitical trends, there may be little reason for optimism that the situation will be much improved 25 years hence.

Peacekeepers operating in the context of UN-mandated peace operations, of course, bear only a portion of the responsibility for protecting civilians in conflict contexts, albeit one that has been particularly prominent in recent decades. In the chapters that follow, I explore in detail the manner in which PoC mandates have been both conceptualised and operationalised at the field level. The next two chapters explore the coercive/non-coercive protection continuum as it has evolved over the first decades of the 21st century, with the next chapter grappling in particular with the vexed issue of 'force in the name of peace' as it has played out both in principle and in practice, while the following chapter critically interrogates the idea of 'protection through peaceful means,' a vision for PoC that is certainly more consistent with traditional peacekeeping norms and values, but may not always be capable of delivering on the promise of protection. The following chapters – on South Sudan, DRC and CAR, respectively – attempt to make sense of how PoC dynamics have unfolded in each of these complex contexts, and with what effects on both conflict dynamics and civilian suffering.

Notes

1 Not everyone felt this way. One young resident of the Juba PoC site told me when I visited in 2019 that living there was like living in a concentration camp; an ethnic Nuer, he stayed because he feared for his life.

2 This paragraph draws on Donais and Murray (2021).

Works Cited

Adler, E. and V. Pouliot (2011) 'International practices', *International Theory* 3(1) 1–36.

Baines, E.and E. Paddon (2012) '"This is how we survived": Civilian agency and humanitarian protection', *Security Dialogue* 43(3): 231–247.

Berdal, M. and D. Shearer (2021) 'Hard lessons from South Sudan', *Survival* 63(5): 69–96.

Bonwick, A. (2006) 'Who really protects civilians?', *Development in Practice* 16(3/4): 270–277.

Boutellis, A. and A. Novosseloff (2017) 'Road to a better UN? Peace operations and the reform agenda', International Peace Institute report, November; Available at: https://www.ipinst.org/wp-content/uploads/2017/11/1711_Road-to-a-Better-UN2.pdf

Burns, J.F. (1993) 'Aid trucks arrive in a Bosnian town after Serbs yield', *The New York Times*, 20 March.

Captier, C. (2003) 'What does humanitarian protection really mean?', *Humanitarian Exchange* 23: 15–18.

Carpenter, C. (2006) *'Innocent Women and Children': Gender, Norms and the Protection of Civilians* (New York/Abingdon: Routledge).

Cornut, J. (2017) 'The practice turn in international relations theory', Oxford Research Encyclopedias (online); Available at: https://oxfordre.com/internationalstudies/display/10.1093/acrefore/9780190846626.001.0001/acrefore-9780190846626-e-113

Craze, J. and N. Pendle (2020) 'A fantasy of finality: the UN impasse at the protection of civilian sites in South Sudan', *African Arguments*, 23 September; Available at: https://africanarguments.org/2020/09/a-fantasy-of-finality-the-un-impasse-at-the-protection-of-civilian-sites-in-south-sudan/

Donais, T. and S. Murray (2021) 'Gender and Protection in UN Peacekeeping: Towards Inclusive Protection Practice', *Balsillie Papers* 4(1), 1–12; Available at: https://balsilliepapers.ca/bsia-paper/gender-and-protection-in-un-peacekeeping-towards-inclusive-protection-practice/

Gao, G. (2016) 'UN peacekeeping at new highs after post-Cold War surge and decline', Pew Research Center, 2 March; Available at: https://www.pewresearch.org/fact-tank/2016/03/02/un-peacekeeping-at-new-highs-after-post-cold-war-surge-and-decline/

Gowan, R. (2015) 'The peacekeeping quagmire', *Georgetown Journal of International Affairs* 16(2): 31–38.

Gowan, R. (2016) 'When should blue helmets walk away from a conflict?', in J. Della-Giacoma (ed.), *Global Peace Operations Review: Annual Compilation 2016* (New York: NYU Center on International Cooperation, 2017), 67–74.

Gowan, R. (2019) 'The security council and the protection of civilians', in L. Sharland (ed.), *Special Report: Evolution of the Protection of Civilians in UN Peacekeeping*; Australian Strategic Policy Institute, July; Available at: https://www.stimson.org/wp-content/files/file-attachments/SR%20140%20Protection%20of%20civilian%20in%20UN%20peacekeeping.pdf

Gowan, R. and S.J. Stedman (2018) 'The international regime for treating civil war, 1988–2017', *Daedalus* 147(1): 171–184.

Holt, V. and T. Berkman (2006) *The Impossible Mandate? Military Preparedness, the Responsibility to Protect and Modern Peace Operations* (Washington: Stimson Center).

Hultman, L. and A.M. Sellstrom (2019) 'WPS and protection of civilians', in S. E. Davies and J. True (eds.), *The Oxford Handbook of Women, Peace and Security* (New York: Oxford University Press), 598–608.

Human Rights Council (HRC) (2021) 'Report of the commission on human right in South Sudan', A/HRC/46/53, 4 February; Available at: https://reliefweb.int/report/south-sudan/report-commission-human-rights-south-sudan-ahrc4653

Jackson, R. (2019) 'Pacifism and the ethical imagination in IR', *International Politics* 56: 212–227.

Kaldor, M. (2012) *New and Old Wars: Organized Violence in a Global Era* (3rd Edition) (Stanford: Stanford University Press).

Kinsella, H. (2005) 'Securing the civilian: Sex and gender in the laws of war', in M. Barnett and R. Duvall (eds.), *Power in Global Governance* (Cambridge: Cambridge University Press), 249–272.

Kirby, P. and L.J. Shepherd (2016) 'Reintroducing women, peace and security', *International Affairs* 92(2): 249–254.

Laurence, M. (2019) 'An "Impartial" force? Normative ambiguity and practice change in UN peace operations', *International Peacekeeping* 26(3): 256–280.

Levine, D.H. (2013) 'Some considerations for civilian-peacekeeper alliances', *Ethics & Global Politics* 6(1): 1–23.

Lund, A. (2013) 'The non-state militant landscape in Syria', *CTC Sentinel* (Combating Terrorism Center at West Point) 6(8): 23–28; Available at: https://ctc.westpoint.edu/wp-content/uploads/2013/08/CTCSentinel-Vol6Iss85.pdf

Mednick, S. (2021) 'UN pullout triggers safety concerns in South Sudan displacement camps', *The New Humanitarian*, 18 May; Available at: https://www.thenewhumanitarian.org/news-feature/2021/18/5/unpullout-triggers-security-concerns-in-south-south-displacement-camps

Metcalfe-Hough, V. (2022) 'Advocating for the better protection of civilians: From stagnation to action', Humanitarian Policy Group Report (London: ODI); Available at: https://odi.org/en/publications/advocating-for-the-better-protection-of-civilians-from-stagnation-to-action/

Paddon Rhoads, E. and J. Welsh (2019) 'Close cousins in protection: the evolution of two norms', *International Affairs* 95(3): 597–617.

Puechguirbal, N. (2010) 'Discourses on gender, patriarchy and resolution 1325: A textual analysis of UN documents', *International Peacekeeping* 17(2): 172–187.

Roberts, A. (2010) 'Lives and statistics: Are 90% of war victims civilians?', *Survival* 52(3): 115–136.

Russo, J. and E. Cinq-Mars (2019) 'POC20: Twenty years of the protection of civilians: Challenges, progress, and priorities for the future', Report, Center for Civilians in Conflict; Available at: https://civiliansinconflict.org/wp-content/uploads/2020/12/Final_POC20-Report_CIVIC_September2019.pdf

Sande Lie, J.H. (2012) 'The knowledge battlefield of protection', *African Security* 5: 142–159.

Slim, H. (2007) *Killing Civilians: Method, Madness and Morality in War* (Oxford: Oxford University Press).

Slim, H. (2016) 'Civilians, distinction, and the compassionate view of war', in H. Willmot et al. (eds.), *Protection of Civilians* (Oxford: Oxford University Press), 11–28.

Smyth, P. (1999) 'Annan accepts UN must carry blame for Serb atrocities at Srebrenica', *The Irish Times*, 7 December; Available at: https://www.irishtimes.com/news/annan-accepts-un-must-carry-blame-for-serb-atrocities-at-srebrenica-1.258443

Stearns, J. (2022) *The War that Doesn't Say Its Name: The Unending Conflict in the Congo* (Princeton: Princeton University Press).

Tardy, T. (2012) 'The dangerous liaisons of the responsibility to protect and the protection of civilians in peacekeeping operations', *Global Responsibility to Protect* 4: 424–448.

Taylor, S. and G. Baldwin (2019) 'The global pushback on women's rights: The state of the women, peace and security agenda', International Peace Institute Issue Brief, September; Available at: https://www.ipinst.org/2019/09/global-pushback-on-womens-rights

United Nations (UN) (2015) 'United our strengths for peace – Politics, partnership and people: Report of the independent high-level panel on peace operations', A/70/95-S/2015/446, 17 June; Available at: https://digitallibrary.un.org/record/795940?ln=en

United Nations (UN) (2024) 'Protection of civilians in armed conflict: Report of the Secretary General, S/2024/385, 14 May; Available at: https://documents.un.org/doc/undoc/gen/n24/110/29/pdf/n2411029.pdf

UN Department of Peace Operations (UN DPO) (2023) 'Policy: The protection of civilians in United Nations peacekeeping (PoC Policy)', 1 May; Available at: https://peacekeeping.un.org/sites/default/files/2023_protection_of_civilians_policy.pdf

UN Department of Peace Operations (UN DPO) (2025) 'Peacekeeping operations fact sheet', 31 January; Available at: https://peacekeeping.un.org/sites/default/files/peacekeeping_fact_sheet_english_january_2025.pdf

United Nations Development Program (UNDP) (1998) *Human Development Report* 1998: *Consumption for Human Development* (New York: United Nations).

Walter, B.F. (2017) 'The new new civil wars', *Annual Review of Political Science* 20: 469–486.

Williams, P.D. (2013) 'Protection, resilience and empowerment: United Nations peacekeeping and violence against civilians in contemporary war zones', *Politics* 33(4): 287–298.

Williams, P.D. (2016) 'The R2P, protection of civilians, and UN peacekeeping operations', in A. J. Bellamy and T. Dunne (eds.), *The Oxford Handbook of the Responsibility to Protect* (Oxford: Oxford University Press), 524–544.

Woodward, S. (1995) *Balkan Tragedy: Chaos and Dissolution after the Cold War* (Washington: Brookings Institution Press).

2 Robust Protection Debates

Introduction

If Srebrenica might be considered at one end of the practice spectrum with regard to the use of force by peacekeepers, to the extent of becoming shorthand for the perils of passivity in the face of ruthless conflict parties, one might place Cité Soleil at the other. The most notorious of the many *bidonvilles* scattered across the lower elevations of Haiti's capital, Cité Soleil found itself in early 2007 as the site of one of the most dramatic armed standoffs in modern peacekeeping history. Several years into its deployment, the UN's MINUSTAH operation – in possession of both a stabilisation and a PoC mandate – found itself needing to come to terms with a metastasising gang problem, with Cité Soleil at its epicentre. Not only did gang violence increasingly pose "an intolerable threat to the peace and stability of the country," as Walter Dorn (2018: 129) has noted, but it was generating a growing number of civilian casualties – including kidnap victims – and eroding the mission's reputation in the eyes of the Haitian population. Under the leadership of Brazilian Major General Carlos dos Santos Cruz, who would later make a name for himself as the spokesperson for hyper-robust peacekeeping, MINUSTAH's uniformed elements planned and executed a series of military operations in the name of restoring law and order. The largest of these operations, *Jauru Sudamericana*, involved over 700 troops and 44 armoured personnel carriers, and was aimed at disrupting and dislodging key gangs while limiting civilian casualties in the crowded slum. Over the course of several months, Cité Soleil was progressively liberated from gang control, over 800 gang members were arrested and eventually the Special Representative of the UN Secretary General (SRSG) in Haiti was able to freely walk through its streets while local residents celebrated the end of a dark and dangerous period (Dorn 2018).

A superficial comparison of the Srebrenica and the Cité Soleil episodes might conclude that the UN successfully drew lessons from the former and applied them to the latter, with better results. While there's some truth to this, it must also be tempered by some hard realities. While MINUSTAH's robust approach of countering violence with violence in an effort to bring armed gangs to heel was an unquestionable success on its own terms, saving lives and creating the conditions for the extension of state authority into previously inaccessible and

DOI: 10.4324/9781003291114-2

ungoverned spaces, from the perspective of early 2025 – as Haiti has once again descended into gang-led anarchy – that success feels more ephemeral than durable. As James Cockayne (2014: 737) has observed, while the Cité Soleil operations clearly demonstrated the capacity of a motivated and determined mission to deploy force at the tactical level to successfully 'neutralise' (in the sanitised language of subsequent Security Council Resolutions) sources of instability and civilian insecurity, "it has not demonstrated an ability to harness the utility of force towards state consolidation." In other words, MINUSTAH's experiment with what Georg Sorensen (1992) once termed 'developmental violence' successfully disorganised and decapitated specific gangs but failed to uproot deeply embedded networks of hidden power, which have re-emerged with a vengeance in recent years and pushed Haiti – and Haitians – into an even darker and more dangerous place than in 2007. More generally, with some specific and controversial exceptions (notably the Force Intervention Brigade (FIB), discussed below), the success of MINUSTAH's war on armed gangs has not been replicated in other peacekeeping contexts, in part because of the nature of the adversaries that peacekeepers were confronting in Haiti (criminal gangs rather than more conventional rebel groups) and in part because of the perception that MINUSTAH forces strayed – even if their cause was just – into the murky terrain of peace enforcement, still widely considered to be a no-go zone for peace operations.

More generally, with regard to the deployment of armed force to protect civilians in the context of peace operations, the UN has spent the better part of the past two decades 'muddling through' the vast grey area between inertia and enforcement (Curran 2017). Three decades on from the Srebrenica and Rwanda debacles, PoC has taken hold as a clear centre of gravity for peace operations and is widely recognised as a core obligation of the UN; robust protection language has become common in both Security Council Resolutions and Secretariat policy guidance, providing a clear green light to peacekeepers to use lethal force when necessary to protect imperilled civilians. In practice, however, missions continue to struggle with the perennially vexed question of when and whether to take lives to save lives, and have often oscillated between innovation and initiative, on the one hand, and retrenchment and retreat on the other. Indeed, just over the past decade the policy debate on the subject has been notable for wide swings of tone and emphasis. While an internal UN report noted in 2014 that UN peacekeepers "almost never use force to protect civilians," by the second half of the decade many analysts were warning that the UN was beginning to lean too far in the direction of enforcement peacekeeping (Andersen 2018; Peter 2015; Karlsrud 2015; UN OIOS 2014). This trend reversed almost as quickly as it emerged, however, and we are currently witnessing what appears to be a full-scale retreat from the very idea of large, multidimensional missions capable of juggling both the short-term protection and long-term peacebuilding imperatives of early 21st-century peace operations. While over the short term the balance of influence appears to be with the forces of retrenchment, it would be premature to write off peacekeeping – either generally or as an instrument of civilian protection – especially in the context of an ongoing and troubling upsurge of armed conflict in recent years. Just as wars will remain a feature of the international system and just as civilians caught up in war will continue to be victimised, deliberately or inadvertently, so too is the debate over the appropriate role of outside actors in responding to both ongoing conflicts and the civilian suffering flowing from them likely to continue; those who wear UN blue are also likely to continue to be central figures in such debates.

In this chapter and the next, I locate shifting PoC practices within the context of two broad approaches to protection, coercive and non-coercive (or, drawing from the language of the HIPPO Report, armed and unarmed). This chapter examines the use of force debate as it has evolved in the context of UN peace operations in recent decades, with an eye on the extent to which the grey area noted above has been reduced and consensus reached on the specific conditions and circumstances in which peacekeepers are permitted – or indeed required – to deploy coercive force in the performance of their duties. To be clear, this debate has just as often revolved around stabilisation tasks as around protection ones, although as the Cité Soleil example suggests it is not always easy to distinguish between the two, especially as the former can usually be expected to contribute to the latter (if not necessarily vice versa). Following a brief excursion through some of the most important policy statements on use of force questions to emerge over the past two decades, I examine some of the key tensions and ongoing contradictions at the intersection of policy and practice that have led many observers to conclude that there remain 'certain inescapable limits' (Berdal 2018) on the ability of UN missions to constructively wield force in the name of peace. Despite some narrowing, many of these tensions remain fundamentally unresolved, and perhaps unresolvable, especially given the diversity of strongly held views on many of these issues found across the relevant components, and member states, of the UN system, which are if anything widening rather than narrowing over time. As a consequence, field-level commanders still enjoy (or perhaps suffer from) wide interpretive latitude in navigating perennially difficult use of force questions, and have continued – with some prominent exceptions – to demonstrate a strong tendency to err on the side of caution.

Protection Debates: Discord and Doctrine

The widely cited Brahimi Report (UN 2000) remains a key reference point for the ongoing effort to modernise peace operations for the realities of the 21st century, and it established some important markers in terms of both the moral imperatives and the practical limitations of force as an instrument of both peace and protection. Emerging as it did in the wake of the protection disasters of the mid-1990s, and at around the same time as the key pillars of the R2P doctrine were being elaborated, Brahimi – named after the Algerian diplomat who chaired the blue-ribbon panel that produced the report – was categorical in its insistence that uniformed UN peacekeepers, be they soldiers or police officers, who witness violence against civilians "should be presumed to be authorised to stop it, within their means, in support of basic United Nations principles" (UN 2000: x). While this authorisation was framed more in terms of a right than a responsibility or an obligation, the report also made it clear that the changing nature of conflict necessitated not only greater mandate specificality with regard to an operation's authority to use force, but also more robust force configurations and a greater willingness to confront 'would-be spoilers.' The ability to project credible force, in other words, was accepted as instrumental to the success of complex peacekeeping missions, even if it was also understood that peacekeepers cannot impose peace through force alone (UN 2000: viii). With respect to PoC in particular, the report flagged the reputational risks to the UN of making promises to vulnerable civilians in the full knowledge that protection demands would almost always outstrip supply. At the very least, it suggested, if an operation was given a PoC mandate, "it also must be given the specific resources to carry out that mandate" (UN 2000: x). At the other end of the use-of-force scale, the report was also eager to clearly delineate even robust forms of peacekeeping from enforcement-type operations: the United Nations, it insisted, 'does not wage war,' and in the circumstances where enforcement action was both justified and authorised, coalitions of the willing, rather than peace operations, should be charged with the heavy lifting (UN 2000: 10).

Some 15 years later, another blue-ribbon panel had another go at clarifying use of force questions in peacekeeping contexts. The report of the High-Level Independent Panel on Peace Operations (HIPPO) (UN 2015) – while insisting that the UN's bedrock peacekeeping principles should never be used to excuse failures to protect and flagging (again) the dangers of using peacekeepers for enforcement (as well as for counter-terrorism) purposes – also pushed back against the idea that in volatile contexts, the more robust a mission the greater the likelihood of success. The HIPPO Report's headline message centred, conversely, around 'the primacy of politics,' which was a reminder both that the UN's *raison d'être* in conflict environments was to encourage and facilitate peaceful solutions among conflict parties and that any use of force – whether for protection or stabilisation purposes – had to be linked explicitly to political solutions if it was to have any meaningful impact. Given the dangers – and the myriad potential unintended consequences – of resorting to deadly force in mandate implementation, the report was also careful to insist that coercive means should always be a last resort, and that "unarmed strategies must be at the forefront of UN efforts to protect civilians" (UN 2015: 37). As Louise Riis Andersen (2018) has argued, at its core the HIPPO Report can be read as a concerted effort to counter the trend towards the militarisation and 'robustification' of peacekeeping, and to reinforce some core premises, namely that peacekeepers were 'soldiers without enemies,' that peacekeeping forces should work with rather than against conflict parties and that the UN should always be seen as an enabler/convenor rather than as an enforcer/implementer.

Beyond the Brahimi and HIPPO Reports, both of which were preoccupied more with the strategic direction of peacekeeping than with the finer details of doctrine, and neither of which fully addressed the contradictions of either enforcement peacekeeping or robust PoC, recent years have also witnessed several other key interventions of direct relevance to use of force debates. Emerging at around the same time as the HIPPO Report, the 2015 Kigali Principles on the Protection of Civilians was a more focused effort, drawing on key troop- and financial-contributing countries (TCCs and FCCs), to clarify the specific modalities of PoC in peacekeeping contexts. In contrast to the HIPPO Report's caution, the 18 Kigali Principles collectively argued for a much less inhibited approach to PoC, with many of the articles aimed at clearing away obstacles – from command-and-control confusion to national caveats to equipment deficits – that prevented full actualisation of the 'all necessary means' imperative in PoC mandate implementation. As a call for troop contributors in particular to commit themselves to using force when and as necessary in the name of protection, the Kigali Principles proved divisive. They were never fully embraced by the UN at an institutional level, and while many prominent TCC's signed on to them, just as many – notably India, Pakistan, Nepal, Egypt and Indonesia – did not (Nadin 2018: 173). No less controversial was the so-called Cruz Report – from the Brazilian general of Cité Soleil fame – which was less about PoC and more about the security of peacekeepers themselves, but which struck a tone which discomfited many within the peacekeeping policy community. Calling out what he saw as an excessively cautious and risk-averse 'Chapter VI syndrome' both within the UN and among its key TCCs, Cruz advocated for a much more aggressive force posture on the part of peacekeeping contingents, including area domination and the use of overwhelming force, on the argument that "hostile forces do not understand a language other than force" (dos Santos Cruz et al. 2017: v, 11). While largely silent on PoC questions, the implication was clear: missions with PoC mandates should not hesitate to use the means at their disposal to neutralise or eliminate threats and should adopt whatever force postures were required to intimidate and deter armed groups, on the grounds that the best defence is a good offence.

Where many observers considered the sentiments around overwhelming or aggressive force expressed by the Cruz Report to be extreme and dangerously at odds with core peacekeeping principles (Ali Khalil 2018), the pendulum appeared to swing back in the opposite direction with Secretary General Antonio Guterres' 2018 Action for Peacekeeping (A4P) initiative. Meant to trigger 'a quantum leap' in collective engagement on the part of member states and to reaffirm their belief in peacekeeping's core value proposition, the A4P initiative, and in particular its Declaration of Shared Commitments, toed a very traditional line in its pursuit of the widest possible consensus among peacekeeping's core stakeholders. Indeed, out of respect for the sensitivities of China and Russia in particular, the Declaration's only reference to the use of force was a negative one, namely the reiteration of conventional peacekeeping doctrine proscribing the use of force except in self-defence or in defence of the mandate (Giffen 2018). On PoC, A4P similarly reiterates the established, differentially interpretable language of Security Council Resolutions, beginning with a boilerplate statement around host states bearing the primary responsibility for civilian protection. While the now-familiar concept of 'all necessary means' was included in the context of PoC, as Jake Sherman (2018: 4) noted at the time this formula seemed increasingly to represent a coded acknowledgement of the persistence of long-standing differences around the use of force, and of the UN's inability to transcend them. Ultimately, while A4P can be viewed in the context of ongoing efforts to strengthen the UN's broader peace and security architecture – efforts which culminated in 2019 in newly created Department of

Peace Operations (DPO) and Department of Political and Peacebuilding Affairs (DPPA) – field-level analysts such as Alison Giffen (2018) were left to wonder whether A4P signalled a retreat from core PoC commitments rather than a renewed resolve to effectively operationalise them.

In light of the persistent yet shifting dissensus at the point where protection of civilians and use of force questions intersect, one can sympathise with the unfortunate Secretariat staff tasked with translating PoC mandates into operational guidance for field-based missions. In each iteration of DPO's *Policy on the Protection of Civilians in United Nations Peacekeeping* (the latest of which was released in 2023), the central organising framework is a three-tiered action matrix. Within this matrix, the provision of physical protection (Tier II) is sandwiched between more conventional, less confrontational strategies ranging from dialogue and engagement with both conflict parties and conflict-affected communities (Tier I) to establishing a 'protective environment' (Tier III), which is shorthand for a set of activities – from security sector reform to anti-corruption efforts to democracy promotion – traditionally associated with peacebuilding. There is no inherent hierarchy or sequencing across the tiers, and each is meant to fit seamlessly with the others as part of a comprehensive, integrated approach "which takes into account and addresses the range of factors that influence and underpin threats to civilians in both the short- and long-term, including political, security and economic factors" (UN DPO 2023: 3). The difficulty with formulating PoC in these terms is much the same one that has bedevilled the operationalisation of the human security concept since its original elaboration: the definition is sufficiently capacious that it is difficult to imagine any activity undertaken by a peace operation that couldn't legitimately fall within one or more of the three tiers. To paraphrase a common criticism of the human security paradigm, if PoC is about everything, then effectively it is about nothing.

That said, it is still possible to distinguish protection responses according to whether the threats involved are proximate and immediate or structural and longer-term in nature, with the use of force being justifiable only in the former case. Tier II, then, is the most relevant in the context of use of force debates, including as it does "activities by uniformed components involving the show or use of force to prevent, deter, pre-empt and respond to threats to civilians" (UN DPO 2023: 12). The most precise guidance comes in para 52, in the context of peacekeepers encountering or responding to situations where physical violence against civilian populations is either 'imminent or in progress.' In such circumstances:

> the mission has a responsibility to act to the full extent of its capabilities by deploying rapidly to secure the civilian population, including through the dispatch of quick reaction forces. Peacekeepers must be ready at all times to act swiftly and decisively … with the full degree of force needed to protect civilians.
>
> (UN DPO 2023: 13)

Here, the guidance seems to rest on relatively safe ground, as the language does little more than update the Brahimi Report's conclusion, that peacekeepers encountering violence against civilians "should be presumed to be authorized to stop it," from a right to a responsibility. More controversial is the guidance around the pre-emptive measures that missions 'must' take in response to concrete and verified threats against civilians, which can run the gamut from reinforced presence and patrolling to 'neutralising' the source of the threat in accordance with the mission mandate (para 51). As Hanna Bourgeois and Patryk Labuda (2022: 62) have argued, in the context of the obligations of peacekeepers to respect human rights law (HRL) the notion of 'imminence' carries considerable weight. HRL, as they note, "imposes strict temporal conditions of imminence for any use of intentional lethal force in self-defence or the defence of civilians," and thus the use of force to 'take out' threatening groups before their threats become manifest may represent violations of the relevant legal regime to which the UN is technically bound (Bourgeois and Labuda 2022: 62; Gilder 2023: 344).

Beyond such legal considerations, however significant, the bulk of the Tier II guidance, which emphasises both the immediate stopping power of uniformed UN elements in reaction to imminent threats or unfolding atrocities as well as the range of actions available to missions to help vulnerable civilians get out of harm's way, leans heavily in the direction of what might be termed 'defensive PoC.' Consistent with the widespread sensitivity across the UN system concerning the risks and perils of enforcement peacekeeping, in other words, as outlined in the 2023 guidelines even robust PoC lays far more emphasis on addressing the downstream consequences of violence against civilians in conflict consequences than on addressing its upstream sources. Harm mitigation, in this sense, can be achieved not only through the mission's own efforts to 'do no harm' – either directly or indirectly – in pursuit of its mandate, but also through defensive interpositioning (between the threatening and the threatened), through the use of UN bases and facilities to shelter civilians fleeing violence (as with the UN's PoC sites in South Sudan) and through protective accompaniment measures to ensure the safe movement of displaced civilians while in transit (UN DPO 2023: 14–16).

While it lays out the full suite of actions that a mission may, should, or must contemplate in order to fulfil mandated PoC obligations, it is also clear that missions – and the military contingents expected to deliver on the robust element of PoC – still possess enormous discretion by virtue of the fact that the range of real and potential threats to civilians in contemporary conflict contexts will always outstrip the capacities of missions to respond to or pre-empt such threats. In this sense, standard mandate caveats limiting a mission's PoC obligations to those "within its capacity and areas of deployment" provide a relatively high degree of plausible deniability for all but the most egregious failures to protect (Donais and Tanguay 2021: 568). It is also the case that while the guidelines acknowledge some of the fundamental tensions that missions must navigate given sweeping and often contradictory mandate imperatives, they provide little concrete direction in terms of how they might be overcome. To take just the most dramatic example, while missions are expected to fulfil their protection obligations regardless of the source of the threat, "it is recognized that a robust response to threats posed by the host state may be beyond the mission's capabilities, may result in insecurity for peacekeepers and can affect the host state's strategic consent for the mission" (UN DPO 2023: 14). Given the extent to which this issue has both plagued and blighted protection efforts across all three of the cases discussed in subsequent chapters, the suggestion that missions might overcome the problem by encouraging better behaviour on the part of state security forces, while being prepared to intervene physically if necessary, comes across as not especially helpful (UNDPO 2023: 14).

Ultimately, then, high-level debates and headquarters-level guidance reveal not only deep and ongoing discord across the UN system on use of force questions, but also the inherent limits of *any* policy meant to equip field-level actors with context-specific direction in the fluid, chaotic and information-poor environments in which peace operations function. While guidance and mandates can, to some extent, hope to shape and frame peacekeeper dispositions, they can never anticipate every potential use-of-force scenario or the myriad consequences – positive or negative – that might flow from a decision to deploy lethal force. It is also the case, moreover, that the UN, and specifically its peace and security infrastructure, operates in ways that depart significantly from any rational-bureaucratic ideal. The institutional configuration of UN peace operations has long precluded the establishment of straightforward hierarchies, with clear chains of command and tasking flowing seamlessly from the top-down and clear lines of accountability flowing from the bottom-up. The broad, ambiguity-laden and sometimes contradictory direction emanating from the centre, combined with the reality that those who bear the brunt of the expectation to deploy force in the name of civilian protection – a mission's military contingents – represent the full spectrum of human diversity, with different military and political cultures, different levels of training and equipment, different risk tolerances, different understandings of their roles and responsibilities as peacekeepers, and different conceptions of the 'to whom' and 'for what' of accountability, means that a field-level perspective is essential in order to generate an accurate depiction of how use of force questions have been answered in recent years, and why. For while it may be possible to sustain ambiguity and discord at the doctrinal level – indeed, this is a crucial part of the skill set of successful bureaucrats, diplomats and mediators – ambiguity, uncertainty, and dissensus inhibit clear, concerted and consistent practice at the operational level (Blyth and Cammaert 2016: 325). Faced with the prospect of having to make life-and-death decisions within extremely narrow timeframes and limited contextual understandings, professional soldiers have long fallen back on their training to provide them with an almost instinctual sense of the particular actions required at particular moments; in PoC scenarios, it remains far from clear that any such clarity – let alone automaticity – yet exists in terms of knowing how to fulfil one's protection obligations. With regard to this specific issue, then, it is fair to characterise UN peace operations as more 'disintegrated' than integrated, with the consequence being that robust approaches to PoC have been applied unevenly or selectively at best and incoherently and haphazardly at worst. In what follows, I elaborate further on some of the core tensions and constraints that lie at the heart of field-level decision-making around the use of force for protection purposes.

Risk Tolerance and Cost-Benefit Analysis

In 2005, with the international peace and security architecture very much still in flux and grappling in particular with the implications of the ongoing US-led war on terror, Tom Woodhouse and Oliver Ramsbotham – in an article in *International Peacekeeping* – laid out a transformative vision for peacekeeping centred squarely on cosmopolitan ideas. Theirs was essentially a thought experiment, which asked what it would take to transform the UN from a creature of an unreconstructed system of sovereign states, dominated by state interests, into a genuine agent of cosmopolitan values, "centred on protecting civilians from violent conflict and on furthering the human security agenda to which the UN is committed" (2005: 142). While fully cognisant of the risks, and the paradoxes, of attempting to harness greater military robustness behind a genuinely cosmopolitan project prioritising the interests of vulnerable human populations ahead of those of powerful states, Woodhouse and Ramsbotham contemplated a range of potential mechanisms – including a UN Emergency Peace Service – through which their vision of cosmopolitan peacekeeping could be actualised. At the heart of this vision was an attempt to find a way to sever the link, in the minds of those tasked with making peacekeeping work, between serving the UN and advancing the national interests of their own states.

Two decades on, not much has become of this cosmopolitan project, but the central paradox that it grapples with – one which has left the UN as a whole underpowered as an agent of both human security and civilian protection – remains crucial to understanding the challenges of translating the good intentions of PoC policy into effective practice at the level where it matters most. This is the same paradox observed by Thierry Tardy (2007), who has written of the UN's dual nature, characterised by persistent tension between the liberal values that animate the system's human rights, peace and development ambitions and the system's realist, state-centric political foundations, themselves premised on the assumption that the system's key constituent components will put their sovereign self-interests above all else. Framed in slightly different terms, much of the UN's entire peace and security *problématique* can be captured by the metaphor of a perennial tug-of-war between human security and state security; peace operations, as Tardy notes (2007: 50), are at the heart of this conceptual tension, as are the dilemmas of protecting civilians through force of arms. Ultimately, the armed forces of TCCs may serve the UN, but they simultaneously serve their own nation, and in case of emergency there is usually little question where their ultimate loyalties lie. As Tardy notes, since the military components of mandates are implemented by the armed forces of member states, "it is these same states who define the use that may be made of their forces, and what is possible, or not, in the domain of the use of force" (2007: 58).

It is thus a truism that the application of force in the context of UN peace operations can never be fully divorced from the interests of those that employ such force, especially given the life-and-death stakes involved (Nadin 2018: 174). As prominent as it may be in mandate language, the protection and preservation of civilian life in conflict contexts is far from the only consideration in the minds of commanders when weighing use of force decisions. While it may be the case, as the Cruz Report argued, that a willingness to project credible force may over the longer term have a protective impact by convincing conflict parties that UN forces are not to be trifled with, in the immediate term the consequences of use of force decisions are inherently difficult to predict or control. Even though soldiers in principle sign up knowing they will be asked to put their lives on the line, action taken to save civilian lives must also be weighed against the risks that lives of personnel may also be lost as a consequence of such action. While such risks may be weighed differently in contexts where important national interests are at stake – Canadians, for example, by and large accepted the limited loss of Canadian soldiers in Afghanistan on the grounds that they were fighting for a just and important cause – the calculation may be entirely different in peacekeeping contexts, where sacrificing the lives of personnel in the name of cosmopolitan values such as PoC might be harder to defend on the grounds of national interest. Patrick Cammaert, a retired Dutch major general who led UN forces across a range of missions, recalls receiving strict orders from his political superiors prior to one deployment to avoid even a single Dutch casualty (*The Economist* 2021).

The reality of risk-aversion tends to be more lamented than analysed in the context of PoC mandates, even though the potential risks involved go well beyond what might be expected in more traditional peacekeeping contexts. Operating in conflict and post-conflict environments is of course an inherently risky proposition – more than 4,000 peacekeepers have been killed in the line of duty since 1948 – but heightened prospects of armed confrontation with conflict parties have revealed a very wide range of views across TCCs concerning the risk thresholds they consider acceptable. As one former SRSG has noted, while risk-averse contingents are a reality with which every peace operation must contend, the imperatives of force-generation often lead the UN to downplay the risks involved in any particular mission in order to not discourage potential contributors. As a consequence, "when robust operations have been required, contingents have responded by saying that they had not signed up for such operations and were not equipped to undertake them" (cited in Berdal 2018: 738).

Given the outsized impact that prominent protection failures have on relations between peacekeepers and peacekept – massacres such as the one that unfolded in November 2008 in the eastern Congolese town of Kiwanja, less than a kilometre from a UN base, very quickly deplete any reserves of goodwill that a mission may have built up with local communities – there's merit to unpacking the rationales of such failures to protect with force. While national stereotyping is prevalent within the UN system no less than in any other large institutional environment, there is no *a priori* reason to attribute failures to protect to simple cowardice, or to believe that the balance between courage and cowardice among either individuals or groups should be a function of either culture or geography. While the psychology of individual commanders clearly matters, a wide range of additional factors feeds into the willingness of national contingents to contemplate lethal force in the name of PoC, including training and doctrine – still far more determined by national militaries than by UN policies – as well as equipment and logistics. The rather dramatic shift in recent decades towards the Global South as the source of uniformed peacekeepers has had a discernible impact not only on the quality of soldiers and equipment available to contingents but also on the availability of key supports such as medical and medevac capacity; ill-equipped and poorly trained contingents and those lacking robust 'back-office' supports, all things considered, are more likely to be risk-averse. In the case of Kiwanja, all these factors and more played a role in the non-response to the massacre. As a Human Rights Watch report on the incident reported, the UN force based in the town was outnumbered and underpowered relative to the rebel threat, divided between two different national units of command, lacking intelligence or even interpreters to facilitate real-time communicate with the local population, and preoccupied with ongoing efforts to protect non-Congolese, including an abducted foreign journalist and dangerously exposed humanitarian workers (HRW 2008: 22–26).

At the same time, for all the emphasis on spontaneous, in-the-moment failures to protect, many of the key impediments to more robust peacekeeping are institutional in nature, in the form of national caveats that troop contributors place on what their forces can and cannot do – such as limiting activities to daylight hours only – as a condition of deployment. Such caveats persist, in part because the demand for peacekeepers continues to outstrip supply, despite an ongoing campaign to eliminate them. In some cases, the insistence on the part of commanders that use of force decisions be signed off by senior authorities in their respective national capitals (a caveat which might be either explicit, hidden, or invented on the spot) means that by the time approvals have been sought and granted, the opportunity to respond effectively has passed and the damage – in terms of lives lost – has been done (*The Economist* 2021). While more difficult to demonstrate empirically, there are also widespread suspicions – not least among those who have sought UN protection – that use of force decisions are often dictated by the strategic interests of the troop-contributing country. In the case of the attacks by government forces on PoC sites in South Sudan in 2016, for example, a widespread view among site residents was that the poor protection performance of Chinese peacekeepers had much to do with China's emerging economic partnership with the Government of South Sudan;[1] a military confrontation in this context would have been diplomatically awkward.

TCC interests can push in the opposite direction as well. The establishment of the FIB as a component of the MONUSCO operation in the DRC – which took the UN well into the no-man's-land of peace enforcement by authorising offensive operations aimed at neutralising named armed groups, including the notorious M23 – had much to do with the strategic calculations of the regional countries willing to contribute to the FIB. As Mats Berdal has noted (2018: 737), South Africa and Tanzania in particular were concerned about the growing threat posed by the Rwandan-backed M23, and saw the FIB primarily as a mechanism to rein in Rwanda's strategic meddling in the eastern DRC. Once the M23 was defeated – temporarily, as it turned out – the FIB quickly lost interest in taking on the other armed groups it was tasked with neutralising (Tull 2018: 178). As Jenna Russo (2021: 3077) concluded in an analysis of the track record of militarised peacekeeping in the DRC, while PoC might be 'at the top of the Christmas tree' in the MONUSCO mandate, "the same is not true for regional troop contributors, whose focus centres on mitigating threats to state security."

Short-Term Protection vs. Long-Term Peacebuilding

The second key tension speaks to the very purpose of contemporary peacekeeping, and concerns whether the emergence of PoC as the headline mandate task of the UN's most important missions has displaced – or even replaced – peacekeeping's original rationale of creating the necessary political space within which the parties to the conflict can arrive at peaceful negotiated settlements. This was, as noted above, a central preoccupation of the HIPPO Report, whose 'primacy of politics' message was at least in part a call to not lose sight of the reality that protecting civilians – however noble – can never be an effective substitute for sustained efforts at conflict resolution (Berdal 2018). At its core, this tension revolves around the question of whether peace operations should seek to address the consequences or the causes of armed conflict, or whether they can in fact do both simultaneously. While the costs of failing to respond forcefully to ongoing or imminent attacks against civilians are now clear, it is also the case that any sustainable exit strategy remains fundamentally dependent not only on a dramatic reduction – if not termination – of armed conflict but also on a coherent strategy for transferring protection responsibilities to the host state, where they rightfully belong. Thus, while forceful interventions to prevent or stop atrocities against civilians represent one end of the PoC spectrum, at the other end are longer term institutional reforms more conventionally associated with peacebuilding and state-building, from security sector reform to rule of law promotion and from the strengthening of human rights mechanisms to the establishment of viable power-sharing formulas.

Fully coming to terms with these short-term/long-term dynamics also means grappling with the concept of 'stabilisation' as it applies to contemporary peace operations. Despite having crept into the mandates, and the titles, of a significant number of peace operations since the turn of the millennium, there is no universally agreed understanding of what stabilisation actually means, or what precisely it implies for the day-to-day work of peacekeepers. Unofficially, however, as Jenna Russo (2021: 3072) has noted, stabilisation

> is generally understood as an approach or a set of activities taking place prior to the full consolidation of peace, comprising a robust force posture, including a willingness to use force to neutralize non-state armed groups and protect civilians, and a focus on bolstering state authority.

It is this latter focus, and in particular its association with the notion of 'extending state authority,' that has raised especially thorny issues for UN missions. On the one hand, the idea of helping state institutions to extend the depth and breadth of their authority is simply a reassertion of the liberal peacebuilding paradigm's insistence that a capable and legitimate state is a necessary requirement for sustainable peacebuilding, in addition to being vital to any viable mission exit strategy.

On the other, however, in the increasingly common absence of credible and inclusive peace agreements within which peacebuilding processes can be grounded, efforts to support state authorities – and especially state security actors – look suspiciously like efforts to support one party to an ongoing conflict at the expense of others, casting serious doubt on the UN's ability to stake out a role for itself as an impartial facilitator.

At the same time, stabilisation and PoC priorities – the two key issue areas where use of force is contemplated by contemporary peace operations – often clash in circumstances where the greatest threats to civilians come from precisely those government forces working to extend, with UN support, the authority of the state. As a means of mitigating such tensions, in 2013 the UN implemented its Human Rights Due Diligence Policy (HRDDP) to guard against the risk that the provision of UN support to non-UN security forces would contribute directly to human rights violations. Despite the good intentions of the HRDDP, however, it remains the case that field-level personnel expected to be both enablers and watchdogs of host-state security actors all too often find themselves in untenable situations (Hirschmann 2020). Given the additional reality that the host state remains not only a party to the conflict but also a veto-holder over the mission's continued presence on its sovereign territory – as the UN was reminded when its MINUSMA mission was evicted from Mali – is perhaps unsurprising that missions are often paralysed by the ambiguities inherent in their role, and default to privileging good relations with the host government over protecting civilians when forced to choose between the two. This has certainly been the case in the DRC, where MONUSCO has been tainted by its association with the Congolese armed forces and their all-too-frequent disregard for the principles of human rights and humanitarian law, and has been forced to tread very carefully as relations with the host government have deteriorated in recent years (de Vries 2015). In the neighbouring Central African Republic (CAR), where a military counter-offensive against an armed rebellion following controversial presidential elections in late 2020 – a campaign in which military 'trainers' from Russia's notorious Wagner Group were deeply implicated – left considerable civilian suffering in its wake, the response from the MINUSCA mission was limited to reporting on human rights abuses (Druet 2023). As elsewhere, numerous factors played a role in the weak response – including COVID lockdowns, government moves to restrict the mission's freedom of movement and a reluctance to be drawn into conflict with forces associated with a permanent member of the UN Security Council – but it nevertheless reinforced the impression that at the crucial junction where PoC, use of force and stabilisation policies intersect, not all conflict parties are treated equally by UN peace operations.

If stabilisation policies have all too often let state security forces off the hook for civilian abuses, serious questions have also been raised about the utility of military operations against non-state security actors absent a clear and direct connection to a broader political strategy. To return to the case of the FIB, Dennis Tull (2018) has made a compelling case that the pursuit of a military solution to the problems posed by armed groups such as the M23 directly undermined ongoing peacebuilding efforts in the eastern DRC. As Tull notes, when the M23 captured Goma in late

2012 it forced a weakened Congolese government to negotiate the Peace, Security and Cooperation Framework (PSCF), which involved national, regional and international players and committed the government to substantial reforms aimed at addressing dysfunction within key state institutions. Once the FIB's creation raised the possibility of resolving the M23 issue by military means, and without requiring difficult compromises on the part of the government, the latter quickly lost interest in PSCF implementation. In this sense, then, it is difficult to avoid the conclusion that "the FIB sounded the death knell to PSCF, which has been the single most important political and diplomatic framework for peace in Congo and the region over the past decade" (Tull 2018: 181).

More generally, peacekeeping traditionalists have long feared that the UN's well-established third-party role in conflict-affected environments – deploying its 'good offices' in support of peaceful negotiated outcomes – may be jeopardised if the use of force comes to occupy more than a niche role in UN peacekeeping practice. John Karlsrud, for one, has argued that the kinds of political considerations that produced the FIB, and which were for a period at least pushing UN peacekeeping in more robust directions, were burdening the UN with tasks for which it was not designed and which would, over the longer term, "have grave consequences, undermining the general acceptance of UN peacekeeping operations as a tool to help states emerging from conflict" (2015: 50). Regardless of the doctrinal gymnastics involved in redefining impartiality to include forceful, proactive interventions in defence of the mandate, such definitional nuances are very likely to be lost on conflict parties who find themselves on the receiving end of live fire from peacekeeping contingents. Not only is the risk of retaliation real – with mission staff and UN agencies more generally increasingly considered fair game by armed groups on the receiving end of robust tactics – but armed groups in such circumstances are also likely to treat with considerable scepticism any effort, by any part of the UN, to subsequently offer itself up as an honest broker in future peace negotiations. As more than one analyst has underlined, the paradoxes involved in peace operations trying to make war and peace simultaneously are legion.

One possible – if somewhat discouraging – rejoinder to the argument that the more peacekeepers are expected to use force in implementing their mandates the less credibility the UN has an impartial arbitrator in conflict contexts is that the UN's influence in the latter area has been on the wane for some time now, making the trade-offs less acute that they may initially appear. Especially across the big four African missions – DRC, Mali, South Sudan and CAR – not only has the proliferation of conflict parties, the intransigence of host governments and the often-unhelpful interventions of neighbouring powers meant that peace agreements have been difficult to negotiate and impossible to sustain, but increasingly the UN has been shunted to the margins of the political process. For better or worse, this ground has been increasingly ceded to regional and subregional organisations and processes – the Intergovernmental Authority on Development (IGAD) in South Sudan, for example – and reconnecting UN field operations to the central enterprise of mediation and conflict resolution is a challenge that goes well beyond any real or imagined trade-offs with robust peacekeeping strategies (Berdal 2018). Indeed, rather than the one coming at the expense of the other it may be just as credible to view robust peacekeeping – with PoC at its heart – as an alternative legitimation strategy for an organisation increasingly hard-pressed to justify its presence in conflict contexts by virtue of the unique role that it plays in shepherding conflict-affected societies towards sustainable peace. While the DRC might be an extreme case, it is increasingly difficult to make the argument – 25 years after peacekeepers first deployed – that MONUSCO's continued presence in the region can be justified on the basis of its track record as a peacemaker.

In light of the foregoing, one increasingly common theme in the peacekeeping literature concerns the questionable utility of military operations absent a clear and direct connection to a broader political strategy. There are, however, several problems with the argument that any use of force in a peacekeeping context must be embedded within a broader political roadmap. First, as hinted at above, while 'the primacy of politics' may be a catchy slogan, it is not at all clear what it means in the context of the ongoing decline in the UN's diplomatic influence at the level of peacemaking and conflict resolution. Even were the UN to regain its role and reputation in this area, it is undeniable that what Gowan and Stedman (2018) have termed 'the standard treatment' for civil wars – negotiating settlements, building state capacity, implementing transitional justice and deploying multidimensional operations involving both security forces and civilian experts – is no longer working. The primacy of politics, in other words, remains little more than an empty catchphrase absent reconsideration of a seriously underperforming peacebuilding template emphasising the deconstruction of armed non-state actors and the reconstruction of state authority based on Weberian ideals about monopolies on the legitimate use of force. Second, current UN doctrine around the use of force has quite explicitly established a firewall between the tactical and strategic levels, in part to allow a doctrinal distinction to be sustained between the strategic uses of force (presumed to violate conventional principles of consent) and tactical use of force (presumed not to violate consent). While this distinction is blurred within the DPO's own PoC guidance, it is laid out clearly in the UN's Capstone Doctrine, which defines robust peacekeeping as involving "the use of force at the tactical level with the consent of the host authorities and/or the main parties to the conflict" (UN 2008: 19). This emphasis on keeping robust measures strictly bounded in terms of time and space, focused on specific and containable threats, and within limits acceptable to the main conflict parties, was reiterated in a 2010 concept note discussed as part of the General Assembly's Special Committee on Peacekeeping Operations (cited in Karlsrud 2015: 43). At least in principle, then, this distinction between the strategic and the tactical would suggest that while the use of force might be permissible to halt or avert attacks against civilians, employment of coercive force is far more questionable as part of a broader strategy to alter the strategic calculations of conflict parties (Nadin 2018). In this sense, then, closely linking the use of force with long-term strategic thinking appears to violate the UN's own peacekeeping doctrine. Finally, in PoC contexts it remains far from clear that responding to attacks against civilians can always be – or need always be – coherently linked to a broader political strategy for conflict transformation. In other words, the particular contexts in which peacekeepers operate may often force them into firefighting mode, responding to the most urgent crises – à la the concept of protection through projection – without necessarily linking such short-term actions to broader strategic considerations. While it may be the case, as Thierry Tardy (2007: 59) has noted, that "one of the basic principles of the use of armed forces is its inscription in a political framework," the frequent disconnect between political strategy and use of force decisions within peace operations may have more to do with the particular tasks that peacekeepers are asked to undertake than with a generalised failure of strategic planning on the part of the UN.

Mandates vs. Resources

A third fundamental tension around use of force questions in contemporary peace operations concerns the persistent gap between what UN forces are expected to do and the resources available to them. While this is a persistent theme in development and peace work more generally, it is particularly pertinent in contexts where peacekeepers are expected to stand and fight, for whatever reason. In this sense, the contrast between the UN's responses in Srebrenica and in Cité Soleil can be understood not only as a product of institutional learning but also as a relative power calculus; the outnumbered and outgunned Dutch contingent in eastern Bosnia faced a quantitatively and qualitatively different challenge than Brazilian-led forces in Haiti, who had the benefit of superior firepower, better organisation and stronger numbers than the gangs they were confronting. All else being equal, therefore, the willingness to use robust means in peacekeeping contexts is directly linked to the extent to which the relevant actors possess proportionately robust capacities in order to allow them to achieve objectives while keeping risk within tolerable limits.

While this issue was raised above in the context of contingent-level risk tolerance, it also applies more generally to both the capacity and the will of UN peace operations to use force for protection purposes. For all the vigorous debate over the past several decades about the appropriate role of coercive force in the context of peace operations, serious concerns persist about whether the UN is, or will ever be, "structurally equipped and politically suited to take on a *coercive* role in internal conflicts and civil-war-like situations" (Berdal 2018: 723). As Eric Tanguay and I have written elsewhere (2020: 73), just as the A4P initiative was launched as a means of making peacekeeping 'fit for the future,' downward budgetary pressures led by key member states, including the United States, were forcing existing missions to fit into shrinking budgetary envelopes. Despite the HIPPO Report's warning in 2015 that many missions with PoC responsibilities were already severely under-resourced, and the Brahimi Report's much earlier concern about matching mandates and resources, the UN's overall peacekeeping budget shrunk from US$8.27 billion in 2015–2016 to US$6.1 billion in 2023–2024. While the raw numbers don't account for the fact that a number of missions have been shuttered during this period, they also don't account for the significant impact of ongoing peacekeeping arrears – withheld portions of assessed national contributions that have created serious cash-flow headaches and play out in delayed reimbursements to TCCs, which can undercut the capacity of mission contingents in the field.

Ultimately, then, robust forms of PoC are very difficult to square with austerity peacekeeping, and in the field the effects on operations have been palpable, despite the UN's avowed commitments to making peace operations more 'field-focused.' In the DRC, where budget cuts forced the mission to shift from presence-focused protection to an emphasis on 'projection,' the fact that cuts also impacted aviation assets – at one point MONUSCO's helicopter contingent was capable of flying no more than an hour a day – led at least one mission official to wonder whether the mission was being set up for failure (Carver 2018; Spink 2018: 13). In the case of MINUSCA, the thinly stretched nature of the mission's military assets meant that when the mission's 450-strong Gabonese contingent was repatriated in late 2021, after failing to take seriously allegations of sexual abuse and exploitation within its ranks, the mission struggled to find the resources to cover the contingent's area of responsibility, which included some of the country's most insecure areas.[2] More generally, as Severine Autesserre has noted (2019), across the full range of UN missions the reality of too few people on the ground "makes it difficult for the UN to even scratch the surface of its mandates."

Peacekeeping's chronic mandate-resource gap has also been central to ongoing debates about improving performance and increasing accountability within peace operations. While both issues are fraught – performance questions are difficult to separate from the deeply contested issue of how success and failure should be defined in peacekeeping contexts, while efforts to improve accountability cannot avoid grappling with the myriad and overlapping lines of authority that are a feature of any peace operation – they have come increasingly to the fore in recent years both in the context of long-standing claims about peacekeeping's 'inefficiency' and in the context of efforts to squeeze greater outputs from peacekeepers without a commensurate increase in inputs. Such questions are even more sensitive given the regionalised division of labour that has become more prominent in recent decades *vis-à-vis* peacekeeping: more than ever, the peacekeeping universe is segregated – in ways that inhibit rather than encourage unity of purpose – among those countries who set peacekeeping budgets, those who establish mandates and those expected to implement them. While important FCCs – overwhelmingly countries from the Global North who at present contribute few front-line personnel to peace operations – push for missions to deliver better value for money, including on PoC, important TCCs – now overwhelmingly represented by countries from the Global South – have grown palpably more frustrated not only by what are perceived to be presumptions of indolence and/or incompetence that underpin such demands, but also by the expectations that they expose their own personnel to risks that their counterparts in the Global North no longer seem willing to countenance (Karlsrud 2015: 50). As the representative of Côte d'Ivoire noted during a 2018 Security Council debate, echoing the frustration felt by many troop contributors, "without the right resources and skills to match their operational environment, it is difficult for contingents to discharge their mandated tasks. We cannot ask for more to be done with less" (UN 2018: 10).

Conclusion

For the better part of the past several decades, the protection of civilians debate has occupied centre stage in discussions around peacekeeping reform. Beyond a baseline agreement that peacekeepers must never again stand idly by as civilians are slaughtered, though, achieving a clear consensus on the meanings of protection and on the expectations and obligations that PoC places on front-line peacekeepers has been elusive. As Alexander Gilder (2023: 318) has noted:

> Those exploring PoC policies for the first time would be forgiven for thinking the UN has crafted a detailed framework, well-grounded in international law, that provides precise mechanisms for *how* and *when* peacekeeping personnel should protect civilians that, in turn, are easily operationalized by forces in the field. This is not the case.

Unlike non-coercive protection mechanisms (the focus of the next chapter), where the key questions surround not whether they are legitimate but whether they are effective, the key controversies surrounding coercive or robust protection strategies surround both efficacy and legitimacy. On the one hand, as Bellamy and Hunt (2021: 143) note, "there is clear evidence that robust peacekeeping operations can improve the protection of civilians," even if this is difficult in practice and can produce unintended negative consequences. While many of these negative consequences are not inconsequential, in circumstances where atrocities against civilians are imminent or in progress, there is a strong case to be made that, where possible, a robust response by a capable and determined peacekeeping contingent is the only viable defence against mass slaughter. Even a willingness to respond with graduated force provides contingent commanders with considerable leverage over the cost-benefit calculations of attackers: all but the most determined will reconsider assaults on civilian populations if they must first fight their way through a robust UN defence (Donais and Tanguay 2021: 570).

As noted above, however, efficacy is a slippery concept in the context of peace operations, and while it might be self-evident that the counter-application of force represents the only effective response to a murderous rampage – just as few question the use of deadly force as a means of neutralising school shooters in the United States – in conflict contexts the use of force can reverberate in unpredictable ways. Unlike the school shooter example, peacekeepers are locked into longer-term, iterative relationships with those conflict parties whose behaviour they seek to impact: robust protection efforts in one locality might render civilians elsewhere – where no peacekeepers are present – more vulnerable, in the same way that civilians may find themselves saved one day only to be re-victimised the next, after peacekeepers have moved on to the next hotspot. The effects of violence, however much practitioners might attempt to mete it out in precise, calibrated doses, almost always generate consequences that are difficult to predict or control, whether in terms of relations with a host state, altering cost-benefit calculations of key conflict actors *vis-à-vis* the pursuit of negotiated solutions, or incentivising retaliatory strategies. Robustness, as the Cruz Report argued, may also have salutary deterrent effects in conflict contexts – making conflict parties themselves re-calculate the utility of aggression against either civilians or peacekeepers. In the volatile contexts of contemporary conflict – in which a proliferation of armed actors has become more the norm than the exception – it remains difficult to draw clear empirical conclusions about the utility of force by peacekeepers based on the existing evidentiary base.

Regarding legitimacy, 25 years after the first PoC mandate was inserted into a mission-specific Security Council Resolution, "the use of force remains the most controversial and problematic of all the UN's peacekeeping instruments" (Nadin 2018: 173), in large part because it throws into question the very purpose and identity of peacekeeping. The holy trinity of peacekeeping principles – consent of the parties, impartiality and non-use of force except in self-defence or defence of the mandate – cannot easily be reconciled with robust peacekeeping, and UN member states, peacekeeping scholars and professional staff across the UN system remain deeply divided on the place of coercive force in contemporary peace operations. And despite considerable experimentation and innovation across different missions in recent decades, fundamental tensions persist around whether the core priority of peacekeepers should be to shield civilians from the consequences of conflict, or to work with conflict parties in search of durable peace; to suggest that there are not quite often difficult trade-offs between these two competing priorities is disingenuous. Indeed, it is precisely at the point where a commander must give orders to open fire on advancing armed groups that such tensions become most apparent, and where questions about the fundamental purpose of peacekeeping must be answered. At an open Security Council debate in 2014, the Permanent Representative of India clearly specified the dilemma as he described the choices faced by a small contingent of Indian peacekeepers in 2013, when the displaced civilians they were protecting at their base in South Sudan were under threat from an advancing column of some 2,000 armed youth:

> The 40 Indian peacekeepers were heavily outnumbered. They had superior fire power and a robust mandate which would have allowed them to use force, not just in self-defence, but also in defence of the mission. Had they opened fire, hundreds of lives would have been lost. Would those lives have been civilian or combatant? And the troops who availed their superior firepower, would they have been peacekeepers or war makers?
>
> (cited in Blyth and Cammaert 2016: 315)

One can sympathise with the commander's dilemma in this case. Not only was he forced to decide under enormous pressure between peacekeeping and war-making, he also had to contemplate the potential unintended consequence of his decisions (or non-decisions) and perform a mental calculus concerning the relative balance of lives taken, lives saved and lives sacrificed. The irony, of course, is that this situation represented among the most clear-cut and least-ambiguous scenarios that field-level commanders can encounter. The hostile intent of the armed youth was clear (even if they more closely resembled an angry mob than an organised 'party to the conflict'), and the fact that the civilians were sheltering at the UN base meant there could be no doubt as the contingent's protection responsibilities. At the same time, the balance of power (if not numbers) favoured the Indians, and there was therefore also no question as to the peacekeepers' capacity to protect. Ultimately, according to the preliminary incident report by UNMISS, peacekeepers came under sustained attack "while trying to open negotiations with the assailants," and by the time the base was secured two peacekeepers and at least 20 of the displaced civilians were dead (UNMISS 2013).

It is of course impossible to know whether a decisive demonstration of firepower on the part of the Indians would have pre-empted the subsequent violence or triggered a bloodbath, and armchair analysts can disagree about whether the failure to respond in a robust manner represented a dereliction of duty or a defensible effort "to resolve the situation by other means" (UN DPO 2023: 13). Indeed, it is precisely this type of scenario that has prompted Alexander Gilder to argue that it is time to move beyond generalised articulations of peacekeeper responsibilities towards the development of a "narrow and easily communicated minimum obligation to be placed on peacekeepers," especially with regard to the obligation to use force to protect civilians in situations of imminent violence (Gilder 2023: 317). Not only would establishing such minimum baselines inject some important clarity into use of force debates, moving beyond the current amorphous policy of 'doing what we can with what we have where we are able,' it would also lay out clear red lines about the kinds of actions that would automatically trigger a robust response on the part of peacekeepers. Such clarity could be useful for civilians, for whom the UN remains a fickle, unreliable and unpredictable protector, no less than for combatants, who would presumably be incentivised to remain on the safe side of any red line.

As desirable as it might be to impose a minimal legal obligation on peacekeepers to use the coercive means at their disposal in certain specified situations of imminent threat, not least in terms of harmonised responses across diverse national contingents and reducing indeterminacy and unpredictability in the way PoC mandates are operationalised, there is little indication at present of any clear motivation on the part of the peacekeeping establishment to move in this direction. Making certain actions obligatory in certain situations may have upsides in terms of predictability and consistency, but these must be weighed against the downsides of reducing flexibility and the ability to engage in real-time problem solving on the part of field-level decision-makers. Tying the hands of field-level commanders in this way might ultimately result in more rigid and less contextually sensitive decision-making, with worse protection outcomes in the end. At the same time, the idea of 'minimum legal obligations' also implies that those entrusted with fulfilling such obligations can and will be held accountable for their actions. Accountability is a deeply fraught question with regard to PoC, and one of the few attempts to hold an individual accountable for command-level failures to protect – the sacking of the Kenyan force commander of UNMISS in the aftermath of the 2016 Juba crisis – prompted a vigorous diplomatic backlash on the part of the Government of Kenya. More generally, accountability questions in the context of PoC raise thorny questions about the practicability of holding individuals accountable for acts of omission – for failures to act rather than for specific actions contrary to laws or regulations. Given the struggles of the UN to date to hold individual peacekeepers accountable for acts of commission, and specifically for the kinds of sexual abuse and exploitation that have tarnished the entire institution of peacekeeping in recent years, it may be the case that the UN system remains institutionally ill-equipped to lower the boom on acts of omission regarding the use of force, especially in the context of deep and ongoing divisions across the UN system on this very question.

Notes

1 Author interview, Juba; July 2018.
2 Author interview, Bangui, July 2022.

Works Cited

Ali Khalil, M. (2018) 'The UN's Cruz Report on improving peacekeepers' security goes too far', *PassBlue*, 20 May; Available at: https://www.passblue.com/2018/05/20/the-uns-cruz-report-on-improving-peacekeepers-safety-goes-too-far/

Andersen, L.R. (2018) 'The HIPPO in the room: The pragmatic push-back from the UN peace bureaucracy against the militarization of peacekeeping', *International Affairs* 94(2): 343–361.

Autesserre, S. (2019) 'The crisis of peacekeeping: Why the UN can't end wars', *Foreign Affairs* 98 (January/February): 101–116.

Bellamy, A. and C. Hunt (2021) 'Using force to protect civilians in UN peacekeeping', *Survival* 63(3): 143–170.

Berdal, M. (2018) 'The state of UN peacekeeping: Lessons from Congo', *The Journal of Strategic Studies* 41(5): 721–750.

Blyth, F. and P. Cammaert (2016) 'Using force to protect civilians in United Nations peacekeeping operations', in H. Willmot, R. Mamiya, S. Sheeran and M. Weller (eds.), *Protection of Civilians* (Oxford: Oxford University Press), 309–328.

Bourgeois, H. and P.I. Labuda (2022) 'When may UN peacekeepers use lethal force to protect civilians? Reconciling threads to civilians, imminence and the right to life', *Journal of Conflict and Security Law* 28(1): 1–65.

Carver, F. (2018) 'With DRC election in December, MONUSCO, squeezed by political and budgetary pressures, labors on', *IPI Global Observatory* (online), 22 August; Available at: https://theglobalobservatory.org/2018/08/monusco-political-budgetary-pressures-labors-on/

Cockayne, J. (2014) 'The futility of force? Strategic lessons for dealing with unconventional armed groups from the UN's war on Haiti's gangs', *The Journal of Strategic Studies* 37(5): 736–759.

Curran, D. (2017) 'Muddling on through? Cosmopolitan peacekeeping and the protection of civilians', *International Peacekeeping* 24(1): 63–85.

de Vries, H. (2015) 'Going around in circles: The challenges of peacekeeping and stabilization in the DRC', Report, Clingendael Institute; Available at: https://www.clingendael.org/pub/2015/going_around_in_circles/
Donais, T. and E. Tanguay (2020) 'Doing less with less? Peacekeeping retrenchment and the UN's protection of civilians agenda', *International Journal* 75(1): 65–82.
Donais, T. and E. Tanguay (2021) 'Protection of civilians and peacekeeping's accountability deficit', *International Peacekeeping* 28(4): 553–578.
Dorn, A.W. (2018) 'Protecting civilians with force: Dilemmas and lessons from the UN stabilization mission in Haiti', in P. Nadin (ed.), *The Use of Force in UN Peacekeeping* (Abington/New York: Routledge), 124–144.
dos Santos Cruz, C.A. et al. (2017) 'Improving security of United Nations peacekeepers: We need to change the way we are doing business', 19 December; Available at: https://peacekeeping.un.org/sites/default/files/improving_security_of_united_nations_peacekeepers_report.pdf
Druet, D. (2023) 'Wagner group poses fundamental challenges for the protection of civilians by UN peacekeeping operations', *IPI Global Observatory* (online), 20 March; Available at: https://theglobalobservatory.org/2023/03/wagner-group-protection-of-civilians-un-peacekeeping-operations/
The Economist (2021) 'UN peacekeeping is hamstrung by national rules for its troops', 21 March.
Giffen, A. (2018) 'The declaration of shared commitments on UN peacekeeping: One step forward – Or twenty years back?', Center for Civilians in Conflict (CIVIC) blog post, 25 September; Available at: https://civiliansinconflict.org/blog/declaration-of-shared-commitments-on-us-peacekeeping/
Gilder, A. (2023) 'The UN and the protection of civilians: Sustaining the momentum', *Journal of Conflict and Security Law* 28(2): 317–348.
Gowan, R. and S.J. Stedman (2018) 'The international regime for treating civil war, 1988–2017', *Daedalus* 147(1): 171–184.
Hirschmann, G. (2020) 'Cooperating with evil? Accountability in peace operations and the evolution of the United Nations human rights due diligence policy', *Cooperation and Conflict* 55(1): 22–40.
Human Rights Watch (HRW) (2008) 'Killings in Kiwanja: The UN's inability to protect civilians', December; Available at: https://www.hrw.org/report/2008/12/11/killings-kiwanja/uns-inability-protect-civilians
Karlsrud, J. (2015) 'The UN at war: Examining the consequences of peace-enforcement mandates for the UN peacekeeping operations in the CAR, the DRC and Mali', *Third World Quarterly* 36(1): 40–54.
Nadin, P. (2018) 'The logic of force in UN peacekeeping', in P. Nadin (ed.), *The Use of Force in UN Peacekeeping* (Abingdon/New York: Routledge), 169–195.
Peter, M. (2015) 'Between doctrine and practice: The UN peacekeeping dilemma', *Global Governance* 21: 351–370.
Russo, J. (2021) 'Militarised peacekeeping: Lessons from the Democratic Republic of the Congo', *Third World Quarterly* 42(12): 3070–3086.
Sherman, J. (2018) 'Action for peacekeeping: Will political consensus lead to change in practice?', Issue Brief, International Peace Institute, September; Available at: https://www.ipinst.org/2018/09/action-for-peacekeeping-will-political-consensus-lead-to-change-in-practice
Sorensen, G. (1992) 'Utopianism in peace research: The Gandhian heritage', *Journal of Peace Research* 29(2): 135–144.

Spink, L. (2018) 'Protection with less presence: How the peacekeeping operation in the Democratic Republic of Congo is attempting to deliver protection with fewer resources', Center for Civilians in Conflict report, 10 January; Available at: https://civiliansinconflict.org/publications/research/protection-with-less-presence/

Tardy, T. (2007) 'The UN and the use of force: A marriage against nature', *Security Dialogue* 38(1): 49–70.

Tull, D.M. (2018) 'The limits and unintended consequences of UN peace enforcement: The force intervention brigade in the DR Congo', *International Peacekeeping* 25(2): 167–190.

UN Department of Peace Operations (UN DPO) (2023) 'Policy: The protection of civilians in United Nations peacekeeping (PoC Policy)', 1 May; Available at: https://peacekeeping.un.org/sites/default/files/2023_protection_of_civilians_policy.pdf

UN Office of Internal Oversight Services (UN OIOS) (2014) 'Evaluation of the implementation and results of protection of civilians mandates in United Nations peacekeeping operations: Report of the office of internal oversight services', A/68/787, 7 March; Available at: https://digitallibrary.un.org/record/767929?ln=en&v=pdf

United Nations (UN) (2000) 'Report of the panel on United Nations peace operations (Brahimi Report)', A/55/305-S/2000/809, 21 August; Available at: https://peacekeeping.un.org/sites/default/files/a_55_305_e_brahimi_report.pdf

United Nations (UN) (2008) 'United Nations peacekeeping operations: Principles and guidelines (Capstone Doctrine)'; Available at: https://peacekeeping.un.org/sites/default/files/peacekeeping/en/capstone_eng.pdf

United Nations (UN) (2015) 'United our strengths for peace – Politics, partnership and people: Report of the high-level independent panel on peace operations (HIPPO Report)', A/70/95-S/2015/446, 17 June; Available at: https://digitallibrary.un.org/record/795940?ln=en

United Nations (UN) (2018) 'United Nations peacekeeping operations', UN Security Council Meeting Minutes, 12 September; S/PV.8349; Available at: https://documents.un.org/doc/undoc/pro/n18/283/35/pdf/n1828335.pdf

United Nations Mission in South Sudan (UNMISS) (2013) 'UNMISS issues preliminary account of Akobo base attack', Press Release, 20 December (on file with the author).

Woodhouse, T. and O. Ramsbotham (2005) 'Cosmopolitan peacekeeping and the globalization of security', *International Peacekeeping* 12(2): 139–156.

3 Non-coercive Protection

Protection by Peaceful Means?

Introduction

Just as with the ongoing debate around the Responsibility to Protect, PoC policy debates have long been dominated by stereotyped, if unrealistic, images of armed international protectors arriving in the nick of time to save beleaguered and defenceless populations from predatory bullies contemptuous of civilian life. In the case of PoC in particular, this vision of blue-helmeted cavalry riding to the rescue stands in stark contrast to the competing stereotype – all too prevalent within host states – of indolent, indifferent peacekeepers failing to act as innocents are slaughtered within earshot of the nearest UN base. For most peace operations most of the time, however, the reality of operationalising PoC mandates is far more prosaic, with successes reflecting instead the understated micro-heroism of timely interventions, respect for and sensitivity to local context and carefully cultivated relationships. In South Sudan's multi-layered conflict as it emerged shortly after that country's post-independence euphoria, for example, one under-reported but consequential protection success story has involved the ongoing efforts by the UNMISS Civil Affairs Division to mediate conflicts between farmers and herders that have all too often turned deadly. While difficult to isolate entirely from other conflict drivers – farmer/herder conflicts often parallel ethnic rivalries and reflect climate-induced pressures on local livelihoods, while cattle ownership in particular has been implicated in elite-level politics – the low-level diplomatic work that has facilitated peaceful dispute resolution has without question saved many lives, and stands as a prime example of the kinds of dialogue and engagement work that has long been the bread and butter of UN interventions in conflict-affected contexts.

Given the structural impediments to robust forms of PoC outlined in the previous chapter, there is merit to a closer examination of unarmed, or non-coercive, protection strategies and the prospects for enhancing or strengthening such mechanisms. Moreover, if the UN, as Conor Foley (2023) has suggested, is in the process of rethinking protection as it reduces its physical footprint and contemplates the end of an era of large, multidimensional peace operations, there are good reasons to believe that much of the focus of this latest period of introspection will be on the non-coercive elements of the protection toolkit. While it has been a decade since the Security Council last authorised a fully fledged UN-led peace operation,

DOI: 10.4324/9781003291114-3

for example, recent years have seen the proliferation of so-called special political missions (SPMs), which are unarmed and civilian led. While only one of 24 existing SPMs has a protection mandate – UNAMA in Afghanistan, although UNITAMS in Sudan had one as well until it was terminated in early 2024 – to the extent that PoC remains a core UN priority there is likely to be growing pressure on SPMs to 'do' PoC, albeit in ways that do not contemplate the potential use of force. Given that the exercise of force in the name of peace remains among the most contentious items on the UN's peace and security agenda, and with distrust and dissensus within the Security Council currently higher than at any point since PoC mandates in peace operations became commonplace (Lilly 2022), it is also the case that rebuilding consensus around more collaborative and less confrontational forms of protection will almost certainly prove to be the diplomatic path of least resistance for the PoC agenda. Indications of such a shift are already apparent in the Secretary General's 'New Agenda for Peace' from 2023, which cautions against burdening future peace operations with unrealistic mandates, calls for further reflection on the limits of peacekeeping, and hints at a future of 'networked multilateralism' marked, in part, by "a new generation of peace enforcement missions and counter-terrorism operations, led by African partners with a Security Council mandate" (UN 2023: 26). While such a vision echoes previous messaging, including from Brahimi and HIPPO, about the unsuitability of UN peace operations for enforcement tasks, it also signals a clear intent to return peacekeeping to more conventional terrain, while leaving the more militarised heavy lifting to others.

Given these trends, this chapter critically examines the HIPPO Report's key contention that the UN should place unarmed strategies at the forefront of its efforts to protect civilians. This involves both unpacking the contents of the unarmed protection toolkit and taking seriously both the limitations of such strategies and their potential to deliver better protection outcomes to vulnerable populations. In other words, while there is some evidence that the sheer presence of peacekeepers in a conflict-affected context mitigates violence against civilian populations (Keating 2017: 120), it is also the case – as Stian Kjeksrud (2016: 329) has argued – that what peacekeepers actually 'do' also matters. Presence may make a difference, as he suggests, but only in combination with actual practice, and therefore "understanding how peacekeepers can best meet the specific threat posed is critical for improving civilian protection." It also remains the case, however – possibly even more so than in the realm of armed protection – that teasing out effective from ineffective unarmed protection practices, let alone clearly identifying what 'works' as a guide to future policy-making, remains very much a work in progress. Despite some notable efforts in this direction in recent years, both data limitations and the long causal chains – especially at the structural end of the protection spectrum – connecting protection actions with protection outcomes continue to represent a serious obstacle to any effort to tally up with any confidence the sum of 'lives saved' by UN peace operations.

A further complicating factor here is the inherent difficulty of clearly delineating armed from unarmed protection efforts. While this distinction provides a useful heuristic, and while there is an obvious distinction between forcefully confronting a hostile armed group and engaging the same group in dialogue with the goal of avoiding civilian harm, there does exist a considerable grey area where armed and unarmed elements of peace operations intersect. Effective early warning systems, for example, are inherently reliant on extensive civil-military relations that connect community-level *detectors* – whether in the form of community alert networks (CANs) or community liaison assistants (CLAs) – with mission-level *effectors* in the form of timely and appropriate responses, whether armed or unarmed, to identified threats (see Chapter 5 for further discussion of the MONUSCO case). Similarly, it is often the case that a mission's coercive capabilities provide the credibility required for mission personnel – civilian or military – to access armed groups and their leadership. In other words, while Tier I (dialogue and engagement) protection efforts may be conceptually distinct from those within Tier II (provision of physical protection), the capacity to conduct the latter may in fact serve as a critical enabler for the former. In this sense, then, it may make little sense to attempt to differentiate too rigidly between the armed and unarmed elements of the protection toolkit, or to even try to evaluate the relative success of one instrument in isolation from others. Indeed, the latter part of this chapter will argue that for all its flaws, the UN has carved out over the past 25 years a unique niche in the protection space that has been enabled by its capacity to *both* project force *and* engage in non-coercive protection diplomacy and capacity-building. Rather than argue for the primacy of one over the other, the focus should be on how the combination of the two can be more effectively leveraged – and tensions between them managed – to ensure more effective protection outcomes in conflict-affected contexts. At the same time, if the end of the current era of large multidimensional peace operations marks a definitive break in the progressive development of PoC doctrine and practice, it is worth wondering – and worrying – about what precisely will replace it in a world where armed conflict and civilian suffering appear to be waxing rather than waning.

The Unarmed Protection Toolkit

The manner in which robust protection debates have long dominated PoC discussions points to what Gilmore and Staples (2019) have termed a 'default militarism' that has tended to characterise not only protection debates but international security scholarship more generally. For Richard Jackson, similarly, the ongoing marginalisation of pacifist thinking and ethics – understood broadly as the ongoing search for practical, functional alternatives to the use of violence – has narrowed the ethical imagination of both theorists and policy-makers, not least in relation to the protection of vulnerable populations (2019: 218). While peacekeeping itself remains an important site of contestation concerning the appropriate balance of carrot and stick in multilateral conflict interventions, recent failures to achieve durable negotiated settlements across a broad range of conflict contexts and a growing list of conflict parties – from al-Shabaab to the M23 – considered too extremist to be viable negotiating partners, has served to reinforce a widespread assumption "that only counter-violence can be effective against most, if not all, forms of violent threat to human life and state security" (Jackson 2019: 218). In the specific context of peace operations, the Cruz Report's lament that "hostile forces do not understand a language other than force" (dos Santos Cruz et al. 2017: iv) is among the clearest manifestations of this broader sentiment.

While there may be merit to the argument, articulated by Dustin Ells Howes (2013: 438), that "actions motivated by good intentions that in practice lead to bad outcomes are just as often the hallmark of those who embrace the use of violence as those who reject it," with advocates of armed solutions no less susceptible to tragic idealism (see Iraq circa 2003) than proponents of non-violence, it still remains incumbent on the latter to offer compelling answers to the question of how to prevent or halt violence in the absence of recourse to counter-violence. The literature on the relative success of non-violence as a political strategy for change has long relied on specific historical cases – notably the campaigns against slavery and for women's empowerment, the Indian anti-colonial and US civil rights movements, and the myriad 'coloured' revolutions of Eastern Europe in the aftermath of the cold war – as well as on the storied legacies of individuals such as Gandhi and Martin Luther King. It has also been given renewed impetus in recent years by empirical work, most notably that of Chenoweth and Stephan (2011), demonstrating the superior track record of non-violent revolutions in comparison with violent ones. While peacekeeping might be considered as part of this wider legacy, given its status as the UN's signature contribution to the non-violent management of armed conflict at both inter- and intra-state levels, there has been considerably less scholarly attention paid to the tools of non-violence as they apply to the specific challenges of civilian protection in the context of specific peace operations. The nature of the challenge has been effectively captured by the hourglass model of intervention popularised by Ramsbotham et al. (2005), which illustrates the narrowing of political space – and the limited opportunities for constructive engagement – in contexts of active large-scale violence. Whereas greater opportunities exist on either side of this constricted space, both in terms of conflict prevention prior to the escalation of violence and peacebuilding once a ceasefire and/or peace agreement are in place, the model assumes that outside actors operating in contexts of open conflict, when threats to civilians are most pronounced, have limited room to manoeuvre and few constructive engagement options at their disposal. Rwanda provides the paradigmatic example; once the genocide began in earnest and the stark choice between standing/fighting and retreating was made in favour of the latter, key international actors such as the UN could offer little more than impotent hand-wringing and feeble calls for the 'conflict parties' to return to negotiations.

While the hourglass model does imply an oversimplified before/during/after linearity to armed conflict – one unavoidable lesson of 21st-century African conflicts is that they are anything but linear – the model does point strongly to the conclusion that many African wars, and by extension those prominent UN peace operations active within them, have become stuck in the narrowest point of the hourglass, which has perhaps reinforced the tendency to consider intervention options in increasingly militaristic terms. Yet despite the emphasis on the need for more robust responses on the part of uniformed peacekeepers to threats against civilian populations in ongoing conflict contexts, there have also emerged a range of unarmed responses, some innovative, others drawing on long-standing peacekeeping practice, that should also be considered essential elements of the UN's protection toolkit. In what follows, I examine three broad categories of such responses – presence/accompaniment, dialogue/engagement and capacity-building – while also probing the causal mechanisms that are presumed to underpin the protective impacts of each.

Presence/Accompaniment

The most elemental form of unarmed protection is presence, and the simple act of bearing witness has been demonstrated to have a deterrent effect on conflict parties, reining in some of their worst inclinations. The moderating impact of international presence suggests that conflict parties are in fact more sensitive than generally assumed to reputational considerations, especially when the costs of committing atrocity crimes – and having their culpability widely publicised – can include diminished international political and material support as well as potential criminal prosecution for responsible individuals (Mahoney 2006; von Einsiedel 2015). As Liam Mahoney (2006: 20) has noted, such reputational considerations mean that proactive presence acts to reduce the perceived political space for perpetrators: "international presence moves the border between acceptable and unacceptable actions, and thus provides real protection." While there are limits to the protective effects of presence – extremist groups with little regard for how the outside world views their actions are unlikely to be swayed by reputational considerations, for example, while the ability to restrict freedom of movement gives armed groups an effective veto over where outsiders can and cannot be present – it remains the case that in most circumstances, presence does have a demonstrable deterrent effect. Indeed, it is precisely this cause/effect relationship that is responsible for the emergence of the small but determined cottage industry of unarmed civilian peacekeeping (UCP), led by international NGOs such as Peace Brigades International and Nonviolent Peaceforce, whose very *raison d'être* is premised on the notion of protective accompaniment. While originally developed as a means of providing protection to especially vulnerable individuals – prominent human rights defenders in contexts such as Colombia, for example, for whom accompaniment provides at least some protection from violence at the hands of opponents who had hitherto been able to count on immunity through obscurity – the basic concept is easily scalable, with protection teams now regularly deployed to vulnerable spaces such as South Sudan's PoC sites.

As scholar-activists such as Sara Koopman (2013) have demonstrated, however, presence by itself means little absent a credible communication chain, both to be able to convey reports of abusive behaviour to outside actors (both government and public) and to be able to convey to potential perpetrators the likely negative consequences of such behaviour (see the longer discussion under engagement, below). The importance of this communications/reporting function recalls the role of the American journalist Webb Miller's reporting at the time of the Dharasana salt raids, one of the key episodes of Gandhi's non-violent campaign against British imperialism. While Miller's reporting – which reached a broad international audience – did not deter atrocities against Gandhi's followers, its graphic depiction of the ensuing violence did impose a significant reputational cost on imperial Britain, weakening its claim to cultural superiority and throwing into question the underlying logic of the colonial-era *mission civilisatrice* (Martin 2012). As Koopman (2013) has noted, however, it is not just public opinion that matters; in the Colombian case, it also mattered that accompaniers had direct lines of communication with officials at the US embassy, given the outsized influence of US support to Colombia's government and, by extension, its paramilitary proxies.

Such dynamics play out in similar ways in the context of contemporary peace operations, albeit with the added wildcard of a mission's capacity or willingness to use force as part of a protection mandate. For Hultman et al. (2013), for example, there is a direct and demonstrable correlation between more boots on the ground and better protection outcomes. The presence of peacekeepers increases the costs for combatants seeking to exploit soft civilian 'targets of opportunity,' through the dynamics of witnessing described above, but also through the long-standing strategy of interpositioning, through which peacekeepers "impose physical barriers between combatants and potential civilian targets, making violence a less attractive way for warring factions to extract support or resources from the civilian population" (Hultman et al. 2013: 876). Given what von Einsiedel (2015: 1) has termed "the notorious reluctance of peacekeepers to use force in the pursuit of PoC mandates," it remains an open question whether the fact that peacekeepers are armed makes a decisive difference with regard to the efficacy of such interpositioning strategies. On the one hand, it is reasonable to assume that all but the most determined armed actors will think twice about assaulting unarmed civilians if they have to first overcome the physical barrier of a peacekeeping contingent, regardless of whether or not that contingent is prepared to respond to provocations with deadly force. In this sense, the protective effects of presence may be seen to hold regardless of whether the nature of that presence is unarmed civilians, civilian UN staff or lightly armed peacekeepers. On the other hand, however, Hultman et al. also find that the presence of *unarmed* UN observers might actually be associated with an *increase* in civilian killings, and theorise that this might be due to the signal of 'weak resolve' that the deployment of observers sends to the conflict parties (2013: 880). While suggestive, this explanation is only partially convincing, given that being armed is only one factor among many that constitutes resolve in the context of international interventions, and that interpositioning strategies have come to be the unique preserve of armed – if differentially robust – peacekeeping contingents.

Approaching the protection through presence question from a somewhat more conventional perspective, a 2024 report from the Effectiveness of Peace Operations Network (EPON) on UN human rights engagement concludes that, on balance, "UN peace operations' efforts to advance human rights contribute to a reduction in violence levels and to longer-term sustainable peace" (Hunt et al. 2024: 8). A key element of this contribution is human rights reporting, which can serve both to deter abuses against civilians and to incentivise broader behavioural change among conflict parties, while at the same time providing "a basis for dialogue and engagement with local and other actors, including government and host authorities, on protection" (Hunt et al. 2024: 34). While there is little question that conflict parties, and host governments in particular, are deeply sensitive to negative human rights reporting that reflects badly on them, the difficulty of specifying impact beyond the rather vague notion of 'contribution' is that – especially in the contexts of ongoing armed conflict – parties are just as likely to respond by shooting the messenger as by improving their human rights records. While EPON cites evidence suggesting that public human rights reporting does not negatively impact mission effectiveness, recent high-profile cases illustrate the fine line the UN regularly has to walk between the imperative of honest and forthright reporting and the competing imperative of maintaining host state consent for the mission's very presence. von Einsiedel (2015: 6) notes, for example, that UNAMID – the joint AU/UN Mission in Darfur – came under heavy criticism for failing to report 'strong circumstantial evidence' of government attacks against civilians, presumably out of concern for maintaining good relations with the Sudanese government (which nevertheless eventually called for UNAMID's withdrawal). A similar dynamic led to the termination of the MINUSMA mission in Mali. As the EPON report cited above acknowledged, "the mission's human rights functions and reporting were the main reasons for the Malian government withdrawing its consent for MINUSMA and requesting its departure" (Hunt et al. 2024: 144).

Dialogue/Engagement

If the simple presence of international actors in conflict-affected contexts has a protective influence for vulnerable populations, it follows that such opportunities should expand as one moves along the spectrum from passive presence to active engagement. While engagement is something of an umbrella concept, covering the full gamut of actions between mute observation of conflict dynamics to full-scale armed intervention, in PoC terms it implies active and ongoing efforts to influence key actors to alter their behaviour in civilian-friendly ways. Dialogue and engagement, to borrow a Churchillian turn of phrase, is the jaw-jaw counterpart to war-war, and lies squarely within the UN's traditional comfort zone of mediation, good offices and peaceful conflict resolution. It is no coincidence, therefore, that dialogue and engagement appear as Tier I of UN peacekeeping's PoC policy, covering a broad and diverse range of mission activity, including:

> Active, structured and regular dialogue with perpetrators or potential perpetrators of violence against civilians; conflict resolution and mediation between parties to the conflict; advocating with the host government, its security institutions and other relevant actors to intervene to protect civilians; local conflict resolution and social cohesion activities; reconciliation initiatives; strategic communication; investigation; advocacy; reporting on human rights and other protection concerns; and other initiatives that seek

to protect civilians through communications, dialogue and direct or indirect engagement.

(UN DPO 2023: 10)

While some of this activity, such as human rights reporting, has been discussed above as part of presence/accompaniment, and other aspects – notably links with host governments and host-state security institutions – are linked with capacity-building (addressed below), for the purposes of this discussion I highlight the potential and limitations of mission-level dialogue/engagement as it impacts both conflict parties and conflict-affected communities. With regard to the former, one key debate revolves around the question of whether armed groups can be either convinced or incentivised to avoid inflicting violent harm on civilian populations, or whether – following the logic of the Cruz Report – the only reliable way of exercising influence over such groups is through a robust show of military counter-force. For certain groups in certain situations – Bosnian Serb forces in Bosnia during that country's civil war or the Rapid Support Forces in Sudan, which emerged from the notorious *Janjaweed* militias in Darfur and are now locked in a vicious civil war with the Sudanese Armed Forces – the dehumanisation of the 'other' and the perceived utility of attacks against civilians combine to render any attempt at dialogue an exercise in futility, especially at the narrowest point of the metaphorical conflict hourglass. It is also the case, however, that not only UCP but the entire enterprise of humanitarian protection relies fully on the idea that armed groups can be dissuaded, socialised and/or incentivised to respect fundamental distinctions between civilians and combatants. Much of the work of the International Committee of the Red Cross at the coalface of conflict, for example, assumes that conflict actors of all stripes can be convinced to embrace, and respect, the fundamental principles of international humanitarian law. The very idea of 'humanitarian space,' within which relief and aid agencies can function even in the most violent of circumstances, attests to the power of such external influence, as does the progress that has been made towards ending the recruitment and use of child soldiers (von Einsiedel 2015: 7). As Mahoney (2006: 29) contends in his review of the impacts of unarmed civilian protection strategies, the question is not "if abusers are sensitive to influence, persuasion or pressure, but rather how sensitive they are, to what kinds of influence, and what are the appropriate channels of persuasion or leverage."

In reality, therefore, just as there is an increasingly kaleidoscopic range of armed actors involved in the contemporary conflicts where UN peace operations deploy – from formal armies to armed gangs, and from religious extremists to ethnically based citizen militias – there is an equally wide range of levels of sensitivity across such groups to external influences. Given this, it is surely just as inaccurate to argue that non-coercive forms of engagement are futile as it is to argue that they represent a panacea for civilian suffering in conflict contexts. The logical answer to the question of how best to engage armed groups, of course, is that such engagement must be planned and calibrated based on a sound understanding of the group in question, its ideological underpinnings, its dependence on support from both external actors and local communities, and its goals and motivations for taking up arms in the first place. Given the fragmentation of armed actors in recent decades, developing an accurate understanding of how and why armed groups operate has without question become more difficult, but it has certainly not become any less important.

Engagement with armed actors on PoC questions, of course, extends well beyond efforts to encourage them to be nicer to civilians. It is well-established that the best and most sustainable PoC strategy must necessarily involve the removal of the key drivers of civilian insecurity through conflict resolution and longer-term peacebuilding (Duursma et al. 2023: 8). As previously noted, however, not only have contemporary conflict dynamics – and in particular the proliferation of armed actors – made the achievement of durable negotiated settlements that much more difficult in recent decades, but the UN itself is no longer the mediator of choice in many ongoing conflict contexts, even where it has peace operations in place. While scholars such as Mats Berdal have made the case for reconnecting the UN presence in conflict-affected contexts to "the central enterprise of mediating and reaching political settlements to conflict" (2018: 746), it is also the case that national-level peace processes are far from the only arena in which mediation can play a constructive role in dampening violence and reducing threats to civilians. In South Sudan, for example, in addition to mediating reductions in farmer/herder tensions (as noted above), UNMISS was central to negotiations over the 2018–2019 period that produced some 160 local- and regional-level *ententes* among armed groups, which have in turn delivered measurable peace dividends by reducing violence, facilitating trade and humanitarian access, and enabling joint action against local criminality (Donais 2020). While such agreements are often fragile, subject to being swept away by shifting conflict dynamics at the national level, they have proven their worth as interim measures capable not only of reducing violence against civilians at the level of individual communities and neighbourhoods, but also laying the foundations for more inclusive and participatory forms of local-level security governance. In the context of the Central African Republic, similarly, Marie-Joelle Zahar and Delphine Mechoulan (2017) have made the case for a more deliberate and strategic effort on the part of MINUSCA to leverage opportunities to support mediation – from local to national levels – as the most sustainable way to achieve the mission's strategic objective of reducing both the presence of, and the threat posed by, armed groups. Consistent with the broader thrust of the so-called 'local turn' in the field of peacebuilding, then, mediation at the local and subregional levels offers considerable scope for expanding peace operations' room to manoeuvre, especially in the context of ongoing and seemingly intractable violent conflict. It is also increasingly clear that another key form of protection-oriented engagement with non-state armed actors in particular – disarmament, demobilization and reintegration (DDR) – is also fundamentally dependent on the establishment of a viable peace process, regardless of whether such a process emerges from the bottom-up or the top-down. Simply put, it is exceedingly difficult to convince fighters to give up their weapons and return to civilian life unless a compelling case can be made that the time for fighting has ended, and that a war-to-peace transition is not only underway but irreversible.

The alternative to PoC-focused engagement with the real or potential sources of threat to civilian populations, of course, is engagement with threatened populations themselves.[1] Indeed, one emerging strand of PoC research has emphasised precisely the agency of 'the protected' in conflict contexts, and has sought to challenge the conventional narrative that PoC is overwhelmingly about the mobilisation of international agency on behalf of voiceless, helpless populations (Baines and Paddon 2012: 232; Levine 2013). In the first place, as Paul Williams (2013: 296) suggests, UN peace operations are, at best, equipped to address "only the tip of the iceberg of civilian suffering in war zones," and peacekeepers often arrive at the scene of atrocities too late to make a life-saving difference. Andrew Bonwick (2006: 270, 274), similarly, has noted that despite the tendency to view protection as an externally provided commodity, akin to humanitarian assistance, "a rarely spoken truth about protection is that the main players in the protection of civilians in conflict are the civilians themselves." Such considerations point to the importance of the hitherto-neglected agency of local communities themselves, who in any conflict context deploy a range of self-protection strategies and demonstrate reserves of resilience that must be acknowledged by any sustainable PoC strategy.

While recent years have certainly witnessed greater attention on the part of both scholars and policy-makers to the ways in which civilians in conflict contexts navigate violence and insecurity, it is also vital to recognise the limits of such strategies, and the wrenching trade-offs they often entail. Civilians may play their cards more or less successfully in their efforts to survive in the often-Hobbesian circumstances of contemporary conflict, but their hands are invariably weak *vis-à-vis* the armed actors who enjoy the power of coercive force over them. As Baines and Paddon (2012) note in an important early contribution to this debate, while civilians caught up in conflict develop repertoires of survival tactics – from attempting to remain neutral to avoiding armed groups to accommodating their demands – their ability to influence specific armed groups or their predatory tendencies, let alone broader conflict dynamics, remains marginal at best; for many, self-protection means sleeping with their shoes on in the hopes of making a quick getaway when the armed men arrive. Justin Corbett, similarly, notes that the basic survival choices forced upon residents of Sudan's South Kordofan region during an earlier phase of that country's civil war – most importantly flight into the remote Nuba Mountains – had terrible downside consequences in terms of starvation, disease and lack of basic services (2011: 24). In the words of Aditi Gorur and Nils Carstensen (2016: 420), then, "community self-protection is never itself a satisfying solution to the wide-ranging and serious abuses suffered by people at risk."

It is, however, a dynamic and ubiquitous element of the broader PoC *problématique*, and effective engagement with conflict-affected communities necessarily entails acknowledgement of, respect for, and at least some accommodation with these coping mechanisms. At a minimum this means taking care to do no harm in the course of introducing externally conceived PoC strategies; more ambitiously, it means concerted efforts to develop integrated protection strategies based on existing local knowledge and practice, with an emphasis on augmenting and complementing existing protection strategies and empowering communities to protect themselves (Gorur and Carstensen 2016: 427). On the do no harm front, mixed or ambiguous messages on the part of international actors can have fatal consequences for civilians targeted by armed actors; unmet promises of protection (whether explicit or implied) that compel civilians to seek shelter at UN bases rather than flee into the bush have in many cases – Srebrenica being only the most egregious example – compounded rather than reduced civilian suffering. Such is the moral hazard of contemporary peace operations with PoC mandates: frightened civilians expect UN protection and will continue to do so notwithstanding any limits or caveats the UN may place on its protection obligations in a given context. Similarly, protection strategies that disrupt or interfere with community protection practices, and the communicative and knowledge networks which underpin them – as in Baines and Paddon's (2012) account of how Uganda's decision to forcibly relocate Acholi civilians into government-run camps undermined community-led protection mechanisms – may also end up doing far more harm than good.

More positively, there have been some notable experiments in community engagement at the field level, including the widespread use of CLAs and CANs in the DRC and elsewhere (Bellamy and Hunt 2015; Gorur and Sharland 2016; Weir and Hunt 2011). Widespread experimentation has in some cases led to the development of relatively sophisticated early warning systems, generating both a better understanding of the dynamics of insecurity in particular areas as well as a set of mechanisms enabling both rapid and contextually tailored responses. Beyond the specific modalities of particular mechanisms, such developments have been the most prominent manifestation of 'people-centred' protection strategies, opening up crucial channels of communication and helping to break down barriers of mistrust and misunderstanding across the protector/protected divide. In some circumstances, such channels may not even involve peacekeepers at all, but rather provide platforms for constructive engagement between community representatives and armed groups. Such engagement strategies have not been without their critics; some have pointed out that the directional flow of information generated by such networks are often one-sided, with missions accused of taking an extractive approach to information received from local communities without necessarily reciprocating in kind. Others, including members of such networks, have complained that beyond initial seed funding to help establish local-level alert networks, the UN and other supporting donors have expected them to be self-sustaining, and have provided little by way of ongoing funding to enable local volunteers to do the work expected of them. In a context such as CAR, where in remote areas even the cost of fuel for motorbikes is beyond the means of ordinary people, resource constraints can seriously hamper a network's ability to function.[2] Security considerations, too, have emerged as a factor; participation in community-engagement fora can result in individuals being marked as collaborators, subject to reprisals by armed groups.

While approaches to effective, community-engaged protection have without question evolved in positive ways over the past two decades, it is fair to conclude that efforts to connect PoC to systematic strategies of community empowerment (Williams 2013) or to rethink PoC in terms of 'protectors-with' rather than 'protectors-from' (Levine 2013) remain at a relatively early stage. The shrinking budgets and resource constraints of recent years have also limited the capacity of

UN missions to fully engage with the communities they are mandated to protect, with the risk that hard-won gains may in fact be reversed if current trends continue. Effective community engagement requires considerable investment in human resources and human relationships to pay serious dividends; to the extent that 'projection' replaces 'presence' as protection practice, hard-earned trust and mutual understanding can be lost; equally concerning – especially in the DRC, where MONUSCO was expected to wind down by the end of 2024 (the mission was in fact extended by an additional year in late 2024) – are questions of transition; it remains unclear whether such mechanisms will even survive the end of the mission's tenure.

Capacity-building

Entrusting peacekeepers with the responsibility of protecting civilians in conflict contexts is, by definition, a time-limited proposition. Missions wind down and peacekeepers depart, and whatever protection tasks they may have assumed are conceptualised – not least in Security Council Resolutions – as temporary aberrations from normal states of affairs, undertaken for a period in which the host state is temporarily unable to uphold its core responsibilities for protecting its own civilians. The so-called monopoly model of security provision – grounded in Weberian definitions of the state and deeply engrained within the state-centric fabric of the UN system – assumes not only a stable negotiated peace as the end state of a peace operation, but also the full transfer of security provision back into the hands of a capable sovereign state. In the context of contemporary armed conflicts across much of the developing world – particularly in Africa and especially in the three country cases that are the focus of subsequent chapters – this 'restoration' model of security provision remains convenient if almost entirely fictional. Of the approximately 120 million souls living on the contiguous territories which now encompass CAR, South Sudan and the DRC, their experiences of the state overwhelming involve some blend of malign neglect and armed predation; in short, the state has never taken seriously its 'primary responsibility' to protect civilians within its territory and subject to its jurisdiction. To take but one example, in CAR the state has historically exerted very limited influence beyond Bangui, and the periphery has long been considered not as a territory populated by citizens in need of both services and security, but rather as a resource to be exploited for the primary benefit of capital-based elites.

It is within this wider context that security sector reform (SSR) – as the functionally codependent twin of DDR (McFate 2010: 11) – has emerged as an essential element of any peacebuilding process, in the recognition that not only do state security forces have to be retrained, reconfigured and resized in the transition from war to peace, they also have to be re-socialised to embrace the protection of civilians as their headline responsibility. In connection to PoC, therefore, successful SSR is a necessary extension of any sustainable PoC strategy; in the words of Arthur Boutellis (2013: 6), "unless there is progress on national SSR, peacekeepers will have no one to hand over their physical protection mandate to as they exit."

SSR has always involved a delicate dance between capacity and accountability, particularly in the context of war-to-peace transitions. Without sufficient capacity – in the form of uniformed personnel (military or police), modern equipment and efficient bureaucratic processes – the state cannot credibly claim a monopoly on the legitimate use of force across its entire sovereign territory. Without accountability, however, and at least some means of shaping, directing, and limiting the uses to which such capacity is put, it may be wishful thinking to imagine that greater capacity will be employed for the purposes of protection rather than predation. The UN Security Council, in a stand-alone resolution adopted in 2014, underlined this dual nature of SSR by reaffirming that an "effective, professional and accountable security sector without discrimination and with full respect for human rights and the rule of law is the cornerstone of peace and sustainable development" (UN 2014). While this vision of SSR has remained largely unchanged since the concept was first popularised at the end of the cold war, the pathways to achieving it – especially in the deeply fraught environments of fragile and conflict-affected states – have remained frustratingly obscure over the intervening years.

In the first place, as highlighted in the previous chapter, in the absence of formal political settlement the unreformed security forces of the host state are yet another armed party to the conflict, and in many cases represent the most serious source of civilian insecurity. This has long been the case in the DRC, where MONUSCO has coexisted uneasily with the Congolese Armed Forces (*Les Forces armées de la République démocratique du Congo*, or FARDC) which – after a quarter-century of international engagement in the country – is still widely viewed as unreformed, unprofessional and deeply corrupt. While SSR efforts have never gained traction in the DRC, in large part due to a lack of enthusiasm on the part of the Congolese government, ongoing efforts to extend state authority and combat the most toxic of the armed opposition groups in the eastern part of the country have inevitably brought MONUSCO and the FARDC together. This has always been a fraught and difficult partnership, however, especially given that the UN's human rights due diligence policy means that support for the DRC authorities must always be tempered by efforts to ensure that the UN neither enables nor is complicit in violations carried out by the Congolese military. This pattern – a mix of awkward collaboration, arms-length coordination, and mutual distrust and hostility – has long strained relations between the government and the mission and severely tested the principle of host-state consent. Despite its acknowledged centrality both for sustainable peace and for civilian security, SSR has faced similar obstacles in both South Sudan and CAR. In the former, support for SSR initiatives was stripped from UNMISS' Security Council mandate in 2014, subsequent to South Sudan's rapid descent into civil war and the associated atrocities carried out by both government and opposition forces. In the latter, the government of CAR's turn towards Russia – and the robust security assistance provided through the Wagner Group – forced a reconsideration of more conventional SSR programming, notably that led by the European Union.

Two additional factors have added to the headwinds that SSR efforts in peacekeeping contexts have faced in recent decades. The first is the political fallout from what Christine Bell and Jan Pospisil (2017) have termed 'political unsettlement,' which describes the persistent pattern of neither war nor peace that has come to characterise many of the environments in which UN peacekeepers now operate. In conditions of political unsettlement, "while forms of political order may continue within the formal and informal institutions, political bargaining will also be undertaken through extraordinary use of violence and extraordinary state responses to it" (Bell and Pospisil 2017: 581). While violence may ebb and flow, and afflict some parts of the state but not others, unsettlement can also imply a certain accommodation on the part of conflict parties to the indefinite perpetuation of the conflict, albeit at lower intensities, and an acceptance of their inability to arrive at a formal political settlement that marks a definitive break between war and peace. The implications of an extended unsettlement interregnum have already been noted above in the context of DDR, as armed actors unable to rely on the signed provisions of a peace agreement to protect their security interests are unlikely to voluntarily disarm. More generally, conditions of unsettlement privilege short-term thinking among conflict parties, as they make and break agreements – including around the integration of fighters into state-level armed forces – according to short-term strategic calculations. For governing elites caught in these conditions, SSR programming – with its necessarily long timeframes – is of limited appeal given the more immediate struggle to impose order, control resources and outmanoeuvre the armed opposition. To the extent that governments in these situations can be convinced to embrace SSR, they invariably tend to prefer the so-called 'train-and-equip' variety, with more emphasis on building up short-term force projection capabilities and less emphasis on over-the-horizon questions such as democratic accountability, respect for human rights and embedding security provision in rule of law frameworks. All too often, as Mark Sedra (2006) has noted with reference to SSR in Afghanistan, the end result is a slide towards expediency, and a privileging of capacity over accountability in ways that may ultimately heighten rather than reduce civilian insecurity, at least in the short term.

Second, the challenges of managing the realities of unsettlement have been exacerbated by shifts in global-level dynamics that not only have led to increasing discord – if not outright paralysis – within the UN Security Council but have also complicated mission/host-state relations. In short, the progressive unravelling of the liberal peacebuilding paradigm that has long provided the template for international intervention in conflict-affected states – as well as for SSR more narrowly – has accelerated in recent years, aided and abetted by both China's and Russia's increasingly assertive and decidedly illiberal stances *vis-à-vis* conflict-affected states. On the one hand, as Rosemary Foot (2020) has argued, China has increasingly sought to shape UN-level narratives around peacekeeping and protection to align with its own state-centric and sovereignty-first views. According to this vision, peacekeeping and peacekeepers should in essence be seen as the extension of the host state government armed forces, and should follow a service provider mentality; in other words less emphasis on human rights and good governance and more emphasis on defeating threats to the host state and enabling the state to consolidate its authority over its sovereign territory. Russian practice has tended to reinforce such messages, in particular through its use of proxy Wagner forces (some of which have now been rebranded as the Africa Corps) in contexts such as Mali and CAR. While securing strategic footholds on the African continent, Russian engagement on the side of host-government armed forces has tended to tip the military balance in favour of the state, to undercut international commitments to human rights and PoC and to encourage host states to defeat their domestic enemies rather than negotiate with them. Together, these twin developments have worked to embolden host states *vis-à-vis* UN peace operations, and to encourage the former to deploy the threat of withdrawing host-state consent as a means of pushing back against the latter. One consequence of this shifting balance of engagement has been that host states find themselves with a different set of options with regard to dealing with armed groups within their territory; if the UN is unwilling to help the state – in the name of extending state authority – fight its own domestic enemies, other bilateral security partners may be more willing to help with the heavy lifting. While the implications of a shifting geopolitical balance are far-reaching, the impact on the prospects for SSR in conflict-affected contexts is already being felt. With the ability to play powerful states off against each other, host states are much better positioned to resist the deep structural reforms inherent in SSR programming, and to insist on more immediately impactful forms of material support. In such a scenario, the prospects for constructively engaging with the security forces of conflict-affected states over the lifetime of a peacekeeping mission in order to ensure that departing peacekeepers can hand protection responsibilities over to professional, accountable and rights-respecting domestic security forces seem, more than ever, like wishful thinking.

Conclusion

Peacekeeping is an imperfect tool, governed by an imperfect global body and operating in a decidedly imperfect world. Peacekeepers are regularly asked to do more with less, to be more nimble, more flexible and more accountable, to uphold global-level norms and values, and to act as first-responders for threatened, vulnerable populations. That UN peace operations inevitably fail to deliver on such expectations has resulted in periodic falls from grace; peacekeeping went through one such episode in the late 1990s, and may currently be going through another. Given its history, peacekeeping has also been subject to a near-constant stream of proposals for its reform, improvement, or reinvention. Ambition has ebbed and flowed, and whereas only a decade ago observers were both lauding and lamenting (depending on one's perspective) a new era of robust, enforcement-oriented operations, more recently a back-to-basics mentality appears to have taken hold, along with a sense that peacekeeping can no longer be the Swiss army knife of international conflict intervention.

Regardless of its source, just about every reform proposal aimed at 'fixing' UN peacekeeping has grappled with the appropriate balance of coercive and non-coercive, armed and unarmed, confrontational and conciliatory, in peacekeeping doctrine and practice. With the rise in prominence of PoC in recent decades, such debates have if anything become more pronounced, given the life-and-death stakes for so many in getting this balance wrong. While the previous chapter canvassed some of the key contributions to the debate on the appropriate uses of force in UN operations, few have gone so far as to contemplate the consequences of a complete renunciation of force by the UN in its field operations. Given the inherent paradoxes of using force in the name of peace, the long-standing discomfort of many important TCCs with the very concept of robust peacekeeping, the downside risks to the UN of straying too far from traditional peacekeeping principles, the rise of unarmed SPMs in lieu of large, multidimensional missions in recent years and the range of unarmed strategies available to external interveners, it is at least possible to carry the logic of the HIPPO Report's 'primacy of politics' injunction to its logical endpoint. Richard Jackson (2019: 224) has noted, for example, that it is not entirely farfetched

> to imagine a situation in which fully resourced unarmed peace forces trained to a similar level of professionalism as modern military forces, combined with local peace committees practiced in conflict resolution, and supported by international mediators and humanitarian agencies, take the lead in a situation requiring civilian protection, thereby obviating the need for armed intervention.

While suggestive, the ideas underpinning Jackson's imagined future for unarmed peacekeeping are impossible, at present, to test empirically, given that no such mission has yet been deployed. One can be sympathetic (as I am) to the broader mantra of 'peace by peaceful means' (as well as to the alternative formulation of 'protection by peaceful means') while at the same time wondering whether Jackson's formulation is excessively sanguine in its view of armed conflict parties and their malleability in the face of international pressure and/or persuasion, just as one can treat sceptically the counterfactual idea that non-violence, framed appropriately and resourced properly, might have provided an alternative and less destructive response to Nazi Germany some 85 years ago. In the specific and contemporary case of peacekeeping and PoC, however, there are sound reasons for suspecting that more would be lost than gained should future peacekeeping adopt an approach explicitly grounded in a 'default pacifism.'

Contemporary Haiti offers the first such red flag. As these lines are written, armed gangs remain in control of most of Port-au-Prince, and a security and humanitarian crisis is deepening by the day as a newly installed transitional council struggles to assert its authority. With the Haitian state having almost entirely collapsed, the so-called Multinational Security Support (MSS) mission – led by Kenya and authorised by the Security Council – was launched in mid-2024 with the aim of helping Haiti's beleaguered and outgunned police push back the gangs and restore order. While operating under a Chapter VII mandate, the MSS was designed primarily as a policing mission, and since its deployment has struggled – underfunded, under-supported and overwhelmed by the chaotic conditions in which it is operating – to make an impact on the broader security situation. To the extent that the MSS can recover from a weak and uninspiring start, its leadership will need to be prepared for a fight, and will almost certainly be studying the tactics deployed by the successful campaign waged by the UN's MINUSTAH mission against an earlier generation of Haitian gangs. While not everyone is convinced that the mission can succeed – a steady stream of weapons from the United States into Haiti has provided the country's gangs with formidable arsenals, while discussions are currently underway about transitioning to yet another UN-led peace operation – few serious observers believe that anything less than a robust international intervention force can have any hope of reversing Haiti's ongoing slide into violent anarchy. Given this depressing fact scenario, then, with the possible exception of an arms embargo – which has been authorised but not yet enforced – it is difficult to avoid the conclusion that placing unarmed strategies at the forefront of international efforts to protect civilians in the current Haitian context is unlikely to make a significant difference. As Stian Kjeksrud (2016: 341) has noted more generally, "in situations of predatory violence, military operations may be the only way to effectively protect civilians, as perpetrators are likely to continue committing acts of brutality, abduction and killings as long as they are able to operate."

The Haiti example also points to a second crucial, if sometimes underappreciated, function of armed force in the context of UN peace operations: protection for those providing the protection. Since peacekeeping's inception in 1948, some 4,370 peacekeeping personnel have been killed on mission, and in specific country contexts such as Mali – where MINUSMA was often described as the world's most dangerous peacekeeping environment – peacekeepers have found themselves directly targeted by armed groups. This was in fact the primary impetus for the Cruz Report, which argued that insufficiently robust peace operations were getting pushed around by armed groups in conflict contexts, with negative effects on mission effectiveness; getting tougher – through more robust defensive posturing, better training, greater intelligence capacity and a greater determination to exercise area domination – would not only save lives but enhance mandate implementation (dos Santos Cruz et al. 2017: 12). At the same time, the more resources that a mission needs to devote to self-protection, the less it is able to offer meaningful levels of protection to vulnerable civilians; MINUSMA's struggles to protect itself had a discernible impact on its ability to fulfil its PoC mandate. This extends, of course, not just to the usual objects of protection – local communities caught in the crossfire, as it were – but also to civilian components of peace operations as well as development and humanitarian workers from the plethora of non-governmental organisations that typically operate in conflict-affected environments. In most conflict-affected contexts, where risks involve not only armed groups but also criminals and bandits, as well as landmines and improvised explosive devices, a mission's civil affairs officers and human rights monitors rely heavily on their force counterparts to escort them into areas where it would otherwise be too dangerous to travel. Likewise, while the humanitarian community has an ambivalent relationship with armed peacekeepers, and prefers to maintain an arms-length relationship in the interest of safeguarding humanitarian neutrality, it also is very often the case that the protective environment of a peacekeeping presence within a specific region is a critical enabler for any humanitarian activity to be undertaken. In short, therefore, the reluctance to even consider applying the principles of UCP to the entirety of UN peace operations reflects a key tenet of realist international relations theory: notwithstanding specific exceptions to the rule, such as Costa Rica, it continues to be the case that unilateral disarmament for actors in rough neighbourhoods – and peacekeepers almost by definition operate in rough neighbourhoods – remains a risky proposition.

It may be, in the end, that armed and unarmed forms of protection stand in relation to each other in the same way that justice and peace do in the context of post-conflict peacebuilding: in tension but ultimately inseparable. Rather than viewing them as alternatives, in other words, a more constructive approach may involve the search for ways to manage the tension and maximise the complementarity. Seen in this light, therefore, multidimensional UN peace operations are unique in that they possess a broad repertoire of armed and unarmed protection tools, which are at least in principle amenable to being scaled, calibrated and combined as necessary to fit the specific conditions in which peacekeepers operate. Twenty-five years into the UN's ambitious experiment with explicitly charging its peacekeepers with PoC mandates, there are important lessons to be learned from the field-level trial-and-error that missions have undertaken in order to maximise the resources at their disposal for protection purposes. Some of these lessons relate to the limits of what can and cannot be expected from individual missions – which cannot offer protection to everyone all the time – but there are more nuanced lessons as well around how both uniformed and non-uniformed elements of peace operations are needed in order to animate effective early warning systems, or to gain access to either reclusive rebel leaders or volatile conflict zones. To return to the hourglass metaphor introduced earlier, it may also be that the range of non-coercive protection strategies available to interveners narrows in relation to the intensity of the conflict, but it is also the case that the presence of armed peacekeepers in such contexts can help to expand the space for effective non-coercive engagement.

While this chapter has focused primarily on the non-coercive and unarmed side of the equation, in light of this discussion it is also worth some additional reflection on the specific nature of 'force' as it is employed and deployed in the context of peace operations. While they remain critical reference points for making sense of core protection dilemmas, both Rwanda and Srebrenica have tended to focus minds on one relatively narrow – and rather rare – scenario, that in which peacekeepers must choose between inaction and deadly force as determined armed groups bear down on unarmed civilians. As the work of Stian Kjeksrud (2016) has demonstrated, however, common sense understandings of force tend to downplay its more supple and intangible dimensions. While the use of force may indeed be brutal and bloody, the art of deterrence, by contrast, involves the subtle and calibrated threat of violence which, if the deterrent succeeds, is never carried out. In a similar way, while most police officers are armed, the deterrent aspect of this reality, in combination with an entire rule-of-law apparatus that a police uniform represents, ensures that police officers are only rarely in situations where they feel compelled to fire their weapons. This is precisely why, of course, it is so difficult to classify the work of armed peacekeepers – whether military or police – as either coercive or non-coercive. The fact of being armed sends clear messages to both conflict parties and unarmed civilians in a civil war context, and the significance and influence of such messages can easily be missed if the focus is placed on the fact that peacekeepers very rarely use force to protect civilians.

In an important contribution to the debate on uses of force in PoC contexts, Kjeksrud (2016: 332) argues that at its core, "there is little utility of force to be found if the function of force employed by the protector does not match the type of violence chosen by the perpetrator." In other words, protecting civilians through force of arms requires a clear-headed understanding of the kinds of violence that perpetrators deploy against civilians, and responding in kind. Drawing on earlier work by both Alexander Beadle and Rupert Smith, the latter a former commander of peacekeeping forces in Bosnia, Kjeksrud lays out both a typology of 'violence types' typically used by perpetrators, and a corresponding typology of four 'force functions' available to contemporary peacekeepers, including amelioration (delivering aid or observing ceasefires), containment (no-fly zones or interpositioning), deterrence/coercion (involving a stated commitment to response in force if certain 'red lines' are crossed) and destruction (as in the MONUSCO Force Intervention Brigade's mandate to 'neutralise' armed groups such as the M23). While Kjeksrud finds some statistical support for his core contention, his study is equally valuable in underlining both the different functions of force in peacekeeping and PoC contexts and the importance of understanding the motivations and strategies of armed groups who threaten civilians. In combination with the point developed above about the importance of 'hybrid' protection strategies which combine both the coercive and non-coercive repertoires of contemporary peace operations, this points to a promising line of inquiry that moves beyond the debate about whether UN peace operations protect (some) civilians and towards a more sustained exploration of what the recent history of PoC practice can teach us about the emergence of hybrid, contextually informed protection strategies that are capable of generating concrete and sustained improvements in protection outcomes.

Notes

1 It is not always possible, of course, to maintain a clear distinction between 'threatening' armed groups and 'threatened' civilians. In the South Sudan case, as discussed in Chapter 4, some of the most important examples of subnational conflict management – such as the Wunlit process of the late 1990s – have involved 'making peace' between neighbouring ethnic communities. In such cases, the line separating civilians from combatants becomes blurred to the point of non-existence.

2 Author interview, Bouar, June 2022.

Works Cited

Baines, E. and E. Paddon (2012) '"This is how we survived": Civilian agency and humanitarian protection', *Security Dialogue* 43(3): 231–247.

Bell, C. and J. Pospisil (2017) 'Navigating inclusion in transitions from conflict: The formalised political unsettlement', *Journal of International Development* 29: 576–593.

Bellamy, A. and C. Hunt (2015) 'Twenty-first century UN peace operations: protection, force and the changing security environment', *International Affairs*, 91(6): 1277–1298.

Berdal, M. (2018) 'The state of UN peacekeeping: Lessons from Congo', *The Journal of Strategic Studies* 41(5): 721–750.

Bonwick, A. (2006) 'Who really protects civilians?', *Development in Practice* 16(3/4): 270–277.

Boutellis, A. (2013) 'From crisis to reform: Peacekeeping strategies for the protection of civilians in the Democratic Republic of the Congo', *Stability: International Journal of Security and Development* 2(3): 48, 1–11.

Chenoweth, E. and M.J. Stephan (2011) *Why Civil Resistance Works: The Strategic Logic of Nonviolent Conflict* (New York: Columbia University Press).

Corbett, J. (2011) 'Learning from the Nuba: Civilian resilience and self-protection during conflict', Local to Global Protection Study, October; Available at: https://www.local2global.info/wp-content/uploads/SK_Nuba_L2GP_report_final.pdf

Donais, T. (2020) 'Protection through peace building: The future of UNMISS' protection of civilians mandate in South Sudan', CSG Policy Brief, No. 21, Centre for Security Governance; Available at: https://www.secgovcentre.org/publications

dos Santos Cruz, C.A. et al. (2017) 'Improving security of United Nations peacekeepers: We need to change the way we are doing business', 19 December; Available at: https://peacekeeping.un.org/sites/default/files/improving_security_of_united_nations_peacekeepers_report.pdf

Duursma, A., S. Lindberg Bromley and A. Gorur (2023) 'The impact of host-state consent on the protection of civilians in UN peacekeeping', *Civil Wars* (online first version): 1–25.

Ells Howes, D. (2013) 'The failure of pacifism and the success of nonviolence', *Perspectives on Politics* 11(2), 427–446.

Foley, C. (2023) *The Protection Paradox: How the UN Can Get Better at Saving Civilian Lives* (New York: Palgrave Macmillan).

Foot, R. (2020) *China, the UN, and Human Protection: Beliefs, Power, Image* (Oxford: Oxford University Press).

Gilmore, J. and K. Staples (2019) 'Introduction: The politics of protection and the limits of the ethical imagination', *International Politics* 56: 141–157.

Gorur, A. and N. Carstensen (2016) 'Community self-protection', in H. Willmot et al. (eds.), *Protection of Civilians* (Oxford: Oxford University Press), 409–427.

Gorur, A. and L. Sharland (2016) 'Prioritizing the protection of civilians in UN Peace operations: Analyzing the recommendations of the Hippo Report', Stimson Centre; Available at: https://www.stimson.org/2016/prioritizing-protection-civilians-un-peace-operations/

Hultman, L., J. Kathman and M. Shannon (2013) 'United Nations peacekeeping and civilian protection in civil war', *American Journal of Political Science* 57(4): 875–891.

Hunt, C. et al. (2024) *UN Peace Operations and Human Rights: A Thematic Study*. Report of the Effectiveness of Peace Operations (EPON) Network. Oslo: Norwegian Institute of International Affairs). Available at: https://www.nupi.no/en/publications/cristin-pub/un-peace-operations-human-rights-a-thematic-study

Jackson, R. (2019) 'Pacifism and the ethical imagination in IR', *International Politics* 56: 212–227.

Keating, T. (2017) 'UN peacekeeping and the protection of civilians' norm', in A. Hehir and R. W. Murray (eds.), *Protecting Human Rights in the 21st Century* (Abington/New York: Routledge), 110–125.

Kjeksrud, S. (2016) 'The utility of force for protecting civilians', in H. Willmot et al. (eds.), *Protection of Civilians* (Oxford: Oxford University Press), 329–349.

Koopman, S. (2013) 'Making space for peace: International protective accompaniment in Colombia', in F. McConnell et al. (eds.), *Geographies of Peace* (London/New York: I.B. Taurus), 109–130.

Levine, D.H. (2013) 'Some considerations for civilian-peacekeeper alliances', *Ethics & Global Politics* 6(1): 1–23.

Lilly, D. (2022) 'The UN agenda for protection: Policy, strategic and operational priorities', International Peace Institute, March; Available at: https://www.ipinst.org/wp-content/uploads/2022/03/UN-Agenda-for-Protection-PDF.pdf

Mahoney, L. (2006) *Proactive Presence: Field Strategies for Civilian Protection*. Geneva: Centre for Humanitarian Dialogue. Available at: https://hdcentre.org/insights/proactive-presence-field-strategies-for-civilian-protection/

Martin, B. (2012) 'How non-violence works', in C. Webel and J. Johansen (eds.), *Peace and Conflict Studies: A Reader* (New York: Routledge), 289–298.

McFate, S. (2010) 'The link between DDR and SSR in conflict-affected countries', United States Institute of Peace Special Report 238, May; Available at: https://static.newamerica.org/attachments/4130-the-link-between-ddr-and-ssr-in-conflict-affected-countries/SR238McFate_DDR_SSR_Conflict.eeed5947b577487bb892e4a782160df6.pdf

Ramsbotham, O., T. Woodhouse and H. Miall (2005) *Contemporary Conflict Resolution* (2nd Edition) (Cambridge: Polity).

Sedra, M. (2006) 'Security sector reform in Afghanistan: The slide toward expediency', *International Peacekeeping* 13(1): 94–110.

United Nations (UN) (2014) 'Security council resolution 2151', S/RES/2151, 28 April; Available at: https://digitallibrary.un.org/record/769811?ln=en&v=pdf

United Nations (UN) (2023) 'Our common agenda policy brief 9: A new agenda for peace', July; Available at: https://dppa.un.org/en/a-new-agenda-for-peace

UN Department of Peace Operations (UN DPO) (2023) 'Policy: The protection of civilians in United Nations peacekeeping (PoC Policy)', 1 May; Available at: https://peacekeeping.un.org/sites/default/files/2023_protection_of_civilians_policy.pdf

von Einsiedel, S. (2015) 'Non-military protection of civilians in UN Peace operations: Experiences and lessons', United Nations University Centre for Policy Research Occasional Paper 3, May; Available at: https://collections.unu.edu/eserv/UNU:3214/unu_cpr_non-military_poc.pdf

Weir, E. and C. Hunt (2011) 'Field report: DR Congo: Support community-based tools for MONUSCO', Refugees International, 3 May; Available at: https://www.refworld.org/reference/countryrep/ri/2011/en/79108

Williams, P.D. (2013) 'Protection, resilience and empowerment: United Nations peacekeeping and violence against civilians in contemporary war zones', *Politics* 33(4): 287–298.

Zahar, M.J. and D. Mechoulan (2017) 'Peace by pieces? Local mediation and sustainable peace in the Central African Republic', International Peace Institute Report, November; Available at: https://www.ipinst.org/wp-content/uploads/2017/11/1701_Peace-by-Pieces.pdf

4 All Necessary Means, with an Asterisk

How UNMISS Has Operationalised Its PoC Mandate

Introduction

South Sudan seems an unlikely location for a PoC success story. Some 14 years after their country became the world's newest independent state, the people of South Sudan remained among the most insecure on the planet. The post-independence civil war is widely believed to have claimed the lives of some 400,000 people, while as of mid-2024 some 4.6 million remained displaced, either inside or outside the country's borders. Fully three-quarters of the country's entire population (estimated at around 12 million) remain in need of ongoing humanitarian assistance, while millions have had their lives disrupted by unprecedented flooding. Hunger and malnutrition are widespread, with at least one major humanitarian agency warning of 'imminent disaster' and 'monumental levels of hunger' (Save the Children 2024). While a shaky peace agreement between the main conflict parties continued to hold as this volume went to press, even if the implementation process remains badly off track, fallout from the ongoing civil war in neighbouring Sudan has not only exacerbated South Sudan's displacement crisis, but has also seriously disrupted its oil exports, the country's principal revenue source, to the point of triggering warnings of an impending economic meltdown (ICG 2024; Francis and Marks 2024). While national elections (the first since independence) were scheduled for late 2024, the electoral schedule was ultimately pushed back a further two years, reflecting a widespread consensus that the current state of peace implementation made it impossible to organise free and fair elections. Absent a profound change of trajectory, however, elections – if and when they do proceed – could easily tip the country back into full-scale civil war.

In sharp contrast to this grim backdrop, however, it is also possible to build a compelling case that the UN Mission in South Sudan (UNMISS), deployed initially to help build capacity across the fledgling institutions of the South Sudanese state, has been among this century's most successful UN peace operations in terms of delivering on its PoC mandate. Indeed, few UN missions can point to as demonstrable an impact as UNMISS in terms of saving civilian lives. As conflict broke out along ethnic lines in late 2013, the mission opened its gates to tens of thousands of terrified civilians, many if not most of whom would almost certainly have perished in the absence of a rapid UNMISS response. Out of this initial decision emerged a

DOI: 10.4324/9781003291114-4

handful of so-called PoC sites, where more than 200,000 displaced South Sudanese found life-saving shelter – and services – through the worst days of the civil war. And despite dire warnings that transitioning the sites back to the control of South Sudan's government meant handing the victims back to the perpetrators, with the exception of one particularly sensitive site in Malakal (which remained under UNMISS control as of early 2025), the transition unfolded as painlessly as could be expected. While the former PoC sites – now government-controlled camps for internally displaced persons (IDPs) – have witnessed increased criminality and could yet become flashpoints for renewed violence (Sullivan 2022), it is beyond dispute that UNMISS has provided life-saving protection to hundreds of thousands of civilians. In this sense, UNMISS might be considered the Oskar Schindler of contemporary African conflict: while incapable of altering broader conflict dynamics, the mission has leveraged its unique position within the conflict context to save those that it could with the means at its disposal.

The UNMISS experience over the past dozen years, therefore, provides a paradigmatic example of the protection paradox, and the inevitably glass half full/glass half empty nature of the protection debate. When I first visited South Sudan in 2018, a common refrain among those I met was that UNMISS was 'not doing its job.' Despite managing security and infrastructure across sprawling PoC sites – the Bentiu site remains the country's second-largest population centre (Day et al. 2019: 63) – the inability of peacekeepers to provide any meaningful protection for the vast majority of vulnerable South Sudanese residing *outside* the sites, as well as numerous well-publicised protection failures within the sites themselves, left the widespread impression that the mission was failing to deliver on its headline mandate, especially as the civilian toll of the conflict continued to mount. For its part, UNMISS officials insisted that despite the rhetoric of all necessary means, there could never be a peacekeeper 'behind every tree,' and that the mission could only offer levels of protection commensurate with its capacity and areas of deployment.[1] What has emerged, therefore – and not just in South Sudan but more generally across UN peace operations with protection mandates – is a chronic perceptual disconnect between the providers and beneficiaries of UN protection. In conflict contexts where peacekeepers are present, insecure and often desperate civilians – understandably – expect peacekeepers to protect them if their lives are endangered, and have little patience for nuanced arguments about capacity and mandate that often determine, and limit, who does and does not receive protection. While this disconnect is often framed in UN reporting as resolvable through better public information or engagement, the more fundamental issue – inherent to PoC in peacekeeping contexts – is that missions make strategic choices, whether conscious or implicit, that have life-and-death consequences for the civilians they are mandated to protect. Since their country's descent into civil war in late 2013, in other words, the life chances of tens of thousands of vulnerable South Sudanese have been contingent on where they live (or where they may have fled), the nature of the threats they have faced, and the identity of those doing the threatening.

This chapter explores those strategic choices as they have been made in the South Sudan context – in the gap between the now-boilerplate mandate language of 'all necessary means' and the standard caveats about capacity and areas of deployment – and examines the consequences of such decisions. Consistent with the theoretical emphasis on protection practices as outlined in Chapter 1, and with Zoe Cormack and Naomi Pendle's observation (2024: 1) that the inherent ambiguity of the protection concept means that the 'practical meanings' of PoC are often established through implementation, the emphasis here is on the manner in which UNMISS' protection mandate has been operationalised – and the terms of protection established – as a result of both key strategic decisions on the ground and shifting contextual circumstances. At the risk of oversimplifying, the UNMISS experience with PoC can be understood as unfolding in two overlapping phases, both of which – unlike in the case of MONUSCO, addressed in the next chapter – have leaned decisively towards the non-coercive end of the protection spectrum. Once the UNMISS mandate was recalibrated to emphasise PoC and de-emphasise state-level institutional support after armed conflict broke out in late 2013, the lion's share of PoC programming, and mission resources, were devoted to the management of six distinct PoC sites. While the sites provided the mission with a clear protection focus, and a compelling protection narrative, they also generated a very clear – and occasionally uncomfortable – boundary between the protected and the unprotected. At the same time, the second key phase of the UNMISS protection story – which has placed a distinct emphasis on local-level, Tier 1 dialogue and engagement activities aimed at managing and ideally resolving conflict at the subnational level – emerged in the shadow of the PoC sites, but has gained additional prominence as the transfer of PoC sites to government control freed up additional mission resources to devote to dialogue and engagement efforts, while also enabling the mission's uniformed elements to extend their presence, whether through patrols or through the establishment of temporary operating bases in conflict hotspots. Here too, however, strategic decisions have come with clear trade-offs, and it remains an open question whether local-level conflict resolution efforts (what I have termed elsewhere 'protection through peacebuilding' (Donais 2020)) are sustainable in the absence of progress towards peace implementation at the national level. This is especially so as it is widely understood that local- and national-level dynamics are closely linked, with state-level governance dynamics, dominated by a patronage system described by the International Crisis Group (2024) as 'rotten to the core,' often identified as the key driver of subnational violence.

Beyond a focus on the specific strategic decisions and the trade-offs involved, this chapter also draws attention to the dangers for the UN – particularly apparent in the UNMISS case – of the contemporary shift in emphasis *towards* PoC as "the defining purpose of the UN in the twenty-first century" (cited in Kilroy et al. 2024: 2) and *away* from more conventional approaches focused on sustainable conflict resolution, rather than viewing the former as an essential, if short-term, complement to the latter. While even the most competent, committed and well-resourced missions will always be vulnerable to the criticism that they do not do enough to protect civilians, of greater concern is the UN's demonstrable inability to advance the cause of sustainable peace in South Sudan over its tenure. Writing in 2021, for example, Mats Berdal and David Shearer (2021: 72–73), the latter having served as the Head of UNMISS from 2017 to 2021, acknowledged that "from its inception UNMISS's influence on internal political processes and conflict actors in South Sudan, especially among the Juba political elites, has been limited." This is, as I have noted previously, part and parcel of an ongoing crisis of peacebuilding, which has left peacekeepers to address – indefinitely in many cases – the downstream consequences of ongoing conflict in the absence of any discernible progress towards long-term peacebuilding or conflict resolution. In South Sudan's case, with the passage of time the dangers of this ongoing disconnect between short-term protection and longer-term peacebuilding (the latter rightfully understood as the only sustainable way to reduce the threat of violence against civilians) – as well as of the wishful thinking involved in trying to nudge conflict actors and political elites towards embracing principles of good governance – are becoming increasingly evident. The reality is that UNMISS remains without a viable state-level partner committed to progressively taking over protection responsibilities, while the ever-present possibility of renewed conflict – with one analysis describing South Sudan as sitting "on the precipice of a period of profound uncertainty and instability" (ICG 2024) – and the combined effects of environment and economic crises risks overwhelming whatever protection successes have been achieved over the past decade.

The PoC Site Era

It would have been a peacekeeper's worst nightmare, akin perhaps to being caught unawares by an approaching tsunami wave.[2] According to one version of the PoC site origin story (Cormack and Pendle 2024: 7), as thousands of desperate civilians converged on the main UN base in Juba after violence broke out on 15 December 2013, it was left to one on-duty UN police officer at the gates to decide how to respond. In the event – and we can only speculate about whether the officer's actions were driven by humanitarian considerations or by the inevitability that the base's perimeter would be breached regardless – the gates were opened, and within hours the UN found itself having taken thousands of terrified civilians into protective custody. This figure would mushroom in the days and months to come, and extend well beyond Juba, as South Sudan's rapid descent into full-scale civil war meant that what senior UN officials expected to be a short-term expedient – a matter of days or weeks at most (Hagemann 2020: 23) – settled into a semi-permanent state of affairs. While UNMISS was in many ways a hostage to circumstance at that moment – as well as to history, given the weight of past protection failures – it is also the case that decisions made by front-line personnel, both at the onset of the crisis and as the realities of feeding, sheltering and protecting large numbers of displaced civilians began to sink in, would profoundly shape both the trajectory and the parameters of the UNMISS protection response in South Sudan for years to come.

Given the inherent ambiguity of contemporary protection discourse – the impossibility of protecting all vulnerable civilians in conflict contexts, the lack of clarity and consensus around how precisely civilians should be protected, and the uncertainty surrounding how to reconcile the protection imperative with other elements of peacekeeping mandates (and indeed with peacekeeping's foundational principles) – making sense of protection interventions requires a close reading of everyday practices (Cormack and Pendle 2024). In other words, as Anine Hagemann (2020: 19) has suggested, it is through the actions of 'street-level' peacekeeping professionals that the tensions, ambiguities, limitations and possibilities of PoC are negotiated. This characterisation of peacekeeper agency draws explicitly from Lipsky's (2010) classic account of street-level bureaucrats, which emphasised how individual discretion in interpreting 'official' guidance – never comprehensive, not always consistent, and typically marked by notable gaps between expected outcomes and allocated resources – shapes in crucial ways the manner in which public policies are delivered to, and received by, their constituencies. This emphasis on everyday practice is especially pertinent in the context of PoC mandates, given the extent to which the nature of Security Council deliberations, combined with ongoing contestation around the very meaning of protection, has precluded the establishment of detailed, fine-grained guidance around the how of protection and has effectively downloaded onto individual missions the responsibility for working out the details of what is and is not possible in challenging environments with limited resources. In the case of UNMISS in particular, at both the micro and macro levels what the mission has actually 'done' to protect civilians has been shaped far more by the cumulative decisions of field-level personnel than by the faithful implementation of grand strategy from the top down.

At the macro level, the decision to accept – however grudgingly – the indefinite presence of tens of thousands of displaced civilians within the perimeters of UN bases shaped the terms of PoC in South Sudan and set the mission on a very different trajectory relative to its sister missions in the region. For better or for worse, the sites very quickly emerged as the face of PoC for both the mission and the broader populace, even as they offered the mission some useful clarity in terms of how precisely its PoC mandate was to be operationalised and who precisely it would be protecting. In this sense, it allowed the mission to skirt awkward questions around how a relatively small force operating in a country the size of France could provide any meaningful degree of protection to civilians caught up in a brutal civil conflict. As Kilroy and Ryan (2024: 140) have noted,

> having the people in need of protection in a clearly designated, accessible area is an easier option for peacekeepers than trying to cover vast geographic areas with limited uniformed personnel, particularly when freedom of movement is often restricted and in the face of serious logistical challenges during the rainy season.

By narrowing its field of vision, the mission could credibly claim that it was delivering on what had become its pre-eminent mandate task. Not everyone, of course, accepted that protecting a relatively small number of IDPs within a handful of PoC sites represented the most efficient or effective use of mission resources. In a 2019 assessment, for example, the Effectiveness of Peace Operations Network (EPON) noted that the management of the sites consumed an outsized portion of the mission's protection resources, tying down upwards of 70 per cent of both its military and policing assets (Day et al. 2019: 60–61). All this to provide assistance to approximately 10 per cent of South Sudan's internally displaced population of some 2 million (the overall population of those in need of protection being much greater; Day et al. 2019: 62). Despite such concerns, and the stark manner in which the perimeters of PoC sites divided the protected from the unprotected, the relative safety enjoyed by those within the sites provided clear evidence of impact, especially since, as Kilroy and Ryan (2024: 147) note, had the sites not existed UNMISS would still have struggled to provide countrywide protection.

At a micro level, the everyday practices of protection within the sites also beget protection policy over time as field-level personnel attempted to stabilise uncertainty and manage ambiguity in response to the unprecedented state of affairs within the PoC sites themselves. According to standard Status of Forces Agreements (SOFA) signed between the UN and mission-hosting states, UN facilities are under the exclusive control and authority of the UN, despite being located on the sovereignty territory of the host state (Cormack and Pendle 2024: 8). In principle, therefore, the Government of South Sudan had neither legal authority over the sites nor permission to enter. With sole responsibility for the maintenance of law and order in the sites, UNMISS quickly discovered that PoC in practice meant not only protecting site residents from external threats, but from each other as well. And while the SOFA gave UNMISS the authority to do policing, it also specified that "people who had been taken into custody by UNMISS must be handed over to national police immediately" (Hagemann 2020: 22). Since the majority of site residents were there precisely because of a well-founded fear of persecution by state authorities, this presented a clear dilemma for the mission. Detention without handover to national authorities was technically illegal, while handing over detainees risked exposing them to serious human rights violations at the hands of state security forces.

As Hagemann has detailed in a discussion of UNMISS detention practices, the PoC site era saw the gradual emergence of detention policies and practices as the mission struggled to come to terms with the responsibilities of maintaining law and order within the sites. As she notes, trial and error practices came first and policies followed; from the first ad hoc improvisations aimed at separating perpetrators from the general camp population – some of the first detainees found themselves incarcerated in UN vehicles and office containers (Hagemann 2020: 25) – detention facilities and policies gradually emerged, including the establishment of holding facilities and the eventual introduction of mobile courts managed by national authorities. Such measures eased the tensions and ambiguities somewhat, but never fully resolved them. Questions around due process, the legality of indefinite detention, and respect for international standards concerning detention lingered, in part because of the mission's insistence that the challenges posed by detention – as well as the sites themselves – were temporary, and would disappear once site residents returned home. This 'insistence on impermanence' (Hagemann 2020: 24) justified a failure to fully institutionalise detention practices as an essential element of protection within the sites, while at the same time relegating the majority of 'holdees' to a kind of legal limbo, largely out of sight and beyond the rule of law.

With respect to the mission's willingness to deploy all necessary means, including lethal force, to protect when necessary, the experience of the PoC sites is also illustrative of a more cautious, conservative posture adopted by UNMISS and its military contingents at a time when pressures to embrace more robust forms of protection were building.[3] In the face of tensions between the Security Council and the UN Secretariat over precisely how robust the UNMISS mandate should be (Millar 2022: 22), on the ground the mission – whether through its responsibility for PoC sites or through the occasional establishment of temporary operating bases in specific hotspots – came to rely heavily on the deterrent impact of its mere presence, and it became clear early on that the mission was unwilling to confront militarily government security forces complicit in civilian abuses. One external report from 2012 cited UNMISS officials as stressing that "no UNMISS peacekeeper ever has – or ever would – shoot an SPLA soldier to protect a civilian being abused by that soldier" (cited in Millar 2022: 56).[4] With regard to the PoC sites specifically, in ordinary circumstances deterrence through presence worked well enough, with UN police patrolling within the sites, the mission's military contingents providing perimeter security, and the Government of South Sudan and its security forces respecting the non-violability of the sites themselves. When this *modus vivendi* broke down, however, the limitations of this reliance of protection through presence were cruelly exposed, as were the sites' inhabitants.

Several incidents in particular were deeply corrosive to the UN's claims about effectively shielding those sheltering within the PoC sites. On the morning of 17 April 2014, a group of mostly Dinka youth approached the gates of the Bor PoC site, in Jonglei state, which was at the time sheltering some 5,000 mostly Nuer IDPs. The situation quickly escalated as a small group breached the site perimeter and opened the main gate to other attackers, who began shooting indiscriminately (Millar 2022: 73). The UNMISS soldiers guarding the site made little effort to repel the intruders before the shooting started, with some reportedly retreating from fortified positions and into the main UNMISS base. A quick reaction force (QRF) eventually arrived and opened fire on the attackers, but by then the damage had been done; 47 IDPs lay dead (along with three perpetrators and three additional 'unknown' victims) (Radio Tamazuj 2015). While after-incident reporting made it clear that South Sudanese security forces – and especially members of the South Sudanese National Police Service – were at the very least complicit in the attack if not active participants, the bulk of the attention focused on the failure of UNMISS peacekeepers to escalate as the nature of the incursion became clear. As Millar notes, the incident highlighted the shortcomings of peacekeeper training with regard to both protection obligations and high-risk scenario planning, the ongoing reluctance of contingent commanders to act outside national chains of command (the battalion commander spent much of the crisis, reportedly, on the phone consulting with his national headquarters), and the more general failure of the mission to prioritise the physical security of PoC sites (2022: 75).

Some two years later, in February 2016, violence broke out among Dinka, Nuer and Shilluk residents of the PoC site in Malakal, and was intensified when attackers wearing uniforms of the Sudan People's Liberation Army (SPLA) breached the site perimeter and joined the fray. The violence left some 30 IDPs dead, more than 120 injured, and resulted in about a third of the camp being burned to the ground. As in the earlier Bor incident, the UNMISS response was criticised as 'too little, too late,' with peacekeepers again demonstrating confusion about rules of engagement and, ultimately, little appetite to deploy lethal force to save civilian lives (Foltyn 2016).

Worse was to come several months later when South Sudan's first Transitional Government of National Unity collapsed. As violence escalated in mid-July and opposition leader (and former first vice-president) Riek Machar fled the capital, UNMISS bases and their affiliated PoC sites increasingly came under fire. Once again, the UNMISS military response was irresolute, with now-familiar reports emerging of peacekeepers retreating into more fortified areas of their bases, leaving vulnerable site residents exposed to incoming perimeter fire; several dozen were killed across the two PoC sites in Juba. In one widely reported incident, SPLA soldiers attacked the Terrain camp, a residential compound near UN House, where they proceeded, in the words of one account of the events, "to rape and gang rape at least five international aid workers, physically or sexually assault at least a dozen others, and execute a South Sudanese journalist – apparently because of his Nuer ethnicity" (Spink and Wells 2016: 6). Despite UNMISS being aware of the attack shortly after it began and orders being given for a QRF to respond, both the Chinese and Ethiopian battalions refused to leave their base. According to the UN's Independent Special Investigation into the crisis (UN 2016), while UNMISS lacked the capacity to offer ironclad protection guarantees to PoC site residents, failure of leadership and chronic risk-aversion made a difficult situation worse and generated a response that was both chaotic and ineffective. Noting that "failure by peacekeepers to act when civilians are attacked rises above the level of simple underperformance," the report called for relevant commanders and troop-contributing countries to be held accountable (UN 2016: 6). In the event, the recently arrived Kenyan military commander of UNMISS, Lt Gen Johnson Ondieki, was ultimately sacked, prompting Kenya to temporarily withdraw its military contingent from South Sudan in protest against what it considered an unjust act of scapegoating (Donais and Tanguay 2021: 571).

These incidents underlined the circumscribed nature of protection practice, at least as operationalised by UNMISS. Not only was the mission only able to offer protection to certain, relatively privileged categories of civilian in certain geographic locations, but it also demonstrated the limits beyond which the mission – and in particular its armed agents – was not willing to go to protect civilian life. Given this, those residing within the camps might have been forgiven for thinking that a protection promise which ended as soon as the shooting began was little better than no protection at all, and that they might have ultimately been better off relying on self-protection strategies, rather than counting on the UN's rather leaky protection umbrella. At the very least, the well-publicised protection failures within the PoC sites punctured the broader UN narrative that the PoC sites were not only safe havens but also exemplars of 'protection done right.'

The paralysis *vis-à-vis* use of force decisions that characterised the UNMISS crisis response across these episodes was also rooted, ultimately, in the mission's complicated relationship with the South Sudanese government. Armed attacks on PoC sites crossed clear, unambiguous red lines, and in retrospect it is easy to condemn peacekeepers for failing to respond robustly to such egregious violations of the *modus vivendi* that had emerged around the sites. While confusion around protection responsibilities and rules of engagement on the part of peacekeeping forces could have – and should have – been resolved in the period between the Bor and Juba PoC crises, the fact that uncertainty and indecision continued to plague the UN response suggests that the failure to use force had deeper roots. Specifically, in each case government security forces – both police and military – were either complicit in the attacks or direct participants, a reality which raised the stakes of using force on the part of mission personnel considerably.

As with its sister missions in neighbouring CAR and DRC, the relationship between UNMISS and the Government of South Sudan was fraught from the outset, and became more so once civil war broke out and the government became a party to the conflict. Having only just gained its independence following a decades-long armed struggle, it was to be expected that the government would be particularly sensitive to sovereignty concerns, and this reality may have flavoured the UNMISS approach in the early post-independence period. Millar (2022: 66), for example, highlights the reluctance of the first head of UNMISS, Hilde Johnson, to push back against government excesses, a posture he also attributes to Johnson's diplomatic and development background, and her personal connections with high-ranking officials such as President Salva Kiir. Structurally, however, it remains the case that any peace operation with a PoC mandate – whose very presence in a host state is conditional on the ongoing consent of that state – finds itself torn between its protection obligations and the imperative of maintaining good relations with the state. Once the UN pivoted, in Adam Day's words (2022: 42), from "the role of building the state to one of protecting the people from it," these tensions became increasingly difficult to finesse.

While these tensions manifest themselves in various ways – most notably through persistent freedom of movement restrictions, in violation of the SOFA, and through the government's consistent refusal to allow UNMISS to use reconnaissance drones – the PoC sites quickly became a major source of friction between the government and the mission. In most cases, the residents of PoC sites were there precisely because they were, from the government's perspective, on the wrong side of the civil war. With the distinction between soldier and civilian difficult to maintain, and with the porous nature of the site boundaries allowing both individuals and weapons to move in and out, the government's default position was that the UN, through the PoC sites, was providing succour and refuge to its enemies. This, perhaps, explains the UN's consistent ambivalence *vis-à-vis* the sites, manifest both in its refusal to consider the sites as anything other than a temporary expedient and its eagerness to wind them down. It also provides at least a partial explanation for the mission's marked reluctance to confront uniformed agents of the South Sudanese state, despite official UN guidance authorising the use of force – in extremis – regardless of the source of the threat. This posture of non-confrontation has, at least to date, enabled UNMISS to avoid the fate of MINUSMA, which was terminated in 2023 after the Government of Mali withdrew its consent for the mission's presence, but it has come at a cost. Not only has UNMISS been accused of double standards in its differential treatment of abuses by government and opposition forces (and the balance of evidence, as in the DRC, suggests that a preponderance of abuses against civilians have been carried out by the former), but the refusal to confront abuses on the part of government or government-allied forces may have indirectly encouraged such abuses on the part of armed elements confident that peacekeepers would not stand in their way. For site residents having to navigate these realities, speculation has also been rife about the motivations of particular military contingents; in Juba's PoC 3 site, for example, it was widely believed that the Chinese contingent's refusal to take action during the July 2016 crisis had much to do with China's growing economic ties to the South Sudanese government; according to this narrative, protecting civilians ranked well below good government-to-government relations in the hierarchy of Chinese priorities in South Sudan.[5]

Ultimately, Kilroy and Ryan's characterisation (2024: 143) of the PoC sites as Janus-like is accurate on a number of fronts. First, as they observe, the sites were held up both as shining examples of UNMISS accomplishments and as impediments to the mission's ability to expand its protection efforts. They were also, for long periods of time, safe havens for those civilians with legitimate fears for their lives, while at other moments they appeared more like shooting galleries, with trapped civilians easy targets for armed assailants. The sites also served as a particularly sensitive focal point for the unavoidable tensions between missions and host governments that all contemporary peace operations must navigate: while stabilisation and extension of state authority were downplayed as mandate tasks once the context changed from state-building to civil war, the ongoing efforts of UNMISS to position itself as a neutral third party and prioritise good relations with the government were consistently undermined by the latter's sense that the former was on the side of the armed opposition. Little wonder, then, that UNMISS insisted on the 'impermanence' of the PoC sites, and consistently sought to unburden itself of the obligations of PoC site management. This emphasis on impermanence generated yet another paradox within the PoC site model, and a persistent source of tension with the humanitarian community, which provided many of the services within the sites themselves: the reluctance of the mission to invest in site upgrades to bring them up to international refugee protection standards, lest the 'superior' conditions within the sites – from the perspective of both security and services – encourage yet more civilians to move in. While there was relatively little evidence of this 'pull factor' growing the numbers within specific PoC sites (Briggs 2017: 53), the wider sentiment contributed to difficult and overcrowded living conditions for those within the sites; in the PoC site context then, UNMISS was simultaneously protecting civilians while deliberately constraining their ability to lead minimally dignified lives.

In the end, the worst fears – many expressed by the humanitarian actors working the PoC sites themselves – about the transition of the sites from UN to government control did not come to pass. In some cases, as in Bentiu, detailed transition arrangements were hashed out in advance among UN representatives, local officials and PoC community leaders, and 'ownership' of the sites was transferred literally overnight.[6] While fear and mistrust are still facts of life for those still living in the newly re-branded IDP camps – memories of wartime atrocities have most certainly not gone away, and neither have the conflict's primary cleavages – threats to physical security within the camps now have more to do with growing criminality than with a renewal of the inter-ethnic violence that led to the creation of the sites in the first place. While continued UNMISS proximity patrolling has provided additional assurances to camp residents, of more immediate concern is the reduction of services within the camps, as many UN agencies and NGOs withdrew with the handover, and in their wake, water and food distribution has been either reduced or eliminated entirely. According to some observers, this reduction of services suits the larger interests of the government in resolving the issue once and for all by encouraging all camp residents to return to their pre-war homes.[7] While numbers have reduced somewhat, the exodus has been slowed, and in some cases reversed, by the country's unprecedented floods, which have inundated pre-war homes (and turned camps like the one in Bentiu into isolated islands). At the same time, returns have also been slowed by the legal and practical challenges of claiming pre-war property. In an echo of post-war Bosnia, for many of South Sudan's displaced the promise of return is stymied by the reality of 'others' now occupying their property; if those 'others' happen to be military officers, for example, the odds of successfully returning fall to almost zero. Ultimately, therefore, while the PoC site transition resolved a major source of friction between the government and the UN, and overcame a situation in which inordinate UNMISS resources were devoted to the protection of a handful of particularly vulnerable civilians, that formerly privileged group has now been thrust into the same scenario of insecurity and precarity as the vast majority of their compatriots.

Dialogue and Engagement: Protection through Subnational Peacebuilding

In parallel with its role in securing and managing PoC sites, UNMISS has in recent years also moved to embrace Tier I protection activities – those focused on dialogue and engagement – as the centrepiece of its PoC strategy. This emphasis is captured in recent reports of the UN Secretary General on UNMISS, which stress the mission's efforts to promote "inclusive dialogue, peaceful coexistence, reconciliation and social cohesion at the national and subnational levels to enhance protection of civilians," and point to the dozens of programmes being implemented by UNMISS aimed at addressing subnational and intercommunal conflict (UN 2024a, 2024b). By contrast, official reporting over the same period makes no reference to the mission's use of force to protect civilians, emphasising instead the standardised patrolling conducted by the mission's uniformed elements and the static presence of temporary operations bases (four at the time of writing) in especially volatile communities.

In its embrace of protection through local-level peacebuilding (now embedded within the mission's mandate), UNMISS finds itself in an increasingly crowded space, if still *primus inter pares* given its unique reach and multidimensional asset mix. Given the contemporary dynamics of insecurity in South Sudan, a growing number of national and international NGOs are now working on local peacebuilding initiatives, on the argument that this is where the greatest protection dividends are to be found. As Jan Pospisal and colleagues (2020) have noted, the armed political struggle across a fractured Sudan People's Liberation Movement (SPLM) tended to obscure more localised violence, "whose causes include perceived marginalization, intercommunal grievances, competition over resources, endemic cattle-raiding and conflict between cattle-keepers and farmers"; with the top-level conflict now largely contained by a still-fragile peace agreement, such subnational conflict dynamics have now come into clearer focus as the greatest threats to civilian life. Even during the PoC site era, UNMISS had enjoyed some success in facilitating conflict-dampening dialogues between herders and farmers, even if they also discovered that agreements reached were also difficult to sustain in the absence of ongoing engagement.[8] Similarly, the 2018 Revitalised Agreement on the Resolution of the Conflict in South Sudan (R-ARCSS) – while a decidedly imperfect document in many ways – did create opportunities for *rapprochements* to emerge among mid-level military and political leaders across the government/opposition divide. In 2019, for example, the UNMISS field office in Bentiu helped broker a local peace deal that ultimately led to a regional co-governance arrangement, public apologies on both sides, and the beginnings of local action against criminality (Donais and Solomon 2022: 59). The deal also likely contributed to the relatively smooth handover of the management of the Bentiu PoC site from UN to government control, as did the fact that the area's primary cleavage was intra-rather than intercommunal, with the region's population being primarily Nuer.

Bentiu might therefore be considered a special case, more amenable to negotiated solutions since it lacked the inter-tribal tensions found elsewhere in South Sudan. It is also the case, however, that many subnational and intercommunal conflicts have features that not only make differences easier to bridge (at least relative to the existential, zero-sum logic of elite power struggle), but also make the benefits of peace immediately tangible to communities on both sides of a conflict. While local-level conflict in Sudan is rarely insulated from national-level dynamics – contemporary cattle-raiding practices, for example, are overlaid by the reality that cattle ownership has become increasingly concentrated in the hands of Juba-based elites, who often stoke local conflict, including through arms provision, as a strategy for mobilising support in their home regions (see the more detailed discussion below) – the motivation to address such conflicts often comes from violence-weary communities themselves. In the words James Ninrew Dong, a Presbyterian pastor who played a key role in facilitating a successful local dialogue process in 2018 across the Nuer-Dinka divide in Payinjiar and Yirol counties, the initiative began with the affected communities asking themselves "if the government and SPLA-IO opposition are not ready to bring peace to our community, why don't we do it ourselves?" (cited in PAX-Protection of Civilians 2023).[9] While the peace and protection dividends emerging from successful local dialogue processes are immediately evident in the form of reductions in violence, it is also the case that the more such dialogues are locally owned, the more likely communities are to be invested in ensuring their sustainability over the longer term. Moreover, in a manifestation of what John Paul Lederach once termed 'middle-out' peacebuilding (1997: 39), local-level peace dialogues are also more likely to draw not only on culturally relevant conflict management practices, but also on respected authority figures – especially traditional chiefs and religious leaders – to lend legitimacy and moral authority to proceedings. For these reasons, over time UNMISS – and particularly its Civil Affairs Division – has attempted to move away from initiating dialogue processes among communities in conflict, and towards leveraging resources to support agreements brokered by local communities themselves.[10] In South Sudan's resource-poor periphery, in other words, to the extent that external actors such as UNMISS can incentivise the organisation and implementation of local peace dialogues through timely injections of resources – whether financial or in-kind – they can support the consolidation and deepening of local agreements.

Despite the promise of the protection through local peacebuilding approach, which has generated some clear and empirically demonstrable benefits in the form of violence reduction, it is also clear that it is no panacea. Indeed, at South Sudan's present juncture, there are several reasons not to be overly sanguine about the prospects for building peace from the bottom up. In the first place, laying the groundwork for successful local dialogue processes is almost inevitably complex and time-consuming (the Payinjiar-Yirol dialogue took three years to bring to fruition), and requires coming to terms with long-running legacies of violence, cultural traditions such as revenge killings that often celebrate violence (especially by young men), and deepening competition for scarce resources, including land and water. The 1999 Wunlit Peace and Reconciliation Conference, for example – which remains for many the gold standard for how to engage communities in conflict in southern/South Sudan, given its impact in significantly easing tensions between Dinka and Nuer communities – required not only extensive community level pre-consultations but also a sound understanding of traditional knowledge and customary ritual. The necessary immersion in cultural understanding and local conflict dynamics is not for the impatient or faint of heart, especially since ill-considered or poorly planned interventions may ultimately do more harm than good (Wild et al. 2019: 666, 669). Such considerations may be relaxed somewhat in the case of community-initiated processes, but such cases require outside actors to be both patient and opportunistic, and may result in a patchwork of interventions that create, at best, disconnected islands of temporary local stability. Particularly in light of increasing evidence of donor fatigue, as external actors grow impatient with the glacial pace of South Sudan's peace implementation process, community-level dialogue processes may appear as isolated drops in a bucket, unable to generate critical mass or sufficient momentum to exert positive pressure at higher levels of the political system. There is little evidence, for example, that community-level peace dialogues have sufficiently empowered local communities to push back against elite-level manipulation (Krause 2019: 489).

It is increasingly evident, therefore, that bottom-up peacebuilding is most effective not as a substitute for top-down processes, but rather as a complement to them. As Lauren Spink has noted (2020: 12), UNMISS has not been oblivious to such concerns, and has made a concerted effort through its programme of work to connect top-down and bottom-up engagement processes. One example of this 'whole of mission integrated approach' can be seen in the mission's response to an outbreak of violence in Tambura, a county in the southwest that had been spared large-scale violence through much of the post-2013 period. As violence surged in mid-2021, UNMISS responded with a multi-pronged approach, which included the deployment of a temporary operating base, engagement with Juba-based elites – whose manoeuvrings over the provincial governorship had triggered the violence in the first place – extensive human rights reporting, intensive engagement with local stakeholders (including community-level peace consultations), and coordinated humanitarian assistance (UNMISS/OHCHR 2021). Consistent with past practice – and a generalised belief across the mission that using force for protection purposes came with unacceptable risks of counterproductive escalation – UNMISS troops did not engage directly with the perpetrators of the violence, but rather focused on deterrence by strategic presence, which included armed escorts of humanitarian workers and vulnerable IDPs (especially women forced to venture out of relatively safe spaces in search of firewood and water). Despite this effort, which represents a good example of a mission bringing to bear all of its multifaceted assets on an emerging protection crisis, as of this writing Tambura remains a conflict hotspot – with a fresh upsurge of violence in mid-2024 – and it is increasingly clear that while the mission's efforts have mitigated ongoing violence, they have not succeeded in disabling its key drivers or addressing its root causes (Sudans Post 2024).

Second, a series of intersecting crises has in recent years has been a severe test of community resilience and may be pushing stressed communities further into conflict with each other. Civil war in neighbouring Sudan, for example, has driven an estimated 800,000 people – many of them South Sudanese who had previously fled north to escape fighting – back south across the border. With South Sudan's capacity to absorb this rapid population influx limited at best, the returnees have increased pressure on local resources and generated tensions with host communities. The effects of war-induced population movements have been compounded by severe flooding that has affected fully half of all of South Sudan's counties and deeply impacted the lives, and livelihoods, of some 1.4 million people (OCHA 2024). While patterns of flood and ebb are a fact of life across much of South Sudan – especially through the vast Sudd wetlands – climate change has seriously disrupted hydrological cycles and those that depend on them; hundreds of thousands have been displaced, and there is growing concern that many of the displaced many never be able to return to their homes (Levi and Stephens 2024). In a country comprised of 64 distinct ethnic groups, each with deep ties to land and territory, the sheer scale of vulnerable populations on the move is not only pushing many to the brink of survival, it is also exacerbating inter-group tensions and fuelling further conflict. Increasingly, therefore, the capacity of dialogue processes to ease local-level conflict may be being undermined by demographic and environmental trends.

Overlaying these worrying trends is a deep economic crisis, which is also linked to Sudan's civil war and the disruption of South Sudan's ability to get its oil to market. Given that oil exports account for some 90 per cent of government revenue, warnings that the country faces an economic meltdown are not exaggerated, although the government hoped to resume oil exports by early 2025 (Ponnie 2025). Somewhat ironically, the 70 per cent of the South Sudanese population who reside outside of the country's main urban centres have been insulated from the unfolding financial crisis by their marginalisation from the formal economy; South Sudan's complex system of patronage has long ensured that most rural residents see little benefit – in the form of government benefits or support – from the country's natural resource endowments. Nevertheless, economic crisis has had ripple effects across the country, both in the form of increased prices for basic goods as the South Sudanese pound depreciates, and in the form of unpaid, hungry, and increasingly disgruntled police and soldiers, whose performance has deteriorated as wage arrears have accumulated.[11] More generally, both rural and urban areas have seen notable spikes in criminality as young men in particular seek alternative means of survival.

Finally, as noted above, national-level political dynamics continue to drive subnational conflict, and there is ample evidence that the often-toxic linkages between elite-level power dynamics and local-level intergroup relations remain firmly in place. In this sense then, the failures to advance the implementation of the peace process – manifest in the announcement that elections, which were to signal the end of South Sudan's transitional period, had been further delayed until late 2026 – have left largely unchallenged a political status quo in Juba that continues to export insecurity into the periphery. While subnational, and especially intercommunal, conflict is generally understood to entail violent contestation that does not involve a direct challenge to the national government, as Jana Krause has observed (2019: 483) such conflicts are nevertheless "fundamentally political and do not take place in isolation from national political processes and the institutional framework of the state." In the specific case of South Sudan, the perverse incentive structures faced by national-level elites *vis-à-vis* local conflict dynamics have long been recognised, with one UN official lamenting as early as 2009 – before the establishment of either UNMISS or an independent South Sudan – that "all our peace conference and reconciliation efforts at the grassroots level are doomed as long as politicians are whipping up their communities" (cited in Krause 2019: 489). The same set of dynamics and incentive structures persist today, with one Juba-based observer noting that at present the 'million-dollar question' in South Sudan is how much progress is possible through local-level, bottom-up peace processes absent commensurate progress in transforming top-down political dynamics.[12]

Ironically, it was the agreement that ended large-scale violence between the main conflict parties in South Sudan's civil war – the R-ARCSS of 2018 – which created the conditions for the perpetuation of the myriad forms of subnational violence that continue to perpetuate human insecurity across the country. At its core, the revitalised agreement was an exercise in elite pact-making, in which rebel groups were encouraged to stop fighting with the promise of key – and ultimately lucrative – government positions for themselves and their most senior deputies. Thus, the revitalised agreement followed the original ARCSS agreement by bringing SPLM-IO leader Riek Machar back into a Government of National Unity as vice-president, with a further entitlement to place a certain percentage of his people into key government positions. As Daniel Akech Thiong (2018) warned even prior to the signing of the R-ARCSS, the strategy of "buying off violent elites with government posts" is doomed to fail, not only because it is anathema to democracy, justice and accountability and does nothing to address either the root causes of conflict or the concerns of ordinary people, but because it incentivises those who find themselves at the top table to constantly manoeuver for an ever-larger slice of the power-sharing pie. The post-2018 period, therefore, has been characterised by foot-dragging on peace implementation, since those most responsible for peace implementation also have the most to lose from the full implementation of the agreement and the most to gain from an indefinite continuation of the status quo. Crucially, this period has also been characterised by 'relevance-signalling' on the part of key elites, who demonstrate their power and influence – and the risks they pose should they choose to defect and play the role of spoiler – through their ability to mobilise 'their' people, and the strongest signals are those which involve the use of violence. In other words, ongoing elite power struggles are regularly manifest through subnational violence, in which ethnic and other cleavages are mobilised and militarised, and pre-existing militias and self-defence mechanisms co-opted and instrumentalised, to further the particular ambitions of elites.

Such power struggles play out in different ways across South Sudan, with violence in Tambura, referenced above, offering one variation on the broader theme. The Tambura crisis emerged directly from the power-sharing dynamics at the core of the R-ARCSS, and specifically from the fact that the SPLM-IO was entitled, as part of the deal, to appoint a certain number of state governors. This included the governorship of Western Equatoria, which encompasses Tambura. Whereas previous governors had enjoyed strong ties with Kiir's SPLM and with the Avungura clan of the Azande tribe – a majority in Tambura county – Machar's SPLM-IO appointed Alfred Futuyo, a former opposition commander who was half-Balanda (a minority in Tambura) (Mednick 2022). Futuyo's appointment destabilised Tambura's *modus vivendi*, triggering fierce inter-group competition as Azande leaders were encouraged to mobilise against their loss of political influence while the Balanda counter-mobilised in response. While the conflict was ultimately about which faction of the misnamed Government of National Unity would control the region, it is also, in the words of a joint UNMISS-Office of the High Commissioner on Human Rights report on the crisis, a paradigmatic case of where pre-existing fractures – in this case between Azande and Balanda – "have been … politicized, exacerbated, and exploited" (UNMISS/OHCHR 2021: 4). Both Futuyo and Gen. James Nando – an Azande who had defected from the SPLM-IO in March 2020 and directed government forces and local militias through the crisis – were ultimately sanctioned by the US Treasury Department for their roles in the violence that ensued, which included hundreds of cases of conflict-related sexual violence and the forcible displacement of some 80,000 civilians (US Department of the Treasury 2023).

Conclusion

As the 15th anniversary of its independence approaches, South Sudan remains firmly ensconced near the top of the Fund for Peace's Fragile States Index. Only Sudan and Somalia are considered more fragile according to the Index's dozen conflict risk indicators, and by this set of metrics the people of South Sudan are worse off than Haitians, Afghans, or Syrians (Fund for Peace 2024). According to one public opinion survey commissioned by UNMISS, South Sudan's fragility is very much evident in the daily lives of its citizens, with more than half of respondents indicating that they felt very or somewhat unsafe. More surprising, perhaps, was the generally positive public perception of the work of UNMISS in protecting civilians and building peace; with the exception of conflict-wracked Jonglei state, UNMISS performance was considered 'very positive' by strong majorities across South Sudan's ten states. Three in four respondents, moreover, felt that the continued presence and activities of UNMISS were making a positive difference on women's security (UNMISS 2022–2023). While a one-off poll might not tell the full story, it does suggest that the people of South Sudan continue to give UNMISS the benefit of the doubt; while the mission cannot protect everyone in need of protection, and cannot build durable peace on its own, the numbers suggest that most South Sudanese believe that their country, and their own security, is better off with UNMISS than without it. This sentiment was seconded by many observers with whom I spoke during a 2024 visit to Juba, who suggested that UNMISS continues to play a crucial stabilising role in a country that remains far from stable.[13]

In terms of the critical questions about protection posed in the introductory chapter to this volume – whether missions with PoC mandates reduce civilian insecurity as much as is realistically possible given their mandates and asset mixes, and whether protection practices evolve over time in a process of 'learning by doing' – the analysis presented here suggests that in the case of UNMISS, the answer is a qualified (or asterisked) yes. On the latter point in particular, UNMISS has successfully navigated the transition from a relatively narrow understanding of protection, focused on securing PoC sites, to a broader perspective that can credibly claim to bring to bear a whole-of-mission approach to the challenges of protection, especially at the subnational level. While this approach has come under increasing pressure as the peace implementation process continues to lag and as multiple intersecting crises exacerbate insecurity and heighten tension, it is difficult to dispute the contention that UNMISS has made, and continues to make, a positive contribution to civilian protection in South Sudan, even if the scale and scope of this contribution remains difficult to quantify. To the extent that the mission has faltered in the implementation of its PoC mandate, it has done so at opposite ends of the protection spectrum: on the one hand with regard to high-level political engagement, and on the other with regard to its response to imminent, ground-level threats to human life.

On the one hand, South Sudan's turbulent post-independence history underlines the reality that for all the recent emphasis on the potential of local and bottom-up peace processes – manifest most dramatically in peacebuilding's 'local turn' – elite-level peacemaking remains an indispensable element of any sustainable peace process. While the current Head of UNMISS – South Africa's Nicholas Haysom – appears to have made some headway towards re-centring UNMISS as a key player in South Sudan's peace implementation process and re-animating the 'primacy of politics' in the mission's work, it remains the case that the peace process has definitively stalled, with further delays to the electoral schedule merely the latest manifestation of foot-dragging on the part of the Transitional Government of National Unity. At its core, the blockage is rooted in the same dynamic that has for decades stymied meaningful Security Council reform: those with the decision-making authority to enact meaningful change have no incentive to do so, as they continue to benefit (and profit) from an unreformed status quo. As Adam Day (2022: 66) has noted, South Sudan's long independence struggle has generated a powerful military aristocracy which retains a firm grip on the key levers of power, with President Kiir sitting atop an ethno-military system of governance that continues to wield power without accountability. South Sudan's considerable oil wealth – at least when the oil flows – has since the start of the drive towards independence been used not for public services or institution-building, but rather, as the International Crisis Group (2024) has noted, to "underwrite a violent patronage network that president Salva Kiir uses to maintain an uneasy overall peace."

Squaring the circle of supporting short-term stability while also laying the groundwork for long-term transformation remains, not only for UNMISS but also the broader international community, a crucial dilemma lacking an obvious solution. As noted above, intra-elite power dynamics drive a great deal of subnational violence, but at the same time Kiir has played the game with considerable skill, weakening challengers (Machar in particular remains vice-president, but his support has fragmented and he remains effectively under house arrest) while deploying patronage in ways that keep political contestation within tolerable limits. Relative stability is maintained, and key players all have a vested interest in keeping the music playing as long as possible. Consequently, writing a new constitution, unifying and reforming the country's armed forces, and organising elections – key elements in South Sudan's peace implementation process – have taken a backseat to the short-term priorities of stability and continuity, especially as succession dynamics (inevitable among an ageing political class) come ever more sharply into focus. Regardless of the president's own political preferences, therefore, both the survival of the transitional government and the stability of the country, at least in the short term, depend on the continued injection of resources to grease the wheels of the patronage machine. It is clear that altering this dynamic – and in the words of one local observer, ensuring that the proceeds of South Sudanese oil, as it begins to flow again, are directed towards building peace rather than provoking conflict[14] – is quite clearly beyond the remit of any single organisation. At the same time, however, deepening donor fatigue is reducing the likelihood of consistent messaging on the part of the international community in support of both good governance and democratisation. If the ultimate solution to protecting civilians – and enabling UNMISS to execute a successful exit strategy – lies in consolidating an irreversible peace in South Sudan, it remains far from clear what it might take to get the country from where it is now to where it needs to go.

With regard to PoC's most visible and dramatic manifestation – protecting civilians in imminent peril – the tendency of the mission's uniformed elements to err on the side of caution has directly contributed to protection failures that have cost lives and tarnished the reputation of UNMISS (even if, as noted above, most South Sudanese civilians continue to view the mission in a positive light). Over the post-cold war era, the UN's most ignominious episodes – from Rwanda to Srebrenica and from Kiwanja (DRC) to Alindao (CAR) – have involved peacekeepers standing on the sidelines as civilians are massacred, and to this list must be added UNMISS inaction in response to attacks on PoC sites in Bor, Malakal and Juba. In his account of these latter events, former UNMISS official Mark Millar is particularly scathing in his assessment of the mission, pointing to failures of both field-level tactics and high-level leadership, and noting that in the aftermath of these episodes, the emphasis "continued to be less focused on creating a robust defence of the civilians within UN bases, and more focused on strategies to close them" (2022: 84).

As detailed in Chapter 2, however, use of force debates in the context of contemporary peace operations remain fraught, and a quarter-century on from the first PoC-mandated mission, consensus on these questions remains elusive. At the extremes, few would disagree with the contention that peacekeepers have both a moral and institutional imperative to use all necessary means – including deadly force – to protect those they have promised to protect at the moments when threat levels are at their most extreme. Inaction on the part of armed peacekeepers in the face of atrocities against civilians, in other words, remains both indefensible and inexcusable. Outside of these very narrow – and rare – scenarios, however, there is considerably less clarity. On the one hand, in the UNMISS context the most prominent exception to the mission's coercion-averse posture is the Mongolian contingent, which has gained a positive reputation for being both fearless and effective. As Berdal and Shearer have noted, as a result of the Mongolians' insistence on standing their ground and their willingness to use lethal force when required, "its troops have been among the most respected and have enjoyed improved and safer relationships wherever they have gone" (2021: 77). On the other hand, however, it is also clear that the relationship between robust military postures and effective peacekeeping outcomes is far from linear. UNMISS leadership has in fact consistently defended the opposite view: that in South Sudan's complex conflict context – where distinctions between combatant and civilian are often fluid and where patterns of violence are cyclical and/or elite-driven – a strategy of countering violence with more violence is rarely superior to one of constructive engagement, despite the ongoing challenge of identifying and influencing the root causes of ongoing violence. Ultimately, then, robust military engagement on the part of peacekeepers has its place in a conflict setting such as South Sudan, as demonstrated both by the positive example of the Mongolian contingent and the negative example of PoC site massacres. It remains far from clear, however, that at this point in the evolution of UNMISS – and especially as threats to vulnerable civilians proliferate and become less military in nature – how much might be gained in PoC terms by a shift to a more coercive protection posture.

Notes

1 Author interview, Juba, July 2019.
2 The analogy is imperfect, since there were plenty of red flags pointing to the possibility of violence in the days leading up to the December crisis.
3 For example, the so-called Kigali Principles, which sought to commit troop-contributing countries to use force when necessary to protect threatened populations, emerged in May 2015.
4 The Sudan People's Liberation Army (SPLA) became the South Sudan People's Defence Forces (SSPDF) in 2018.
5 Author interview, Juba PoC site, July 2018.
6 Author interview, Juba, October 2024.
7 Author interviews, Juba, October 2024.
8 Author interview, Juba, July 2019.
9 The SPLA-In Opposition (SPLA-IO), is the main armed opposition faction, led by Riek Machar; its political arm is the Sudan People's Liberation Movement-in-Opposition (SPLM-IO).
10 Author interview, Juba, October 2024.
11 Author interviews, Juba, October 2024.
12 Author interview, Juba, October 2024.
13 Author interviews, Juba, October 2024.
14 Author interview, Juba, October 2024.

Works Cited

Berdal, M. and D. Shearer (2021) 'Hard lessons from South Sudan', *Survival* 63(5): 69–96.

Briggs, C. (2017) 'Protection of civilians sites: Lessons from South Sudan for future operations', Report, Norwegian Refugee Council, 31 May; Available at: https://www.nrc.no/globalassets/pdf/reports/poc-sites_lessons-from-south-sudan-copy.pdf

Cormack, Z. and N. Pendle (2024) 'Everyday protection: Learning from United Nations protection of civilians sites', *Journal of Intervention and Statebuilding* 18(1): 1–18.

Day, A. et al. (2019) *Assessing the Effectiveness of the UN Mission in South Sudan (UNMISS)*. Effectiveness of Peace Operations Network (EPON) Report. Oslo: Norwegian Institute of International Affairs.

Day, A. (2022) *States of Disorder, Ecosystems of Governance: Complexity Theory Applied to UN Statebuilding in the DRC and South Sudan* (Oxford: Oxford University Press).

Donais, T. (2020) 'Protection through peace building: The future of UNMISS' protection of civilians mandate in South Sudan', CSG Policy Brief, No. 21, Centre for Security Governance; Available at: https://www.secgovcentre.org/publications/csg-papers-no.-21-(may-2020)

Donais, T. and E. Tanguay (2021) 'Protection of civilians and peacekeeping's accountability deficit', *International Peacekeeping* 28(4): 553–578.

Donais, T. and A. Solomon (2022) 'Protection through peacebuilding in South Sudan', *African Security Review* 31(1): 51–65.

Foltyn, S. (2016) 'UN says response to violence in its South Sudan camp marred by confusion', *The Guardian*, 22 June; Available at: https://www.theguardian.com/global-development/2016/jun/22/malakal-camp-south-sudan-un-united-nations-says-response-violence-marred-by-confusion

Francis, O. and S. Marks (2024) 'A broken oil pipeline plunges South Sudan's capital into chaos', *Bloomberg News*, 18 October; Available at: https://www.bloomberg.com/news/features/2024-10-18/south-sudan-s-juba-sent-into-chaos-after-oil-pipeline-breaks (last accessed 5 November 2024)

Fund for Peace (2024) 'Fragile States Index 2024: Global Data'; Available at: https://fragilestatesindex.org/global-data/

Hagemann, A. (2020) 'Understanding intervention through multiplicity: Protection politics in South Sudan', *Globalizations* 17(3): 498–515.

International Crisis Group (2024) 'South Sudan on edge as its neighbour's war disrupts oil exports', Statement, 15 May; Available at: https://www.crisisgroup.org/africa/horn-africa/south-sudan/south-sudan-edge-its-neighbours-war-disrupts-oil-exports

Kilroy, W., S. Podder, and A. Duursma (2024) 'Civilian protection in theory and practice', *Civil Wars* 26(1): 1–15.

Kilroy, W. and K. Ryan (2024) 'Institutionalising an emergency response: "Protection of civilians" sites at UN bases in South Sudan as a way to deal with violence against communities', *Civil Wars* 26(1): 126–159.

Krause, J. (2019) 'Stabilization and local conflicts: Communal and civil war in South Sudan', *Ethnopolitics* 18(5): 478–493.

Lederach, J.P. (1997) *Building Peace: Sustainable Reconciliation in Divided Societies*. Washington: United States Institute of Peace Press.

Levi, J. and L. Stephens (2024) 'South Sudan may see the first permanent mass displacement due to climate change', *Wired*, 14 September; Available at: https://www.wired.com/story/south-sudan-floods-the-first-example-of-a-mass-population-permanently-displaced-by-climate-change/

Lipsky, M. (2010) *Street-Level Bureaucracy*, 30th *Anniversary Edition: Dilemmas of the Individual in Public Service* (New York: Russell Sage Foundation).

Mednick, S. (2022) 'How South Sudan's peace deal sparked conflict in a town spared by war', *The New Humanitarian*, 16 February; Available at: https://www.thenewhumanitarian.org/news-feature/2022/2/16/South-Sudan-peace-deal-sparked-conflict-town-war-tambura

Millar, M. (2022) *The Peacekeeping Failure in South Sudan: The UN, Bias and the Peacekeeper's Mind* (London: Zed Books).

Office for the Coordination of Humanitarian Affairs (OCHA) (2024) 'South Sudan: Floods Snapshot', 1 November; Available at: https://reliefweb.int/report/south-sudan/south-sudan-floods-snapshot-1-november-2024

Pax-Protection of Civilians (2023) 'Building our peace – people to people peace processes in South Sudan', Documentary, 26 June; Available at: https://protectionofcivilians.org/video/building-our-peace-people-to-people-peace-processes-in-south-sudan/

Ponnie, S. (2025) 'South Sudan announces plan to resume oil production', *Voice of America News*, 9 January; Available at: https://www.voanews.com/a/south-sudan-announces-plan-to-resume-oil-production/7930709.html

Pospisal, J. et al. (2020) 'South Sudan's Transition: Citizens' Perception of Peace', Analysis, *United States Institute of Peace,* 19 March; Available at: https://www.usip.org/publications/2020/03/south-sudans-transition-citizens-perception-peace

Radio Tamazuj (2015) 'Document: UN releases details of April Bor massacre', 11 January; https://www.radiotamazuj.org/en/news/article/document-un-releases-details-of-april-bor-massacre

Save the Children (2024) 'South Sudan on the Brink of Famine as it Braces for Worlds Floods in 60 Years', Press Release, 10 July; Available at: https://www.savethechildren.org/us/about-us/media-and-news/2024-press-releases/south-sudan-brink-famine-it-braces-worst-floods-60

Spink, L. and M. Wells (2016) 'Under Fire: The July 2016 violence in Juba and UN response', Report, Center for Civilians in Conflict (CIVIC); Available at: https://civiliansinconflict.org/wp-content/uploads/2017/09/civic-juba-violence-report-october-2016.pdf

Spink, L. (2020) 'Protection through dialogue: How UNMISS is linking local engagement with a national peace process in South Sudan', Policy Brief, Center for Civilians in Conflict, June; Available at: https://civiliansinconflict.org/wp-content/uploads/2020/06/UNMISS-Peace-Brief-Single-Page.pdf

Sudans Post (2024) 'UN ramps up patrols in Tambura after fresh violence', 10 May; Available at: https://www.sudanspost.com/un-ramps-up-patrols-in-tambura-after-fresh-violence/

Sullivan, D.P. (2022) 'Do not forget: Aiding and protecting civilians in South Sudan', Refugees International Report, January; Available at: https://www.refugeesinternational.org/reports-briefs/do-not-forget-aiding-and-protecting-civilians-in-south-sudan/

Thiong, D.A. (2018) 'South Sudan: Buying off elites to stop fighting won't work. Here's what might', *African Arguments*, 12 March; Available at: https://africanarguments.org/2018/03/south-sudan-buying-off-elites-to-stop-fighting-wont-work-heres-what-might/

United Nations (UN) (2016) 'Executive summary of the independent special investigation into the violence in Juba in 2016 and the response by the United Nations Mission in South Sudan', S/2016/924, 1 November; Available at: https://www.securitycouncilreport.org/atf/cf/%7B65BFCF9B-6D27-4E9C-8CD3-CF6E4FF96FF9%7D/s_2016_924.pdf

United Nations (UN) (2024a) 'Situation in South Sudan: Report of the Secretary General', S/2024/572, 26 February; Available at: https://www.securitycouncilreport.org/un-documents/document/s-2024-572.php

United Nations (UN) (2024b) 'Situation in South Sudan: Report of the Secretary General', S/2024/188, 29 July; Available at: https://www.securitycouncilreport.org/un-documents/document/s-2024-188.php

United Nations Mission in South Sudan (UNMISS) (2022–2023) 'UNMISS perception and public opinion survey 2022–23', Available at: https://unmiss.unmissions.org/sites/default/files/unmiss_perception_survey_-_4_page_summary.pdf

United Nations Mission in South Sudan (UNMISS)/Office of the High Commissioner for Human Rights (OHCHR) (2021) 'Attacks on Civilians in Tambura County', Report; Available at: https://www.ohchr.org/sites/default/files/2022-03/Tambura-Report.pdf

United States (US) Department of the Treasury (2023) 'Treasury sanctions two South Sudanese officials responsible for conflict-related sexual violence', 20 June; Available at: https://home.treasury.gov/news/press-releases/jy1552

Wild, H., P. Fallavier, and R. Patel (2019) '"Lost Generation" in South Sudan: A broader approach toward peace urgently needed', *Disaster Medicine and Public Health Preparedness* 13(4): 663–671.

5 MONUSCO

Innovation without Transformation?

Introduction

The last week of July 2022 might ultimately be remembered as the beginning of the end of UN peacekeeping in the Democratic Republic of the Congo (DRC). That week, anti-MONUSCO protests in Goma and elsewhere – led by demonstrators upset at the UN's failure to stem ongoing violence in the country's east, and calling for the mission's departure – turned violent, and the subsequent unrest would claim the lives of four peacekeepers and dozens of Congolese civilians. While the mission had been under pressure for years, weakened by budget cuts and a tense relationship with the Congolese government – the July protests appeared to send a clear signal that the mission had outlived both its welcome and its usefulness. As he campaigned for re-election in 2023, DRC President Felix Tshisekedi reinforced this message, lamenting the UN's decades-long failure "to cope with the rebellions and armed conflicts" and calling for the mission's accelerated withdrawal (Al Jazeera 2023). As of mid-2024, MONUSCO's exit strategy was, accordingly, well-advanced, although the mission's mandate was ultimately extended by the UN Security Council for an additional year in December 2024.

Of the many ironies surrounding MONUSCO's fraught relations with the DRC's government and its citizens illustrated by these developments, two in particular stand out. The first surrounds the loss of civilian life that flowed from protests against a mission with an explicit mandate to protect civilians. While the majority of civilian deaths in Goma came at the hands of Congolese security forces, an unreformed, corrupt, and abusive set of institutions that is nevertheless expected to take full responsibility for protecting civilians once MONUSCO departs (Verweijen and Vogel 2023), there is still something fundamentally paradoxical about UN peacekeepers having to protect themselves against those they are supposed to be protecting. Second, the pressure for MONUSCO to exit the Congolese scene has increased at precisely the same time that the security situation in DRC's eastern provinces – and especially in North Kivu, where Goma is located – has experienced a marked deterioration. Driven in large part by the resurgence of the so-called M23 movement, which managed to briefly capture Goma in 2012, eastern DRC has again been pitched into crisis, with thousands killed and millions displaced (Townsend 2024). While UN officials have long insisted that

DOI: 10.4324/9781003291114-5

MONUSCO's withdrawal should be conditional on measurable and sustainable security improvements, the chronic violence and insecurity that have characterised most of the mission's tenure in eastern DRC will almost certainly continue well into the post-MONUSCO period. For all the criticism of the UN's myriad protection failures in the DRC over its long history, then, there remains considerable apprehension that in the wake of MONUSCO's departure, life for many Congolese civilians will become even more dangerous and difficult.

As one of the UN's largest and most ambitious peace support operations winds down, this chapter takes stock of a quarter-century of civilian protection efforts on the part of UN peacekeepers in the DRC, spanning both the MONUC (1999–2010) mission and its re-branded MONUSCO (2010–) successor (although with an emphasis on the latter). It is a complicated story to tell, given the long and multifaceted nature of the Congolese crisis and the persistence of conflicting interpretations of what the UN has and has not achieved in the DRC. However, several key elements have dominated. First, it is widely recognised that MONUSCO in particular became something of a laboratory for PoC practice, with many of the key innovations implemented by the mission – including the establishment of community liaison assistants (CLAs), community alert networks (CANs) and local protection committees (LPCs) – subsequently replicated in other missions. In many ways, therefore, PoC as a specific set of peacekeeping practices evolved – necessity being the mother of invention – in the cauldron of the DRC's long-running conflict, and often in tension with competing mandate imperatives. Second, PoC efforts in the DRC have unfolded in an environment in which the linkage between protection and peacebuilding has been almost completely absent. Although the conflict has been far from static, the DRC's particular conflict complex has worked against efforts to negotiate a durable framework for long-term peace, while for its part the Congolese government has shown little commitment to the idea that peace – and sustainable reductions in civilian insecurity – will emerge only with the establishment of capable, accountable, legitimate and responsible state institutions, including those responsible for public security provision. Third, the MONUC/MONUSCO missions have been very much test cases for the principles of robust peacekeeping. Despite some highly publicised protection failures, for better or for worse UN forces in the DRC, in the words of Emily Paddon, "engaged in some of the most combative enforcement action in the UN's history in order to protect civilians" (2014: 161), a trend which culminated in the establishment of the Force Implementation Brigade (FIB) in 2014. While distinguishing the use of force for PoC purposes is often impossible to separate from use of force as a stabilisation tool ('neutralising' spoiler groups in principle advances both goals), MONUSCO in particular regularly tested the boundary between assertive impartiality and peace enforcement. While the record has been both mixed and contested, the UN's experience with robust protection in the DRC also reads as a cautionary tale regarding the tensions, contradictions, and inherent limitations of the idea of peacekeepers using force for PoC purposes; the use of force, as it turns out, offers no easy shortcut to effective civilian protection.

Ultimately, the central argument to be advanced here is two-fold. First, it is possible to speak of both innovation in and evolution of PoC practice, and over the course of some 25 years the UN's protection practices in the DRC demonstrated both, underlining in the process the ways in which creative collaboration between civilian and uniformed elements of the mission was essential to improving protection outcomes. While the balance between the mission's coercive and non-coercive elements was always unstable – with budgetary pressures ultimately leading mission leadership to emphasise the former over the latter – over time the mission did manage to up its game in terms of both refining its PoC strategies and improving outcomes, even if contextual factors always shaped what was and was not possible in protection terms, and despite the reality that successes were always underreported relative to high-profile protection failures. Second, with hindsight it is clear that given the DRC's persistent conflict dynamics and the UN's structural and operational limitations as a force for good (understood in both protection and peacebuilding terms), the latter's presence in the DRC was never – despite the often creative and innovative use of protection tools – going to be able to protect more than a small fraction of those Congolese civilians in need of protection. In this sense, at least in the DRC context PoC remains the 'impossible mandate,' and the mission could never live up to expectations, especially once PoC became the UN's core *raison d'être* in theatre. PoC may be used to justify a mission's presence, but a mission's ability to either persuade or coerce armed actors to respect civilian life and/or to enable civilian self-protection strategies remains limited, and often wholly inadequate, in the face of armed groups who view civilian populations as not especially innocent and who consider killing, raping, or otherwise abusing them as useful, necessary or inevitable in pursuit of their strategic objectives (Slim 2007: 3). The DRC experience makes it clear that for peace operations, protecting civilians is no substitute for sustained long-term conflict resolution efforts.

DRC's Conflict Complex

Making sense of the protection challenge in the DRC requires at least some understanding of the drivers of violence in the country, which have for nearly three decades resisted all manner of attempts to overcome them. Of course, civilian suffering in the DRC has a long history, dominated first by a particularly ruthless form of Belgian colonialism and second by the plunder and predation visited on the country through the long, dictatorial reign of Mobutu Sese Seko (Paddon 2014: 164). In 1996, however, the combination of an exhausted, hollowed-out Mobutu regime and the de-stabilising effects of the demographic displacement triggered by the 1994 Rwandan genocide tipped the DRC (still known as Zaire at the time) into full-scale civil war. Across two phases between 1996 and 2003, what became known as Africa's World War (Prunier 2011) involved a shifting cast of internal rebel groups, drew in armies from most of the DRC's neighbours, and ultimately claimed the lives of some 5 million people. While a series of incremental peace agreements culminating in the Global and Inclusive Agreement of 2002 officially ended the war and helped establish a unified transitional government, ongoing violence – particularly in the east, involving (still) a diverse and evolving cast of both domestic and regional players, and deployed in pursuit of both material greed and ethnic grievance – has remained perhaps the most durable feature of contemporary Congolese politics (Ahere 2012). Most Africans alive today, 60% of whom are under the age of 25, have never known a period when the DRC has been at peace.

For Jason Stearns, a long-time observer of the Congolese conflict, the continuation of variable but persistently high levels of violence in the DRC's eastern provinces in the post-2003 period – notwithstanding a peace agreement and the presence of peacekeepers – remains something of a mystery. The conflict simmers, and occasionally boils over, in his words, "despite billions in international aid, a national army of 130,000 pitted against ragtag rebel groups, and the largest UN peacekeeping operation in the world" (2022: 3/310).[1] While deeper structural factors – combining complex ethnic dynamics, economic incentive structures, and the particular historical trajectory of state-society relations in the DRC – have prevented the emergence of sustainable peace, the proximate cause of the failure of the Global and Inclusive Accords to fully take hold was the RCD (*Rassemblement congolais pour la démocratie)*, a Tutsi-dominated and Rwandan-backed group whose influence diminished considerably once electoral politics threatened to displace armed conflict as a mechanism for allocating power. Increasingly marginalised after national elections of 2006, the RCD leadership eventually reneged on an agreement to integrate their fighters into a new national army and launched a renewed rebellion under the *Congrès National pour la Défense du Peuple* (CNDP) banner and the leadership of General Laurent Nkunda. As Stearns notes (2022: 8/310), the Nkunda-led insurgency prompted countermobilisation by at least a dozen other groups, effectively derailing the project of creating an integrated national army as well as the peace process more generally.

With regional variations, this process of mobilisation/countermobilisation among armed groups has continued for the better part of the past two decades, both enabled by, and contributing to, ongoing state weakness. Particularly in the east, 1,000 miles and a world away from Kinshasa, the footprint of the national government has varied between light and non-existent. By contrast, informal mechanisms and networks of governance have long dominated, both as a means of resource and wealth extraction and as a way of maintaining conflict within tolerable limits; for Kinshasa-based elites – or what Judith Verweijen terms 'the presidential power circle' (2016: 17) – violence that did not threaten their core interests was of marginal concern at best. Over the course of several decades of armed conflict, not only did the absence of anything resembling a state monopoly over the legitimate use of force or the rule of law prompt the proliferation of armed groups in a localised version of realism's security dilemma, it also generated a plethora of localised, militarised protection rackets, as armed groups found clever and lucrative ways to monetise their coercive capacities in the resource-rich eastern provinces. More generally, these dynamics also led to the emergence of what Stearns (2022: 11/310) refers to as a military bourgeoisie, which controls large parts of the economy in the eastern DRC, which has cultivated deep links with political elites across the country, and which has developed a strong vested interest in the status quo. Regional dynamics overlay and reinforce this domestic state of affairs, with Rwandan influence in particular at play in key moments, notably the CNDP rebellion during the MONUC era and the two M23 offensives over the past dozen years. Within this larger context, where perpetual conflict has become a way of life – and a path to wealth – for many key protagonists, and where the state remains largely indifferent to either peacemaking or state-building, it is little wonder that the familiar liberal peacebuilding prescriptions advanced by the UN and other international actors in the DRC have over the course of the past 25 years generated little discernible traction.

Adam Day (2022) offers a systems-level explanation for both the persistence of the DRC's conflict dynamics and the inability of decades of international intervention to alter the fundamental structures, mechanisms and interests that shape the DRC's very particular system of armed politics. Drawing on complexity theory, Day suggests that while the DRC is often portrayed as a paradigmatic example of a failed state, in reality it has evolved its own complex system of governance, dominated by the informal networks of power noted above. These networks not only exist independently of formal state institutions, they have successfully coopted them, stripping them of capacity while at the same time using them as conduits through which resources and rents can be captured by key power-holders. This governance architecture first emerged during the Mobutu era, taking the form of institutionalised kleptocracy aimed at keeping resources flowing from the periphery to the centre, while neither goods nor services flowed in the opposite direction. Citizens, accordingly, were left largely to fend for themselves, while "those asked to govern were expected to extract from the population and feed resources upwards, enriching Mobutu and his coterie but never establishing a national budget that could be used to build schools, police stations, or courthouses" (Day 2022: 85).

Like other complex systems, the DRC's underlying governance structure has proven remarkably resilient, bending and adjusting but not breaking even as the centre collapsed and all hell broke loose in the mid-1990s. As armed groups mobilised to defend themselves, their ethnic communities, and their interests, Mobutu's fend-for-yourself ideology (captured by French expression *se débrouiller*) prevailed, and over time militias inserted themselves into existing governance networks, drawing on links with patrons in Kigali, Kinshasa or Kampala to establish themselves as *de facto* governing authorities and wrest control of key natural resources and transborder trade routes. While the restoration of state authority, especially during the presidency of Joseph Kabila, led to a partial restoration of the sprawling patronage networks of the Mobutu era, the ability of armed groups in the east to consolidate their governance roles – and enforce them through the rule of the gun – has meant at best an uneasy, unstable coexistence with central state authorities in recent years. As Day argues (2022: 107), despite ongoing shifts in local balances of power armed groups became – and remain – "integral aspects of an interdependent system of governance that secured and marketed natural resources, provided protection for communities, participated indirectly in national-level political jockeying, and entered into long-standing disputes over land and local authorities."

Whether understood as a complex system or through the lens of the incentive structures faced by key conflict actors that keep the wheels of violence in eastern DRC turning, both the Day and Stearns accounts underline the persistent mismatch between how violence is perpetuated in the DRC and the externally driven prescriptions for ending it. While much has been made of the need for 'political will' on the part of conflict belligerents – and the Congolese government especially – in order to finally end the war and establish a durable peace, it should by now be apparent (a) that the DRC's problems run much deeper than could be addressed through the discovery of unknown reserves of political will among its elite class, and (b) that the main parties to the conflict in and around the DRC read the conflict, and its stakes, in radically different terms than do international diplomats and peacekeepers. This is evident at the level of individual training, where efforts to inculcate norms of professional conduct among police officers dissipate as soon as the latter return to active duty and are reminded that the system still expects them to 'pay' their commanders (Day 2022: 119). It is also evident at the level of national-level efforts to reform the Congolese security sector; these efforts made little sense, and almost no progress, in a system where underpaid, undertrained and underfed soldiers were a feature of the system, not a glitch. Ultimately, local and international actors have arguably been speaking past each other in mutually unintelligible tongues since the first MONUC peacekeepers hit the ground in 1999. As recently as 2019, a UN-commissioned independent strategic review of MONUSCO (UN 2019) still expressed optimism that under a newly elected president the necessary political will could be mustered to finally put in place the pillars of an emerging liberal democratic state, including thorough reform of the security sector, expanding democratic space, improvements to human rights, and a deepening commitment to good governance and the rule of law across the DRC's entire sovereignty territory. As MONUSCO continues to wind down, much of the strategic review's original optimism has dissipated, even if the worst of the violence has now been confined to the Kivus, where the DRC's current round of troubles began, and where civilians continue to pay the highest price.

PoC Practice – Innovating on the Fly

It is within this wider conflict context – with the shocking numbers of civilian deaths in the early years of the war a stark reminder of the widespread failure of armed groups to embrace the niceties of international humanitarian law – that the UN Security Council made protecting civilians a core component of peacekeepers' job descriptions in the DRC. PoC was first inserted into the MONUC mandate in 2000 – the second UN mission to be given such a mandate – with the Security Council eventually elevating it in the MONUSCO era as the 'key priority task' for peacekeepers, with PoC supposed to take precedence "in decisions about the use of available capacity and resources" (Levine-Spound and Jorgensen 2023). Precisely how this mandate was to be operationalised, however, was largely left for the field to sort out (even as PoC guidelines were being developed and refined by the UN Secretariat), and during the MONUC period the mission's responses to the violence with which it was surrounded oscillated between war-making, including robust special forces combat operations, and paralysis (Murphy 2016; Williams 2023). By 2010, however, a growing number of high-profile protection failures – including the Kiwanja massacre of 2008 and the Walikale incident in 2010, in which some 400 civilians were systematically raped over the course of four days in proximity to a MONUSCO forward operating base – exposed the UN's hitherto-unsystematic (some might say unserious) approach to protection, and prompted a more concerted effort "to ensure that UN peacekeeping missions had the capability and willingness to prevent and rapidly respond to threats of violence against civilians" (Levine-Spound 2021: 1).

While debates about robustness have tended to dominate both the scholarly and policy discussions about PoC in the DRC, it is notable that MONUSCO's earliest and arguably most impactful innovations aimed at closing the protection gap emphasised community engagement. This was both a preview of what the HIPPO Report was later to characterise as 'people-centred peacekeeping' – the idea, as Fred Carver (2022: 9) has noted, that missions should take all available steps "to put the people in whose interest peace is to be kept at the heart of what the mission does" – as well as an affirmation that PoC requires not just 'effectors' in the form of specific protection tools and instruments, but also 'detectors' in order to better understand and anticipate the situations, circumstances and developments that require a response in the first place (Hood and Margetts 2007). Any effective PoC strategy, in other words, must be grounded in the twin imperatives of early warning and rapid response (EWRR), and the crucial linkages between the two. As Daniel Levine-Spound has noted (2021: 4), EWRR in the context of peace operations "is intended to allow missions to gather information regarding emerging or imminent threats of violence against civilians and take actions to prevent or mitigate these threats."

MONUSCO's first key move to improve its situational awareness (intelligence still being a sensitive concept in peacekeeping contexts) was the deployment of CLAs, national staff embedded in military contingents as a bridge between the mission's uniformed elements and the communities they were mandated to protect. In this bridging role, CLAs were expected to perform a number of key functions. In addition to being conduits for information flowing between contingents and communities and crucial sources of information and analysis on conflict-related developments, CLAs were also expected to help manage the local population's expectations about the kinds and levels of protection the UN could offer as well as sensitise peacekeepers about the existence and specifics of community self-protection strategies. At the same time, CLAs were instrumental in the emergence of two additional innovations in the protection toolkit, CANs and LPCs. CANs are technology-facilitated early warning instruments, in essence 'crisis hotlines' through which community members can relay – through phone call or SMS message – information to MONUSCO about emerging or imminent protection concerns. LPCs, conversely, are meant to serve as both community-level focal points on security matters and drivers of local-level responses to protection concerns; with support and training provided by the UN (other LPCs are NGO-funded), the hope was always that LPCs would emerge as independent civil society counterparts to local administrative and security services, and a key pillar of participatory, accountable, local-level systems of security provision that would persist into a post-MONUSCO era. While this theory is currently being put to the test as the mission's geographic footprint shrinks, in combination these three core community engagement tools – CLAs, CANs and LPCs – have provided the backbone of a relatively coherent early warning and rapid response framework, and the model has been exported, with variations, into other mission contexts, including Mali, South Sudan, and CAR. According to UN figures, as of September 2018 MONUSCO oversaw more than 40 LPCs, involving some 3,700 community members, along with some 86 CANs with a geographic reach across some 2,400 villages; the mission also engaged somewhere between 140 and 200 CLAs as part of this emerging network (Carver 2022: 15).

While it is generally accepted that MONUSCO has led the way in the development of community-engaged PoC, even at its height the mission's early warning and rapid response network remained a work in progress. On the one hand, the kinds of relationship-building implied by community-centric PoC is slow and resource-intensive, while the reality of contemporary peace operations is that most missions, as the HIPPO Report underlined, are seriously overstretched and under-resourced. Resource constraints are therefore always a factor in the build-out of early warning and rapid response systems, and have become more so in recent years as budget cuts have forced missions – and MONUSCO in particular – to re-work their engagement strategies. Thus, while MONUSCO appeared to trial-and-error its way into a reasonably effective formula for operationalising PoC, the system was never robust enough nor widespread enough to have any hope of effectively eradicating violence by non-state armed actors (let alone abuses carried out by the Congolese Armed Forces, the FARDC)[2] in the mission's areas of responsibility, even if it did enable it to successfully respond to more protection crises more of the time. On the other hand, MONUSCO's PoC strategy necessarily involved a great deal of learning by doing; while this implies a regular process of refinement and improvement as EWRR mechanisms were adjusted to real-world circumstances and constraints, it also meant a series of growing pains – some of which the mission never fully managed to overcome – that prevented the system from reaching its full potential.

One of the key areas where the 'work in progress' nature of the EWRR system has long been evident is the linkage between MONUSCO's civilian-centric 'detectors' and its military-centric 'effectors.' This challenge is partly inherent in the nature of the exercise; as one mission official noted, "translating intelligence and community-based warnings into actionable information within hours is the difference between an effective POC response and one that comes too late" (cited in Levine-Spound 2021: 4). While various experiments in field-level joint operations and tactical operations centres have been put in place to strengthen analytical capacities and shorten response times, the realities of imperfect, fragmented, and sometimes-contradictory information and the inevitable uncertainties around the selection of appropriate responses means that the risk of 'getting it wrong' can never be entirely eliminated. This is even more so in contexts where cumbersome bureaucratic procedures lead to delays in responding, and where different military contingents bring to the mission different risk tolerances – and national caveats – that constrain the menu of available responses. For local actors participating in early warning networks, in many cases at considerable personal risk, the more that responses remain 'highly fragmented, slow, or non-existent' – and ensuring consistent and timely responses given the nature of UN missions and the variability of the conflict environment was always going to be an enormous challenge – the less confidence local interlocutors are likely to place in the system (Buskie and Ferguson 2021: 37).

A related issue – also connected to questions of trust and confidence-building across the local/international divide – concerns the manner in which information flows across the EWRR continuum. Ideally, as Buskie and Ferguson (2021) have suggested, a fully 'linked-up' early warning/early response system would involve robust, regular, and consistent two-way flows of information between local communities and peace operations, with each node feeding information to the other about both risks and responses. Rather than information flowing upwards from communities and responses flowing downwards from the mission's uniformed elements, there are strong arguments for involving communities themselves in crafting responses to threats, not least because

> local actors are more likely to be able to identify key stakeholders and local influencers, use their established relationships to bring together these key influencers for dialogue, mobilise nonviolent community action, source witnesses, and evaluate the impact of any interventions.
>
> (Buskie and Ferguson 2021: 38)

Such relationships have rarely emerged in the context of community-engaged PoC, however, in part because of the persistence of the idea that conflict-affected communities bring little agency to bear in defence of their own security, and in part because of long-standing military traditions that treat information as a resource to be protected rather than distributed, lest it fall into the wrong hands. As a consequence, in the MONUSCO context there have been persistent complaints on the part of CANs and LPCs that their uniformed partners on the MONUSCO side see them as little more than sources of information to be milked in service of a wider PoC strategy, rather than as full and valued partners in community-level protection (Spink 2018: 5). Such sentiments reinforce not only an implicit hierarchy between the mission and its local interlocutors, but also the idea that the default response to protection threats is not only externally driven but also military-led.

At the same time, MONUSCO's PoC efforts have been complicated, and occasionally compromised, by its fractious relationship with the DRC's domestic security forces, and in particular the FARDC. Notwithstanding the UN's own mantra about host states bearing ultimate responsibility for protecting civilians, efforts to reform and professionalise the FARDC in recent decades have borne little fruit (as noted above); as a consequence, not only have historical patterns of predation persisted in the relationship between Congolese soldiers and citizens, but the army is widely considered to be responsible for more than half of all human rights violations committed in recent years. In short, for a great many insecure Congolese civilians the national army remains more problem than solution. While the UN implemented its Human Rights Due Diligence Policy (HRDDP) over a decade ago as a means of ensuring that any support it provides to domestic security forces doesn't facilitate human rights violations, it remains the case that MONUSCO is trapped in a difficult partnership with the FARDC, and cannot fully separate this relationship from its own PoC policies and responsibilities. The reality that many local communities both fear and distrust local security forces has a predictably corrosive impact on community-mission collaboration, further undermining the relationships of trust that underpin effective early warning; citizens have openly expressed frustration, for example, over cases when the mission deferred protection responses to Congolese security forces (Carver 2022: 23). Such concerns have only deepened as MONUSCO's footprint has shrunk, which has by default meant that PoC responsibilities fall increasingly to domestic security forces. As Lauren Spink (2019: 13) has noted, one of MONUSCO's most pressing dilemmas as its exit strategy takes effect involves ensuring that its departure "does not leave civilians trapped between violent armed groups and abusive state security forces."

Transition issues have, of course, been front-and-centre throughout MONUSCO's lifespan, driven both by the Congolese government's ambivalence to the mission and by downward budgetary pressures emanating from UN Headquarters in New York. As early as 2016, as MONUSCO's budget was beginning to contract, its protection strategy – which had up to that point focused on expanding its presence across insecure areas through the establishment of small bases – was proving unsustainable, with the mission struggling to provision this network of bases with sufficient capacity to meaningfully impact the security environment (Spink 2019: 6–7). In subsequent years, with the MONUSCO budget cut by nearly a third, the mission had little choice but to replace its presence-focused PoC strategy with one focused on projection. This meant significant and progressive reductions in the number of permanent MONUSCO bases as well as a transition to a more mobile operational stance. In part this has meant the deployment of so-called standing combat deployments, temporarily dispatched to conflict hotspots, which have enjoyed some success in preventing or stemming violence (Spink 2019: 7), and in part this has meant a greater reliance on air assets – helicopters especially – as a means of facilitating rapid response in areas without a permanent mission presence. In many cases, however, the reality has been that budgetary restraint (as well as other factors, such as the withdrawal of Ukrainian aviation assets subsequent to the Russian invasion of 2022) has also precluded the mission from obtaining additional resources to enable it to seamlessly transition from presence to projection (Donais and Tanguay 2021). The mission's reduced field presence has also had an inevitable impact on the detector side of the EWRR equation, both in terms of situational awareness and in terms of community engagement and relations with both CANs and LPCs. Not only are there legitimate concerns that PoC strategies emphasising projection – with armed peacekeepers swooping in via helicopter before quickly departing for the next hotspot – invariably privilege coercive over non-coercive responses and short-term bandaids over longer-term resolutions, there is also some evidence that the broader shift in approach comes with significant downside risk for local partners. In Masisi and Nyabiondo, two communities in North Kivu where MONUSCO shuttered its local presence in 2017, local civil society leaders cited by researchers from the Center for Civilians in Conflict (CIVIC) reported feeling abandoned by the mission amidst a deteriorating security situation (Spink 2018: 10). Not only did local alert networks break down after the mission departed, but in Nyabiondo several members of the local LPC were forced to flee after they were targeted by armed actors (Spink 2019: 9).

MONUSCO's experience with PoC through EWRR demonstrated the promise of one particular model for making the most of the unique assets of UN peacekeeping to deliver on an exceedingly challenging mandate in an exceedingly challenging conflict environment. It also demonstrated – with some notable caveats – the importance of effective community engagement to any wider PoC strategy. Ultimately, however, MONUSCO ran out of runway, and budget cover, at a point when this strategy was beginning to demonstrate its potential. While no mission has an unlimited window to refine its operational practices, it seems increasingly clear that presence-centric protection strategies will be difficult to replicate, not only in the DRC context but across peace operations more generally. While never enough to turn the tide of violence against civilians in the DRC's troubled eastern provinces – it remains the case, as Paul Williams (2013: 296) has emphasised, that UN peace operations as currently configured can at best "deal with only the tip of the iceberg of civilian suffering in war zones" – the evolution of MONUSCO's protection toolkit did allow the mission to make a credible claim that not only were its protection efforts saving lives, but that they represented a relatively efficient use of the mission's asset mix in support of the mission's primary mandated task. With hindsight, it is not clear that the same claim can be made for the more budget-driven 'projection' strategy that has been prominent in recent years. At the same time, however, even the long-running UN presence in the DRC is a reminder that no peace operation lasts forever, and that in the absence of both a coherent transition plan and a viable partnership with domestic security forces, not even the most coherent and carefully constructed PoC strategy can offer meaningful levels of protection as a mission winds down and eventually departs.

Protecting without Peacebuilding in the DRC

Despite incremental progress in improving local-level PoC practice, at a more macro level MONUSCO has long struggled to cope with a serious structural problem rooted in the disconnect between protection and peacebuilding. Peacekeepers, even with the best of intentions, will always be imperfect, inadequate agents of civilian protection, and mission-level PoC mandates can never be more than temporary measures aimed at filling gaps in security provision until such time as the fighting stops and domestic security forces are willing and able to take on their responsibilities for public security. In the case of the eastern DRC, however, state weakness and the particular configuration of regional and domestic dynamics described above have conspired to thwart the establishment of a lasting peace, and have left in their wake a legacy of failed development and reform projects. Nearly 30 years on from the outbreak of the First Congo War, the country remains stuck in a cycle of low-intensity warfare, which continues to generate considerable misery for those caught in its currents, but which appears to have been accepted as an undesirable if not intolerable status quo for the Congolese government, its regional neighbours, and the broader international community, none of whom seem currently prepared to invest political capital in large-scale peacemaking.[3] Violence, meanwhile, has been normalised as an instrument of politics, a reality which for the better part of the past two decades has relegated UN peacekeepers to the role of firefighters confronting an arson epidemic. Not even the most finely tuned early warning system can hope to extinguish each spark that might become a conflagration, while absent any viable means to control the arsonists, the protection exercise inevitably runs up against hard limits in terms of the depth, breadth and duration of the protection it can offer.

This is, of course, a challenge that extends well beyond the Congolese context. Contemporary conflict dynamics have shifted to the extent that what Gowan and Stedman have termed the 'standard' international treatment for civil wars – "mediation and the use of peacekeepers to implement peace agreements" (2018: 171) – no longer appears to be working. While a range of factors are at play in this growing disconnect between condition and prescription, including uncooperative (and sometimes hostile) host states, the fragmentation and proliferation of armed groups, Security Council discord, and a more general global-level retreat from liberal principles and values, the result has been a growing crisis of confidence in peacekeeping as an institution. At the same time, rather than serving as a complement to peacekeeping's core long-term business of facilitating and overseeing efforts to end wars and restore peace, increasingly PoC has come to be viewed – in DRC and elsewhere – as the very *raison d'être* of peacekeeping itself. Beyond creating an open-ended responsibility for protecting civilians that not even the most well-endowed mission could sustain, these trends significantly increase the dangers of UN missions – condemned to dealing with the downstream consequences of conflicts over which they have little control – overstaying their welcomes and taxing the patience of host state governments and citizens alike.

These dynamics have been very much in evidence in the DRC over MONUSCO's lifespan and help to explain why the mission is under pressure to wind down even as violence in the east is once again ramping up. The central tension for the UN, arguably, revolves around its relations with the host state, with protection efforts both complicating these relations and being constrained by them. Allard Duursma and colleagues (2023: 22), for example, have referred to the potential of PoC mandates creating a strong 'loop effect' that regularly brings missions into conflict with government counterparts sensitive both to real or perceived infringements on their sovereignty and to criticism over human rights violations perpetrated by state actors. In the DRC case, this loop effect has had several particularly consequential impacts for the operationalisation of the mission's PoC mandate. First, as elsewhere it has meant that peacekeepers almost always err on the side of caution when it comes to threats to civilians emanating from host state security forces. While UN policy is clear that a mission's protection responsibilities apply "regardless of the source of the threat," the potential cost of confronting abusive state security forces – including the nuclear option of the withdrawal of state consent for the mission's very existence – has meant that UN forces almost never use force to repel attacks on civilians by state forces (UN DPO 2023: 5; Duursma et al 2023: 8). As noted above, at an operational level the loop effect has also placed peacekeepers in an exceedingly awkward relationship with the FARDC in particular; reputationally the UN cannot be seen as working too closely with one of the DRC's most abusive institutions, yet it has also committed itself to ongoing joint operations as a means of neutralising armed groups. While there may be some merit to the argument that Congolese soldiers behave better when accompanied by peacekeepers, and while the HRDDP provides a means of allowing the UN to avoid complicity with the most egregious army commanders, it remains the case that, in PoC terms at least, close collaboration with the FARDC comes with serious downside risks for the UN, and has done little to enhance the mission's reputation among Congolese civilians.

Second, not only do the strategic realities of peace operations mean that protection threats posed by rebel groups will always be prioritised over those committed by state security forces, but the mission's ability to progressively re-orient the behaviour of their domestic security counterparts has also proven to be marginal at best. In other words, not only has MONUSCO been unable to prevent abuses by state security forces, but the mission has also been unable to leverage its long-term partnership with the FARDC in the interests of security sector reform (SSR). This is not just a UN problem, of course, and it would be naïve to expect that the level of professionalism exhibited by Congolese soldiers could be significantly enhanced by the relatively thin socialisation potential of UN accompaniment; this is especially so since, as discussed previously, deeply entrenched patterns of informal governance have proven highly resilient to reform. As a consequence, as Adam Day has noted, "nearly twenty years of SSR and hundreds of millions of dollars in international funding resulted in essentially none of the hoped-for transformations;" the patronage systems are the heart of the sector remain largely intact, while the risks to civilians posed by state security forces remain largely undiminished (Day 2022: 115). At the same time, whether by default or by design MONUSCO's PoC strategy has placed more emphasis on the Tier 2 priority of immediate physical protection than on the Tier 3 priority of addressing the security governance shortcomings of the Congolese state (Labuda 2020: 40). Indeed, in the context of planning a responsible exit strategy, the 2019 strategic review recommended reversing these priorities, arguing that "MONUSCO should stop operating as a firefighter and instead invest political capital in incubating a robust political strategy aimed at ensuring that State actors fulfil their primary responsibility to protect" (UN 2019: 21).

Third, since well before transition from MONUC to MONUSCO – which crucially involved the insertion of the term 'stabilisation' into the mission's title – it has been clear that the Congolese government has a particular understanding of MONUSCO's role that sits awkwardly with the mission's own interpretation of its mandate. For all the discussion of so-called 'Christmas tree' mandates – with missions like MONUSCO tasked with too many responsibilities across too many issue areas (even if PoC remains the star atop the tree) – the Congolese government's own expectations of the mission have been clear, singular and unambiguous: peacekeepers are present on Congolese territory in order to help the government defeat its enemies. As Emily Paddon (2014: 175) has noted, President Joseph Kabila, whose term in office spanned much of the MONUC/MONUSCO era, "saw the UN force as an appendage to further his own interests," while the introduction of a stabilisation mandate – with its implications around support for the extension of state authority – was driven in large part by the Congolese government as a means of binding the peace operation more closely to the host state (Labuda 2020). While few observers have given Congolese political elites much credit for being attentive to broader PoC considerations, there is of course a certain logic to a force-first stabilisation agenda from a PoC perspective: civilian security should improve if key threats to civilians can be neutralised or removed entirely. This was indeed the underlying logic that led the UN Security Council to authorise the creation of the Force Intervention Brigade with a mandate to neutralise key rebel groups, notably the M23, as a means of advancing peace, stability, and security in the DRC's eastern provinces. While in many ways the UN's hand was forced on the issue – the pressures to act militarily against powerful armed groups were such that if the robust force that became the FIB wasn't incorporated as part of MONUSCO, if would have been established outside of the UN structure – for a period at least the fact that its presence did help to neutralise the threat posed by the M23 led many to believe that it represented the future of peacekeeping (Dorn 2023).

The flaws in such a strategy quickly revealed themselves, however. Rather than working systematically to neutralise armed groups and enable the progressive extension of state authority, both the DRC government and the leading troop contributors to the FIB revealed themselves to be quite selective in their choice of targets. The Rwanda-backed M23 was a particular preoccupation because it was one of the few groups with the strength to pose a genuine threat to the government, while the FIB's regional backers were keen to contain Rwanda's growing influence; once the threat receded the regional consensus underpinning the FIB, and its collaboration with the FARDC, gave way to drift and discord. After the successful M23 campaign, for example, the FIB turned its attention to joint operations against the FDLR (*Forces démocratiques de libération du Rwanda*), a Hutu-dominated rebel group with whom the FARDC had occasionally collaborated in the fight against the Tutsi-dominated M23. Cynically, the Kabila government appointed two UN-blacklisted generals to lead its side of anti-FDLR operations, knowing full well, as Mhango and Kithatu-Kiwekete have noted (2023: 39), "that MONUSCO would disengage from the campaign on account of its adherence to the Human Rights Due Diligence Policy." Moreover, the resurgence of the M23 as a serious military actor underlines the limits of a peace through victory strategy in a context as complex as that of the Great Lakes region; in retrospect, it is clear that the original 'victory' against the M23 was more of a tactical retreat than a comprehensive defeat, while the underlying political dynamics that animated the movement remain firmly in place. As John Karlsrud (2015: 45) has noted, MONUSCO's joint military operations with the FARDC in general, and the FIB experience in particular, have also placed the UN in a strategic no-man's land between presenting itself as a neutral third party working to facilitate peaceful conflict resolution, on the one hand, and an active party to the conflict on the side of the government on the other. In trying to play both roles simultaneously, the mission risked collapsing under the weight of contradictory visions. One manifestation of this, noted previously, revealed itself when the successful campaign against the M23 let the government off the hook in terms of its commitments under the Peace, Security and Cooperation Framework (PSCF). Having leveraged MONUSCO assistance to weaken its most dangerous rival, the Kabila government quickly lost interest in the compromises required of it in order to keep the PSCF on track (Tull 2018: 180). There is a strong case, then, that the mission's stabilisation mandate directly undermined its mandate to advance political solutions to the broader Congolese crisis.

With the passage of time, it also seems clear that the UN's leverage over host states, whether to inspire them to embrace the key principles of liberal peacebuilding or to compel them 'to fulfil their primary responsibility to protect,' is waning. While the power of liberal ideas to shape peace processes in conflict-affected societies was never as great as the proponents of such ideas wished them to be, a broader crisis of liberal internationalism has seriously weakened the claim that peace must necessarily be constructed on a foundation of democracy, the rule of law, and free markets. More concretely, the actions and postures of both China and Russia in recent years have – tacitly or otherwise – encouraged states like the DRC to push back against the more intrusive aspects of international intervention, and to insist that peace operations should be more about enabling sovereign states to restore their authority than about engineering good governance or accommodating the grievances of an armed opposition (Foot 2020; Lewis 2022). Russia, for its part, has actively worked to displace the influence of both former colonial powers and multilateral institutions like the EU and the UN in conflict-affected contexts such as Mali and the Central African Republic, offering robust military assistance to beleaguered governments, who are in turn encouraged to believe that conflicts can be resolved through unconditional victory rather than through difficult and painful compromise at the negotiating table. In short, over the past decade it has become increasingly clear that the UN is no longer the only game in town for conflict-affected states seeking external support. Just as the FIB could have come into existence as a non-UN entity, the DRC has been experimenting in recent years with different configurations of regional military support – first from the East African Community and more recently from the Southern African Development Community – in the hopes of finding a more robust, less conflicted military partnership that will allow it to achieve peace via the 'annihilation' of its enemies (Russo 2023). This too, ultimately, is a manifestation of the contemporary crisis of peacekeeping; disillusionment with the idea that international intervention can 'make peace' in terms favourable to the host governments has prompted the latter to actively searching for other means, and other fora, through which their core goals can be achieved.

Evaluating Robust Protection

While far from neutral, the UN Secretary General's regular reporting on the activities and developments of specific peace operations provides one source of continuous accounting of the activities undertaken in the name of PoC, even if the claims made about the effectiveness of any specific intervention remain difficult to verify. These reports also provide insight into what missions consider to be core PoC activities, given the reality that the broad understanding of PoC adopted by the UN means that most mission activities could be construed as protection-related. To take just one recent report – covering the period December 2023–March 2024 (UN 2024a) – MONUSCO's reported protection interventions included the maintenance of blocking positions around Goma in order to deter the M23 from attempting to re-capture the city; at the same time, the mission also, 'with varying degrees of success,' worked with the FARDC in support of civilian harm mitigation, especially with regard to the use of mortar and artillery fire in the ongoing conflict with the M23. Further north, in Ituri province, the mission also reported that its forces intervened on 30 separate occasions, including with live fire, in order to thwart 'impending or ongoing' attacks by CODECO elements against civilians; separately, a joint MONUSCO/FARDC operation led to the capture of two CODECO strongholds in Djugu territory. Two small armed groups were convinced to sign the Aru Act of Commitment on peaceful coexistence between communities during the same period, while the mission's police component undertook a range of SSR-related activities with their Congolese counterparts. Across Ituri and two Kivu provinces, the early warning system received over 1,000 alerts, two-thirds of which generated responses, whether by MONUSCO, state security forces, or humanitarian actors. Across the same region over the same time period, the mission recorded 597 separate security incidents, causing a reported 531 civilian fatalities.

This snapshot of activities underlines the extent to which both 'warrior' and 'firefighter' modes continue to coexist in MONUSCO's ongoing efforts to fulfil its protection mandate. While on some fronts the mission continues to be at war – alongside the Congolese government – with a subset of the rebellious factions that remain active in the east, on others the MONUSCO mindset is defensive in nature, with more emphasis on defending the threatened than on neutralising the threatening. In short, MONUSCO continues, as it has for the better part of its mandate, to deploy force across the full spectrum in fulfilment of its core mandated tasks. In both defensive and offensive modes, MONUSCO – and before it MONUC – remains one of the most combative peace operations of the 21st century, and has regularly tested (and occasionally traversed) the boundary between robust and enforcement peacekeeping. It is decidedly less clear, however, what the overall impact of this more robust stance has been on the security of those Congolese civilians the UN is mandated to protect; while there is little doubt that in specific cases peacekeeping passivity has cost civilian lives, it doesn't necessarily follow that the shift to a more robust stance – and especially the introduction of mandate language around 'neutralising' spoilers – has improved MONUSCO's protection record. In a major study of the mission's overall effectiveness, for example, the Effectiveness of Peace Operations Network (Novosseloff et al. 2019: 14) hedges its own conclusions, noting only that MONUSCO's PoC performance "varied widely across both space and time, and has produced a mixed record."

Indeed, gauging the effectiveness of the use of force as an instrument of civilian protection remains a major challenge, because of data limitations, ongoing ambiguities around the very meaning of the word protection, and the unpredictable and often unforeseeable ramifications of deploying armed force in the midst of an already volatile conflict environment. In the first place, not only is the eastern DRC a difficult place to access for independent researchers specifically because of ongoing insecurity, the UN's own newly installed performance-evaluation system – the Comprehensive Planning and Performance Assessment System, or CPAS – remains a work in progress and is at present not well suited to measuring impact.[4] Thus, as Walter Dorn (2023: 32) has noted, it remains the case that "instances of peacekeepers acting with force are seldom described," while the outcomes of such instances are rarely scrutinised. Not only is no one keeping score of lives saved vs. lives lost as a result of particular kinds of PoC-inspired interventions, but use-of-force decisions generate ripple effects that can extend out across both time and space. Evaluating 'efficacy' from a protection perspective, therefore, requires weighing not only the consequences of the immediate protective action – including live-fire engagement with armed groups to disrupt 'ongoing or impending' attacks on civilians – but also subsequent 'reactions' by the group in question. While Dorn contends that there is a strongly positive correlation between robust protection measures on the part of peacekeepers and civilian lives saved, he also acknowledges that in specific cases – notably the joint MONUSCO/FARDC effort to neutralise Allied Democratic Forces (ADF) rebels in 2014 – the offensive may ultimately have generated more violence against civilians than it prevented, given that the ADF subsequently sponsored dozens of attacks against civilians, killing hundreds in the process (2023: 42).

Indeed, it is precisely this ripple effect that has led many students of both peacekeeping and the DRC to call into question the extent to which a greater willingness to use force translates unproblematically into superior protection outcomes. During the MONUC period, for example, joint military offensives against groups such as the FDLR and ADF led to what Emily Paddon Rhoads (2016: 180) has described as 'vicious retaliation' on the part of the targeted groups against civilians in nearby communities. The logic of such retaliation, while ruthless, was unimpeachable: given the UN's sensitivity on protection issues, military operations against armed opposition groups that produced more rather than fewer atrocities against civilians would lead, invariably, to a re-consideration of the value of robust action. This strategy of "if you attack us, it will be the civilians who pay," (Paddon Rhoads 2016: 181) proved difficult to defend against, and has plagued the UN into the MONUSCO era as well. As Mats Berdal (2018: 739) has noted, while tactical victories may have provided a temporary measure of protection for some communities, "the effect elsewhere was an increase in predation and violence targeting civilian populations, and a consequent surge in the number of IDPs." Others have questioned the extent to which even the highest-profile case of neutralisation – the 2013 campaign that addressed, albeit temporarily, the threat posed by the M23 – can be attributed to the utility of superior force. As Stearns (2015: 7) has argued, in the wider context of questioning the value of violence as a solution to violence, at least as influential as the introduction of the FIB in this case was the weight of diplomatic pressure on Rwanda by Western donors; once its Rwandan sponsors 'pulled the plug,' the M23 had little alternative but to withdraw from the field of battle.

Given the current state of knowledge about the relationship between robust peacekeeping and civilian protection, and the very different conclusions that scholars have come to on this issue, it is therefore difficult to avoid the conclusion that generalised statements of causation should be treated with caution. We remain, as Stian Kjeksrud has suggested (2024: 41), largely ignorant "of the conditions leading to successful outcomes when force is used to protect." It may be, too, that even with better data the question of whether robust PoC generates better protection outcomes may still be too blunt; more nuanced approaches may be required to tease out precisely the circumstances in which the use of force (or the threat of the use of force) may have protective effects.

This takes us back to the work of Kjeksrud, who has generated some of the most careful empirical analysis yet undertaken on the utility of force for civilian protection purposes in the context of UN peace operations. Drawing on a dataset of some 200 cases of UN protection operations in Africa from 1999 to 2017, Kjeksrud's starting premise is that "UN troops *can* provide protection to civilians under the right conditions;" (2024: 43) he then proceeds to explore what precisely these conditions might be. Crucially, the analysis brings back into focus the armed groups posing the threat in the first place and moves beyond the overly simplistic assumption that PoC dynamics are primarily about the interactions between protectors and protected. It also underlines the central importance for any effective protection response of understanding the nature, motivations, and sensibilities of the armed groups in question. As discussed in Chapter 2 – and at risk of stating the obvious – not all armed groups are alike, and while some may be deterred from abusive intentions by the mere presence of international observers, for others nothing less than brute force will compel them to alter their behaviour.

Kjeksrud's key finding, which remains more suggestive than definitive, is that there is explanatory power to the idea that the use of force for protective purposes is most effective when it 'matches' the level of force deployed by the perpetrator. In other words – if perpetrator violence can be disaggregated according to the function it serves, from impairment at the lower end to destruction at the higher – protective responses need to be carefully calibrated in order to meet the threat on its own terms. As he notes (2024: 42), "it is not enough to be in the right place at the right time to intervene before perpetrators attack, the use of force must simultaneously be tailored to the threat civilians are facing." In a context such as the eastern Congo, where it is regularly reported that upwards of 130 different armed groups remain active, this conclusion offers both a promising path forward for PoC research as well as a daunting challenge for peacekeeping policy makers. On the one hand, it adds crucial dialectical context to use of force debates in peacekeeping contexts, insisting – rightly – that what matters is not only what peacekeepers do but also how armed groups respond to what peacekeepers do; if protecting civilians is the ultimate goal, this demands careful analysis of whether a robust response is likely to end the threat without deleterious longer-term consequences, or to trigger retaliatory responses that cost the lives of more civilians than the original intervention may have saved. On the other hand, it also sheds light on what remains serious gaps between the information-intensive demands of any 'matching' PoC strategy and the current state of peacekeeping intelligence. While the UN has had a comprehensive intelligence policy in place since 2017, it remains the case that mission-level capacities on this front – subject to the same budgetary pressures affecting peace operations more generally – remain inadequate to meeting the challenge of gathering and analysing data on armed groups at a sufficient level of granularity to be able to predict with any confidence their future behaviour. All this, of course, requires a serious effort to upgrade and enhance the capacities of peace operations across a range of fronts in an era of shrinkage and entrenchment.

Conclusion

While there is little indication that PoC itself is in danger of being downgraded or even abandoned as a peacekeeping priority – as a principle, the protection norm appears well-entrenched and broadly accepted across the UN system, including both within the Secretariat and across member states – MONUSCO's ultimate legacy may have been to demonstrate the limits of how far a robust protection strategy can be pushed. In particular, the DRC's turn towards non-UN security partnerships even as MONUSCO's exit strategy unfolds foretells a re-inscription of the long-standing red line between traditional peacekeeping principles and the perennially controversial concept of peace enforcement. In a case of policy learning from practice, the Secretary General's 2023 'New Agenda for Peace' took a page directly out of the Brahimi playbook in calling not only for peace operations to be freed from the burdens of 'unrealistic mandates,' but also for enforcement operations to be subcontracted out to regional organisations – and particularly the African Union (AU), which has for years now been attempting to carve out a more proactive role for itself in continental peace and security matters (most notably in the Horn of Africa) – underwritten by Security Council mandates (UN 2023: 24, 26). Ultimately, future scholars studying the impacts of robust, highly militarised protection strategies may find themselves much more focused on regional and subregional peace support efforts than on those undertaken under the rubric of conventional UN peacekeeping. Given the extensive experience that the UN has developed with regard to the full gamut of PoC activities in recent decades – and the organisation's still-unique ability to mix civilian, military, diplomatic and developmental in its protection activities – it is certainly worth asking whether rebuilding such capacities in still-nascent and under-resourced regional organisations such as the AU is the most logical way forward for the protection agenda. Regardless of such considerations, however, in the current geopolitical context this particular trend appears to have substantial momentum behind it.

While the precise shape and function of a new model of partnership peacekeeping has yet to come into focus, there is a danger that in seeking to offload more offensive forms of protection onto regional or subregional organisations, the UN also loses the capacity to deliver on the kinds of defensive PoC strategies pioneered and field-tested by MONUSCO. The UN's 2024 'Agenda for Protection' (UN 2024b), which was released with relatively little fanfare, certainly seems to point in this direction, as it self-consciously shifts attention away from the militarised dimensions of protection and towards a vision that is simultaneously holistic and system-wide while also focused on a narrower agenda of defending human rights and supporting conflict prevention. While the Agenda may reflect a new, more diminished reality for the UN in an era when the twin crises of Gaza and Ukraine have paralyzed the Security Council and sidelined the UN as a key player in international peace and security, it also reads more as a document designed to generate broad political support rather than one which builds on hard-earned lessons learned about how to protect vulnerable civilians at imminent risk in zones of conflict. As this chapter has suggested, while protection through neutralisation may be remembered as a bridge too far for the political and operational apparatus of UN peacekeeping, the mission's less publicised and less dramatic experiment in constructing a community-engaged system of early warning and rapid response – while decidedly imperfect – was both functional and represented a reasonably efficient use of the unique mix of capacities available to contemporary peace operations. While it could only address the consequences and not the causes of civilian violence in the eastern DRC, on its own terms it stands as a significant if unheralded success story which, if properly resourced and effectively linked to other elements of the peace promotion toolkit, could still be a model for future protection efforts. Amidst the rapidly shifting geopolitical terrain of the mid-2020s, it seems beyond debate that the UN's long-standing presence in the DRC – even with an imperfect and often-underperforming protection operation – remains preferable to its absence in neighbouring Sudan, where civilians have been left largely to fend for themselves as the country is torn apart by civil war.

Notes

1 Pagination is from the kindle version of this book.
2 *Les Forces armées de la République démocratique du Congo.*
3 The exception to this may be the most recent M23 crisis, ongoing as of early 2025, which the Congolese government increasingly considers to be 'intolerable' as a threat to the country's sovereignty.
4 Author interview, New York, April 2024; Dorn (2023: 32) also posits that the UN may itself be reticent to analyse its own use of force, not wanting to showcase "the violence committed as it works to enhance peace."

Works Cited

Ahere, J. (2012) 'The peace process in the DRC', *ACCORD Policy and Practice Brief*, 6 December; Available at: https://www.accord.org.za/publication/peace-process-drc

Al Jazeera (2023) 'DR Congo President Tshisekedi seeks withdrawal of UN peacekeepers this year', 21 September; Available at: https://www.aljazeera.com/news/2023/9/21/dr-congo-president-says-un-peacekeepers-to-begin-withdrawal-this-year

Berdal, M. (2018) 'The State of UN peacekeeping: Lessons from Congo', *The Journal of Strategic Studies* 41(5): 721–750.

Buskie, A. and K. Ferguson (2021) 'Linked up and linked in: Networking local-international early warning and early response in eastern Democratic Republic of the Congo', *Protection Approaches*, May; Available at: https://protectionapproaches.org/linked-up-and-linked-in

Carver, F. (2022) 'Linked up peacekeeping: Community early warning of atrocity risks as MONUSCO prepares to withdraw', *Protection Approaches*, July; Available at: https://protectionapproaches.org/linked-up-peacekeeping

Day, A. (2022) *States of Disorder, Ecosystems of Governance: Complexity Theory Applied to UN Statebuilding in the DRC and South Sudan* (Oxford: Oxford University Press).

Donais, T. and E. Tanguay (2021) 'Protection of civilians and peacekeeping's accountability deficit', *International Peacekeeping* 28(4): 553–578.

Dorn, W. (2023) 'Peacekeepers in combat: Protecting civilians in the D.R. Congo', *Journal of International Peacekeeping* 26: 31–54.

Duursma, A., S. Lindberg Bromley, and A. Gorur (2023) 'The impact of host-state consent on the protection of civilians in UN peacekeeping', *Civil Wars* (online first version): 1–25.

Foot, R. (2020) *China, the UN, and Human Protection: Beliefs, Power, Image* (Oxford: Oxford University Press).

Gowan, R. and S.J. Stedman (2018) 'The international regime for treating civil war, 1988–2017', *Daedalus* 147(1): 171–184.

Hood, C. and H. Margetts (2007) *The Tools of Government in the Digital Age* (New York: Palgrave Macmillan).

Karlsrud, J. (2015) 'The UN at war: Examining the consequences of peace-enforcement mandates for the UN peacekeeping operations in the CAR, the DRC and Mali', *Third World Quarterly* 36(1): 40–54.

Kjeksrud, S. (2024) 'Finding the utility of force to protect civilians from violence: Exploring outcomes of United Nations military protection operations in Africa (1999–2017)', *Civil Wars* 26(1): 41–73.

Labuda, P. (2020) 'With or against the state? Reconciling the protection of civilians and host-state support in UN peacekeeping', *International Peace Institute*,May; Available at: https://www.ipinst.org/2020/05/reconciling-poc-and-host-state-support-in-un-peacekeeping

Levine-Spound, D. (2021) 'Early warning and rapid response takes root in UN peacekeeping', *Center for Civilians in Conflict Policy Brief*, January; Available at: https://civiliansinconflict.org/early-warning-and-rapid-response/

Levine-Spound, D. and J. Jorgensen (2023) 'MONUSCO's 2022 mandate: Streamlined, but missing key protection language', Center for Civilians in Conflict blog post (undated); Available at: https://civiliansinconflict.org/blog/monuscos-2022-mandate-streamlined-but-missing-key-protection-language/#:~:text=In%20challenging%20circumstances%2C%20the%20Council,security%20sector%20reform%20(SSR)

Lewis, D. (2022) 'Contesting liberal peace: Russia's emerging model of conflict management', *International Affairs* 98(2): 653–673.

Mhango, G.A. and A. Kithatu-Kiwekete (2023) 'Peace enforcement in the Democratic Republic of the Congo: Reflections on the Force Intervention Brigade', *Strategic Review for Southern Africa* 45(1): 28–48.

Murphy, R. (2016) 'UN peacekeeping in the Democratic Republic of the Congo and the protection of civilians', *Journal of Conflict & Security Law* 21(2): 209–246.

Novosseloff, A. et al. (2019) 'Assessing the effectiveness of the United Nations mission in the DRC/MONUC-MONUSCO', Effectiveness of Peace Operations (EPON) Network Report 3; Norwegian Institute for International Affairs, April; Available at: https://www.nupi.no/en/publications/cristin-pub/assessing-the-effectiveness-of-the-united-nations-mission-in-the-drc-monuc-monusco

Paddon, E. (2014) 'Peacekeeping in the Congo: Implementation of the protection of civilians norm', in A. Betts and P. Orchard (eds.), *Implementation and World Politics: How International Norms Change Practice* (Oxford: Oxford University Press), 160–176.

Paddon Rhoads, E. (2016) *Taking Sides in Peacekeeping: Impartiality and the Future of the United Nations* (Oxford: Oxford University Press).

Prunier, G. (2011) *Africa's World War: Congo, the Rwandan Genocide, and the Making of a Continental Catastrophe* (Oxford: Oxford University Press).

Russo, J. (2023) 'East Africa's troops are leaving the DRC: What went wrong and what comes next', *The Conversation*, 11 December; Available at: https://theconversation.com/east-africas-troops-are-leaving-the-drc-what-went-wrong-and-what-comes-next-219500

Slim, H. (2007) *Killing Civilians: Method, Madness and Morality in War* (Oxford: Oxford University Press).

Spink, L. (2018) 'Community engagement by MONUSCO with reduced field presence', *Center for Civilians in Conflict Policy Brief*, May; Available at: https://civiliansinconflict.org/publications/policy/monusco-reduced-field-2/

Spink, L. (2019) 'Charting a future for peacekeeping in the Democratic Republic of Congo', *Center for Civilians in Conflict Policy Brief*, October; Available at: https://civiliansinconflict.org/wp-content/uploads/2020/10/CIVIC_PKReport_Final3_Web.pdf

Stearns, J. (2015) 'Can force be useful in the absence of a political strategy? Lessons from the UN missions to the DR Congo', *Congo Research Group*, December; Available at: https://s42831.pcdn.co/wp-content/uploads/2022/11/crg_publication_monusco_en.pdf

Stearns, J. (2022) *The War That Doesn't Say Its Name: The Unending Conflict in the Congo* (Princeton: Princeton University Press).

Townsend, M. (2024) 'Children executed and women raped in front of their families as M23 militia unleashes fresh terror on DRC', *The Guardian*, 21 December; Available at: https://www.theguardian.com/global-development/2024/dec/21/children-executed-and-women-raped-in-front-of-their-families-as-m23-militia-unleashes-fresh-terror-on-drc

Tull, D.M. (2018) 'The limits and unintended consequences of UN peace enforcement: The force intervention brigade in the DR Congo', *International Peacekeeping* 25(2): 167–190.

UN Department of Peace Operations (UN DPO) (2023) 'Policy: The protection of civilians in United Nations Peacekeeping (PoC Policy)', 1 May; Available at: https://peacekeeping.un.org/sites/default/files/2023_protection_of_civilians_policy.pdf

United Nations (UN) (2019) 'Transitioning from stabilization to peace: An independent strategic review of the United Nations Organization Stabilization Mission in the Democratic Republic of the Congo', S/2019/842; Available at: https://documents.un.org/doc/undoc/gen/n19/337/60/pdf/n1933760.pdf

United Nations (UN) (2023) 'Our common agenda policy brief 9: A new agenda for peace', July; Available at: https://www.un.org/sites/un2.un.org/files/our-common-agenda-policy-brief-new-agenda-for-peace-en.pdf

United Nations (UN) (2024a) 'Report of the Secretary-General on the United Nations organization stabilization mission in the Democratic Republic of the Congo', S/2024/251; Available at: https://documents.un.org/doc/undoc/gen/n24/068/18/pdf/n2406818.pdf

United Nations (UN) (2024b) 'United Nations Agenda for protection: Strengthening the ability of the United Nations system to protect people through their human rights', *Office of the High Commissioner for Human Rights*, February; Available at: https://www.ohchr.org/en/documents/tools-and-resources/united-nations-agenda-protection-strengthening-ability-united-nations

Verweijen, J. (2016) 'Stable instability: Political settlements and armed groups in the Congo', Usalama Project, Rift Valley Institute; Available at: https://riftvalley.net/wp-content/uploads/2018/06/Stable-Instability-by-Judith-Verweijen-RVI-PSRP-Usalama-Project-2016.pdf

Verweijen, J. and C. Vogel (2023) 'Why Congo's M23 crisis lingers on', International Peace Institute (IPI) Global Observatory, 30 May; Available at: https://theglobalobservatory.org/2023/05/why-congos-m23-crisis-lingers-on/

Williams, P. (2013) 'Protection, resilience and empowerment: United Nations peacekeeping and violence against civilians in contemporary war zones', *Politics* 33(4): 287–298.

Williams, P. (2023) 'How peacekeepers fight: Assessing combat effectiveness in United Nations peace operations', *Security Studies* 32(1): 32–65.

6 Protecting Civilians and Expanding State Authority in the Central African Republic

Introduction

Given the centrality of protection of civilian mandates in UN peace operations, it is no small irony that in the centre of Bangui, the capital of the Central African Republic (CAR), the statue honouring armed protectors of unarmed civilians features Russian mercenaries rather than UN peacekeepers. Installed in 2021 near the University of Bangui, the memorial depicts four soldiers – two of whom appear to be members of Russia's Wagner Group – in a protective semi-circle around a mother with two small children.[1] The message, that armed threats to civilians are best countered by the application of greater force, is unambiguous, and evocative of the old realist adage about peace through strength. The fearsome reputation of Wagner, known more for its scorched-earth tactics and cavalier attitude towards human life than for its concern for the fate of women and children caught in the crossfire, imparts this particular *mise-en-scène* with a further sense of irony; this is an organisation, after all, which boasts that 'death is our business.' Still, it is hard to deny that – much as it did in Syria a decade ago – the application of Russian military muscle in support of state security forces, starting with its role in repelling rebel forces that threatened to take the capital in early 2021, has tipped the scales in the state's favour in its struggle against armed groups. It has also subsequently, if not necessarily sustainably, enabled the state to reclaim control of much of CAR's territory, allowed significant numbers of displaced civilians to return home, and created at least an opening for CAR to escape a long-term and vicious cycle of armed conflict and instability.

The memorial, and the continued presence of Wagner Group forces operating alongside those of the *Forces armées centrafricaines* (FACA) and in parallel to MINUSCA peacekeepers, also represents a rejoinder of sorts to the UN's own vision for peace, stability and civilian well-being in CAR. Operational since 2014, MINUSCA has a decidedly mixed reputation among those it was deployed to protect. As elsewhere in the region, well-publicised protection failures – and a reputation for inconsistency and inaction at precisely those moments when imperilled civilians are most in need of help – have tarnished MINUSCA's reputation, as have equally well-publicised cases of widespread sexual exploitation and abuse (SEA) committed by peacekeepers themselves against local women and girls

DOI: 10.4324/9781003291114-6

(Whalan 2017; Debout 2024). Anti-MINUSCA sentiment, however, coexists with a broader sense that the mission continues to play a crucial stabilising role in an unstable environment. Through its widespread presence across CAR's territory, MINUSCA continues to engage in a broad spectrum of protection activities, enables and facilitates the work of humanitarian actors and provides support for the expansion and consolidation of state authority, even if it has not been a game-changer in terms of wider conflict dynamics. For MINUSCA, the protection-peacebuilding continuum has long comprised a defensive-oriented, deterrence-through-presence posture accompanied by ongoing efforts to advance and render irreversible a negotiated peace between the Government of CAR and the myriad collection of armed groups aligned against it, coupled with capacity-building efforts aimed at laying the foundations for the emergence of a fully democratic, rights-respecting set of state institutions. The growing prominence of Wagner forces in CAR, however, has become the elephant in the room *vis-à-vis* both protection and peacebuilding, and provides a clearly differentiated counter-narrative with regard to meeting the challenge of liberating Central Africans from the chronic insecurity that has been their lot for decades. As David Lewis has argued (2022: 654), Russia offers not only armed support to beleaguered conflict-affected states, but also an increasingly coherent vision of contemporary conflict management premised on "the primacy of sovereign norms, the need for strong states and political order, and the rights of governments to suppress internal conflict using any means necessary." It is a vision, in short, of a peace that can be imposed by force rather than nurtured through negotiations.

It is within this broader context that this chapter examines the ongoing protection record of MINUSCA, the United Nations Multidimensional Integrated Stabilisation Mission in CAR, launched in 2014. Moving beyond the big-picture question of whether the mission 'saves lives' – PoC has been MINUSCA's headline mandate from the outset – this chapter explores two related questions. The first concerns the mission's ability to adjust its protection practices to the very different conflict context that has emerged in recent years; in other words, has the mission been able to effectively adapt to a rapidly evolving situation in ways that have enabled it to maximise its ability to protect the vulnerable? The second question concerns the relationship between PoC and the extension of state authority (another key mission mandate), and the role of mission-centric PoC as an important if limited stopgap measure in the interregnum until the state recovers (or develops) the capacity to fulfil its 'primary protection responsibility' *vis-à-vis* its own citizens. While the two objectives are often treated in isolation, in practice – and in the continued absence of stable negotiated solutions that address the root causes of violence and insecurity – strengthening the link between mission-provided PoC on the one hand and state-provided security on the other constitutes an important metric for the success of any civilian protection strategy, and indeed provides perhaps the only sustainable exit strategy for peace operations with PoC mandates.

On both fronts, I make the case that MINUSCA has found itself increasingly pushed to the margins. While it continues to have significant protection resources at its disposal – indeed, between its robust military capacities and extensive civilian resources MINUSCA remains almost certainly the most capable institutional actor in CAR (UN 2024) – the mission's centrality to the country's transition has shrunk discernibly in recent years. Although it retains the capacity to protect civilians at the margins of CAR's shifting conflict landscape, to support life-saving humanitarian assistance, and to deter attacks against civilians within fixed geographical spaces (especially where it has forces based), MINUSCA simultaneously appears to have lost ground in terms of its ability to influence either armed actors (especially those in the employ of the state) or the wider conflict trajectory. While many of the developments that have led to the present moment – among them shifting strategies on the part of those armed groups that defected from the most recent peace agreement and a growing determination of the CAR government to vanquish rather than accommodate the armed opposition – are well outside of MINUSCA's control, they pose difficult dilemmas with regard not only to the mission's short-term protection strategy, but also with regard to what kind of peace, and what kind of state, may ultimately emerge in CAR.

The Peace/Protection Context in CAR

The events of January 2021, when a coalition of rebel forces led by former President François Bozizé tried and failed to capture Bangui in the aftermath of contested national elections, now stand as a critical moment in CAR's long-running conflict, even if it remains premature to pinpoint this episode as a decisive turning point in the country's transition from war to peace. Until that moment, however, CAR seemed to have settled into a pattern familiar to the UN's other large African missions. As in neighbouring DRC and South Sudan, in CAR the norm has long been stasis periodically interrupted by crisis, with the constant threat of a full return to violence, chaos and anarchy lurking in the background. Given the seeming inability of any constellation of external interveners and domestic actors to make a peace that endures, let alone generate momentum behind a genuine and inclusive peacebuilding process, CAR found itself 'stuck' – to borrow a term used by one Bangui-based civil society activist – in an uncomfortable interregnum between war and peace.[2]

Overshadowed first by the global pandemic and the war in Ukraine, and more recently by escalating conflict in the Middle East, CAR's latest peace process partially unravelled over the course of several years. Signed in February 2019, the Agreement for Peace and Reconciliation in the Central African Republic (APPR) included the signatories of 14 armed groups, with the inclusion of rebel group representatives in government institutions being the *quid pro quo* for a cessation of hostilities.[3] The parties' commitment to the APPR was severely tested (and found wanting) in the lead-up presidential elections of late 2020, and in particular by the aspirations of former President Bozizé to reclaim his old job. Disqualified from running by CAR's constitutional court due to war crimes charges against him, Bozizé emerged as the head of the Coalition of Patriots for Change (CPC), leading a handful of APPR signatories to defect from the peace agreement and ultimately spearheading an assault on Bangui in an effort to reclaim by force the position he had been denied the opportunity to pursue via the ballot box. In the aftermath, whether the APPR – shored up by the so-called Luanda Joint Roadmap of September 2021 – can be resuscitated as a viable framework for peace in CAR remains an open question. On the one hand, MINUSCA continues to engage those groups, 8.5 strong by some counts, who have remained loyal to the process, including through the APPR's disarmament, demobilisation and disarmament (DDR) provisions,[4] and the UN continues to call on all parties to the conflict to remain engaged in the political and peace process (UN 2024). On the other hand, it is apparent that CAR's government – seemingly convinced of the fecklessness of the armed opposition and buoyed by the strategic advantages it now enjoys thanks to its Russian partners – now sees military victory rather than negotiated settlement as a more viable and more attractive way to escape the country's long-running cycle of violence.

On the ground, therefore, it is undeniably the case that war has resumed, and continues, between government forces and APPR defectors, even if fighting remains localised and sporadic. With the support of 'other security personnel' – the generic term generally used to refer to Wagner mercenaries, although Rwanda also has an important bilateral military presence in CAR – the FACA have over the past several years been endeavouring to re-capture and hold towns and territory previously held by armed groups (Bax 2021). For their part, the disaffected rebel groups – while the CPC itself has been fractured and weakened, several of its constituent elements, including *Retour, reclamation et réhabilitation* (3R), *Unité pour la paix en Centrafrique* (UPC) and *Le Front populaire pour la renaissance de la Centrafrique* (FPRC), remain active (UN 2024: 10) – have increasingly adopted guerrilla-style hit-and-run tactics, targeting roads (including through the growing use of improvised explosive devices) and FACA forces in particular before retreating to the relative safety of the bush. This fluid game of *cache-cache* among armed groups, MINUSCA, FACA and bilateral forces – in which civilians, as always, find themselves regularly caught in the crossfire – runs in parallel with an ongoing struggle to control CAR's mining sites, and the gold and diamond wealth they contain. While control of mining sites has provided armed groups with a means of survival and sustenance, larger sites – including the major Ndassima gold mine in central CAR – have reportedly been promised by the CAR government to the Wagner Group as payment for services rendered, with the latter increasingly focused on strengthening its grip over these sites (Bax 2021; The Sentry 2023: 26, 29).

There is little doubt that CAR's rebels are on the defensive, and have been increasingly fragmented, marginalised and driven into the bush by the ongoing government offensive. Indeed, President Faustin-Archange Touadéra – who has held office since 2016 – boasted to foreign journalists in late 2023 that whereas armed groups once controlled 80 per cent of CAR's territory to the government's 20 per cent, those numbers have now been reversed (Adegoke 2023). Broader structural factors, however, caution against excessive optimism with regard to CAR's medium-term trajectory. There continues to be much truth to the popular joke that the state ends at PK12, the outer borough where Bangui ends and the country's vast periphery begins (Schnieder 2013). Simply put, the central state has historically shown very little concern for, and very little interest in, socio-economic development outside the capital. As Louisa Lombard (2016: 4) has observed, "if the solution is a government that provides services and a private sector that provides jobs, we must at the very least recognize that CAR's every historical tendency has worked against these ideals." Writing about Africa more generally, Tom Burgis (2015: 80) has also noted how the combination of state-level corruption and absence of economic opportunity collectively act as 'recruiting sergeants' for armed groups, and this dynamic has been very much in play in CAR in recent decades. Ongoing political and socio-economic exclusion continues to drive frustrated young men towards armed groups, which have demonstrated themselves time and again to be the country's most reliable vehicle for airing grievances and for gaining access to both resources (not least through DDR processes) and political positions. As Lombard (2016: 1) has noted, "leading an armed group has become a surer way to power than standing in elections." Despite continuing to enjoy the upper hand in military terms, then, it remains unclear whether the current government possesses either the capacity or the political will to begin to confront the corrosive, destabilising impacts of these long-standing trends. Amidst a persistent economic and fiscal crisis, the government continues to struggle with the fundamentals of public administration, such as paying soldiers' salaries and stipends, while efforts to extend state authority remain limited to major population centres. Of equal concern, the government's top priority for an extended period has involved engineering constitutional changes to enable Touadéra to circumvent term limits and remain in power indefinitely. Deepening economic relations with its Russian partners – and a deepening appreciation of the reality that "Wagner's men … have penetrated the heart of power in Bangui and established an economic stranglehold in return for the protection they provide the authorities" (Bensimon 2023) – have also fed fears that the country's political trajectory is tilting rapidly in an authoritarian direction. Such fears have been exacerbated by debates concerning the passage of a 'foreign agent' law – inspired by similar Russian legislation, in place since 2012, that has been widely used to repress government critics, especially those with international connections (Barrons 2024). While the legislation was still being debated at the time of writing, many have taken it as a precursor to a further constriction of civic space in CAR, which already languishes near the very bottom of Freedom House's (2024) annual global rankings of the state of respect for political rights and civil liberties in the world. As one Bangui-based activist lamented, for a citizenry which has long considered itself to be subjugated (*assujetti*), such developments offer little promise of a better future.[5]

Throughout the current period of instability, meanwhile, civilian casualties have continued to mount; one study has suggested that fully 5.6 per cent of the country's population died in 2022, a mortality rate twice as high as any other country in the world (Mailman School 2023). The hit-and-run tactics of rebel groups have taken a particular toll on civilians, and as territory shifts hands those stuck in the middle have often been subject to exactions by re-occupying forces. Especially troubling has been the wholesale lack of respect for civilian life demonstrated by FACA and its Russian partners over the course of the latest anti-rebel campaign. One Human Rights Watch report (2022) cited 'compelling evidence' that

"Russian-identified forces supporting the Central African Republic's government have committed grave abuses against civilians with complete impunity," including cases of torture, summary executions and unlawful detention. A 2023 report by the investigative group *The Sentry* (2023: 3) reached a similar conclusion, contending that "under the cover of a counter-offensive against anti-Touadéra armed groups, Wagner, Touadéra, and his inner circle have perpetrated widespread, systematic, and well-planned campaigns of mass killing, torture, and rape throughout the country." More recently, *The Guardian* (Obaji 2024) reported that sexual assaults committed by 'white soldiers' in the vicinity of Bouar, in CAR's restive northwest, have become sufficiently widespread that women and girls now avoid tending their crops or attending markets, with food shortages beginning to emerge as a result. As of late 2021, the ongoing violence had pushed CAR's internally displaced population beyond 700,000, with a similar number living abroad as refugees, out of the total population of some 5 million (Bax 2021). More recent figures suggest that the success of the ongoing anti-rebel campaign has created the conditions for some IDP returns, bringing the overall national figure down below 500,000 as of September 2024 (UNHCR 2024). While returns may provide some grounds for cautious optimism, it continues to be the case, as the International Crisis Group (2024) has noted, that "instability and violence continue to fester," at significant cost to civilian populations.

Protecting Central African Civilians

In 2020, the Effectiveness of Peace Operations Network (EPON) published perhaps the most comprehensive independent assessment of MINUSCA's performance in CAR since the mission's inception (Howard et al. 2020). The report walks a fine line between noting the mission's many positive achievements – despite an extremely challenging operational environment – and acknowledging that the prospects for sustainable peace and sustainable improvements in human security in CAR were in many ways no better in 2020 than they were in 2014. On the one hand, the mission "has saved countless lives and contributed to a more stable regime," in addition to making important contributions to building state capacity, helping to establish the rule of law, and supporting local-level peacebuilding (Howard et al. 2020: 26). On the other hand, at the time of publication there were in fact more formalised armed groups active in CAR than in 2014, holding sway over upwards of 75 to 80 per cent of the country's territory; while the mission enjoyed some notable successes in pushing some armed groups out of key population centres, it has been unable to defeat, disarm or disband them. Ultimately, then, "despite important and indisputable points of progress, nearly six years after MINUSCA's deployment, insecurity and instability remain palpable" (Howard et al. 2020: 120).

One conclusion to be drawn from this analysis is that while MINUSCA's presence has not been a game-changer in terms of sustainably advancing the cause of peace in CAR, in its absence the situation in the country would almost certainly have been immeasurably worse; in this sense, helping to prevent CAR's slippage from fragile state to failed state might be considered MINUSCA's signature achievement. A slightly different reading of EPON's assessment might note an implicit distinction within the report between peacekeeping and peacebuilding, a distinction that the UN itself has blurred through the adoption of the language of peace support operations (which are meant to both keep and build peace). On the basis of this distinction, one might reasonably conclude that while MINUSCA has been successful at a range of key peacekeeping tasks, it has been unable to move the needle on the broader peacebuilding challenge. Bringing down death rates, for example, is a different kind of success – perhaps more in line with the mission's capacities – than addressing violence and instability's root causes. With regard to PoC, however, this distinction is difficult to sustain, since the protection imperative straddles both short-term peacekeeping and longer-term peacebuilding; successful PoC means not only protecting civilians against immediate, life-threatening security threats but also laying the foundations for the state to re-assume, over the longer term, its primary responsibility for protecting its citizenry. In this sense, restoring the state's capacity and willingness to assume its protection responsibilities is arguably just as crucial to PoC as pre-empting or deterring civilian atrocities.

Events since 2020, however – and in particular the confluence of COVID, contested elections, and the increasingly assertive influence of 'other security personnel' – have in many ways re-shuffled the deck in terms of both the broader political environment in CAR and MINUSCA's role in supporting peace and protecting civilians. While the pandemic's impact on CAR – a country whose health infrastructure ranks near the bottom of world rankings – was mercifully modest, during the period before and after the December 2020 presidential elections it did have the secondary effect of limiting UN activities, both in terms of mobility and in terms of interaction with the local population (de Coning 2020). At the same time, Bozizé's armed challenge to the election results was a serious blow to the APPR accords, and appeared to convince Touadéra and his closest advisors to put peacebuilding on the back burner in favour of a renewed effort to eliminate the armed defectors once and for all.[6] To this end, and given the continuing weakness of the FACA, the military trainers from the Wagner Group took on an increasingly prominent, and brutal, role in the counter-offensive against the rebels and those civilians seen to be harbouring sympathies towards them. This period was also characterised by a deterioration of relations between MINUSCA and the CAR government, with the latter both limiting cooperation with the mission and seriously restricting peacekeepers' freedom of movement.[7] In this sense, then, 2021 represented something of a lost year for MINUSCA, whose forces were increasingly confined to base and whose leadership was unable to make full use of its capacities to influence unfolding political dynamics.

As MINUSCA has sought to regain its footing, it has struggled to adapt to this new operational environment, especially with regard to the protection of civilians. On the one hand, the mission's ability to reach and defend vulnerable populations remains constrained. The new reality of conflict, with rebel groups increasingly adopting hit-and-run tactics and operating from the relative safety of the bush, has exposed MINUSCA's military components as too big, too slow and too heavy to respond effectively.[8] With armoured personnel carriers confined to the few main routes, with the increased prevalence of improvised explosive devices (especially in the western region), and with limited helicopter support, the mission's PoC efforts are insufficiently nimble, and despite the presence of some forward operating bases much of the mission's protection effort involves static protection of populations in urban centres. Somewhat ironically, efforts to address the negative reputational impacts of earlier scandals involving SEA of local populations have also impacted MINUSCA's operational capacity. In September 2021, the mission's entire Gabonese contingent (at one point some 450-strong) was sent home following credible reports of its members abusing local girls. While consistent with the UN's new and harder line on SEA – which has been a particular problem in CAR – the repatriation had knock-on effects on an already-stretched mission's operational capacities, further reducing its abilities to respond to threats to civilians (UN News 2021). Confronting threats to civilians emanating from *within* the mission, in other words, has increased the broader PoC burden for those peacekeepers who remain.

On the other hand, MINUSCA has also struggled to come to terms with the deepening security partnership between the CAR government and the Wagner Group, which at one point had upwards of 2,500 personnel in CAR (current estimates put Wagner's strength at 1,500–2,000 personnel). While the details of this arrangement remain murky –Wagner's very existence was long shrouded in mystery, even though in the aftermath of founder Yevgeny Prighozin's death the Russian government has exerted more direct control over the organisation's activities – over time Wagner's presence has become more pronounced and more overt, and the mercenaries are widely understood to have been at the very vanguard of the counter-offensive against rebel groups that began in 2021 and was ongoing at the time of writing. As noted above, Wagner's involvement in CAR's conflict has been accompanied by a decidedly cavalier attitude towards human rights, as well as towards the distinction between combatant and civilian, and many of the worst atrocities against civilians during this period have been attributed to Wagner personnel, operating in conjunction with (and often leading) FACA forces (Bensimon 2023). According to *The Sentry* (2023: 3), Wagner-led military operations outside of Bangui have operated under a 'leave no trace' principle: "in other words, kill everyone, including women and children." For MINUSCA, this new reality has presented a painful dilemma: while robust PoC activities are always politically sensitive when the threat to civilians comes from government forces – given the imperative to maintain host-country consent, missions have long been reluctant to confront abusive state armed forces in the name of PoC (Labuda 2020) – the political sensitivity becomes even more pronounced when effective PoC means confronting armed forces with close links to a permanent member of the Security Council, the body responsible for the mission's very existence. This rather unprecedented situation for UN peacekeeping has effectively paralyzed the mission's ability and/or willingness to confront the most egregious threats to civilians. The result, according to one Bangui-based analyst, is a deepening popular perception that MINUSCA is failing where it matters most: "people feel they are doing nothing."[9]

Beyond the coercive, force-first dimensions of PoC, MINUSCA has also been working to reset its diplomatic relations with the Touadéra government, while also maintaining constructive relations with a wide range of grassroots peace committees – some of which it was responsible for creating – which continue to support bottom-up peacebuilding in CAR. In February 2022, Rwanda's Valentine Rugwabiza was appointed as Special Representative of the Secretary General (SRSG) in CAR, and head of MINUSCA. Rugwabiza's appointment reflects, in part, Rwanda's growing influence in CAR, both as a bilateral partner and as a key contributor (with some 2,500 uniformed personnel) to MINUSCA. The Wagner factor, however, has continued to represent a key stumbling block to a full diplomatic reset. Even though the Ukraine conflict prompted a partial (and seemingly temporary) drawdown of the Russian presence in CAR, Wagner's continued influence on both military training and operations and government policy remains hard to reconcile with the broader objectives of sustainable peacebuilding, just as its brutal battlefield tactics remain difficult to reconcile with the ongoing emphasis of MINUSCA on PoC and respect for international humanitarian law. The non-transparency of the government's financial arrangements with the Russians has also thrown into question essential assistance from the international financial institutions, while the European Union Training Mission (EUTM) – which provides non-operational support on security sector reform (SSR) – scaled back its activities in response to Wagner's growing influence over the FACA, and as of late 2024 has re-calibrated its entire approach.[10]

With the broader security environment in CAR having shifted dramatically under the cover of the pandemic, the prospects for significantly scaling up local mediation and peacebuilding initiatives as a PoC strategy have also dimmed. Writing in 2017, Marie-Joelle Zahar and Delphine Mechoulan proposed that, given the comparative advantage of its country-wide presence, MINUSCA should consider shifting from a reactive and ad hoc approach to supporting local mediation efforts to a more strategic vision, involving more expertise, more resources and a more concerted effort to connect top-down and bottom-up dynamics (Zahar and Mechoulan 2017). In different parts of the country, local peace committees have helped win 'small battles' – often involving temporary *ententes* among various armed groups to avoid direct confrontations – that have demonstrated their potential as instruments of peace and protection. Such local success stories continue; in Bouar, for example, the local peace and reconciliation committee had a hand in facilitating the peaceful withdrawal of CPC forces which had occupied the town as part of Bozizé's failed insurrection.[11] More generally, however, the challenge of transforming the sincere hunger for peace and security that exists among local populations across CAR's 16 prefectures into a genuine, locally grounded infrastructure for peace appears largely unmet. While there has been an impressive proliferation of local initiatives for peace – from NGO-funded and UN-facilitated social cohesion initiatives to the government's own network of local peace and reconciliation committees – the vast majority remain dependent on volunteer labour and on their ability to attract external funding, an increasingly scarce commodity in CAR. They are also expected to develop income-generation activities as a means of becoming self-sustaining, a tall order given CAR's precarious economic circumstances, and one which in any event would divert considerable energies away from core peace promotion activities such as engaging in dialogue with local armed groups. And as CAR's economic situation remains precarious, committees become increasingly paralysed by the most quotidian of dilemmas, such as lacking funds to pay for petrol for donated motorcycles.[12] It is also the case, as Zahar and Mechoulan (2017: 32) have noted, that local pacts and national dynamics remain almost entirely unconnected; while the successes that have been achieved have "never been leveraged to foster a national discourse on reconciliation," in recent years there has been a palpable sense of lost momentum, as well as a sense that whatever positive agency grassroots peace efforts might once have had was beginning to wither.

Ultimately, then, it is hard to avoid the conclusion that MINUSCA's PoC strategy has struggled to keep up with the changing conflict context in CAR. To a large extent, this is less a failure of imagination or tactics on the part of mission itself and more a factor of the tectonic geopolitical shifts that are dramatically altering the strategic context in which peacekeepers operate; in other words, given the geopolitical considerations involved, individual missions such as MINUSCA possess very little space to evolve practical responses to such problems through field-level practice. Despite the clear overarching goals of PoC – saving civilian lives and creating the conditions for greater human security among populations at risk – the manner in which the dynamics of conflict have shifted in CAR in recent years has rendered conventional assumptions about the protection-peacebuilding continuum, and the practices flowing from them, increasingly questionable. It is clear that MINUSCA continues to protect civilians in harm's way in CAR, and that in the mission's absence the situation would almost certainly be worse. That said, it is also clear that MINUSCA's protection efforts – whether of the coercive or non-coercive variety – function increasingly on the periphery of CAR's conflict complex, while the mission's ability to affect the wider political context of conflict appears to have diminished over time. Such a situation is hardly unique to CAR; similar dynamics prevail in neighbouring DRC, where MONUSCO's increasingly visible marginalisation has increased pressure on the mission to withdraw, even as the government seeks regional partners capable of helping it defeat its internal enemies. If it is the case that the marginal utility of PoC efforts has appeared, at least in the case of CAR, to decline over time, then this is all the more reason to think carefully about the linkages between PoC and the extension of state authority. It is to this question that this chapter now turns.

PoC vs. Extension of State Authority

In resolutions mandating peace operations to protect civilians, the UN Security Council consistently invokes the 'primary protection responsibility' of the host state *vis-à-vis* its own population. In the case of CAR, such language has long existed in a realm somewhere between the aspirational and the fictional, given not only the reality that the majority of CAR's territory was until recently under the control of armed non-state actors, but also the history of the state's conspicuous absence from the vast periphery beyond the capital and the ongoing uncertainty around whether state actors even consider themselves to be in the business of protecting civilians.

In principle at least, MINUSCA's mandated responsibility to support the extension of state authority is meant to progressively alter these underlying conditions, enabling the state to gradually displace and replace non-state security actors and to establish (for the first time in the country's history) a country-wide monopoly on the legitimate use of force. In other words, mission activity under the extension of state authority rubric is meant to serve as a bridge between short-term, reactive, people-centred PoC and long-term, structural, state-centric PoC; the UN's own PoC policy acknowledges as much in its emphasis on mission support to host governments, and in principle PoC and host-state support are meant to be 'complementary objectives' (Labuda 2020: 5, 39).

In practice, however, as Patryk Labuda has written, the tensions between these two sets of activities are legion and are particularly pronounced in situations where state security forces aggravate rather than ameliorate civilian insecurity. In Labuda's words, "in supporting state actors who violate human rights and prey on civilian populations, the UN may unwittingly exacerbate the very POC problems it is meant to resolve" (2020: 5). Mission personnel are of course well aware – often painfully so – of such tensions, but possess few instruments to overcome them.[13]

In CAR's current context, there are at least two critical manifestations of this dilemma, both of which have been rendered more acute, and more intractable, by the Wagner factor. First, as noted above, the government's counter-offensive against CPC-affiliated forces has been marred by frequent and well-documented human rights violations perpetrated by a coalition of Russian and Central African forces "that had no qualms about killing anyone in its path" (Le Cam 2024). Given the diplomatic sensitivities and freedom of movement restrictions with which MINUSCA has had to contend during this period, the mission has had little ability to influence – let alone mitigate – the humanitarian consequences of such operations. At the same time, as Vianney Ingasso and colleagues (2023) have written, despite the accompanying human rights violations the counter-offensive has remained widely popular among ordinary citizens, many of whom have also suffered from the predatory behaviour of armed groups, and who viewed their elimination as a vital prerequisite to longer-term stability. In this case then, it is at least plausible to argue that this is an instance of 'developmental violence' (Sorensen 1992), involving a necessary dose of short-term violence as a fundamental condition for extending state authority and establishing long-term security and stability.

The current context of CAR – in which UN peacekeepers operate in awkward cohabitation arrangements with 'other security personnel' – is neither unique nor unprecedented. The French-led Operation Sangaris, which was terminated in 2016, operated as an enforcement operation in CAR for the first several years of MINUSCA's existence. The operation's robust posture was credited with encouraging a more conciliatory stance among armed opposition groups, while its withdrawal – premature in the view of some analysts – "coincided with a progressive resurgence of violence throughout the country" (Di Razza 2016). In neighbouring DRC, similarly, MONUSCO has had to contend with such a wide and shifting variety of bilateral and sub-regional military presences – over and above the myriad Congolese armed groups active in the country's turbulent Eastern provinces – that considerable efforts have had to be devoted to so-called 'de-confliction' efforts in order to avoid inadvertent contact, and accidental conflict. The reality that UN peace operations are no longer the only game in town when it comes to international or regional conflict management efforts was explicitly acknowledged in the UN Secretary General's 'New Agenda for Peace' (UN 2023), which called for "a new generation of peace enforcement missions and counter-terrorism operations," particularly in Africa and led by African partners. The role that Wagner forces have been playing in CAR in recent years is therefore a variation on this theme, even though the specific nature of this intervention poses difficult – and unresolved – questions about not only the relationship between enforcement operations and subsequent (or coterminous) peace operations, but also about the link between enforcement and PoC. While Wagner's military tactics are clearly abhorrent from a human rights perspective, there is at the same time an unavoidable logic – akin to MONUSCO's Force Intervention Brigade being tasked with 'neutralising' certain armed groups in the Congolese context – to the idea that defeating armed groups, rather than simply defending the vulnerable from the threats that they pose, may over the long term represent a more sustainable solution to the civilian protection challenge in conflict-affected contexts. Given the persistent ambivalence across the UN system – noted in Chapter 2 – on the question of the use of force for protection purposes, it seems fair to conclude that as an institution, UN peacekeeping has yet to fully internalise the consequences of Wagner-style enforcement operations for either peace or for protection, or fully process the implications of such operations for its own protection mandates.

A second, longer-term manifestation concerns the extent to which the state in CAR is not only capable of but also committed to ending the war (whether by victory or by negotiated settlement), establishing a durable peace, extending its authority across CAR's entire geographical expanse, and working towards improving security and reducing poverty for the country's 5 million citizens. While the very notion of extending state authority is premised on the venerable Hobbesian notion that bringing territory under the control of a central authority is key to escaping the state of nature and entering the realm of order, stability and justice, it remains very much a matter of debate whether this progressive, monopolistic vision is shared by CAR's political elites, past, present or future. Indeed, the ongoing controversy over constitutional reform, and the affiliated prospect of additional terms for the sitting president, seems tailor-made to further inflame grievances across CAR's underdeveloped periphery as political power becomes increasingly concentrated within Bangui's Renaissance Palace, the president's official residence. It is also the case that most of those who have exercised state power in CAR's recent history – the current incumbent being no exception – have understood that what really matters is control of Bangui, and have tended to view the periphery less through the lens of national development and social inclusion and more through the lens of resource extraction. Ongoing struggles over the control over mineral resources – gold mines in particular – fit all too comfortably within this wider narrative (Salih and Burke 2023). Given CAR's own history and the history of other African states which have experienced wild west-style goldrushes, there are reasonable grounds to believe that the struggle to control resource riches will generate much civilian suffering and little sustainable human development. There is, in short, no necessary or inevitable correlation between a state's growing capacity to control territory and its willingness to protect the people who reside there.

At the same time, the principal flaw in the 'developmental violence' argument noted above is that even with ongoing Wagner support CAR's security forces continue to lack the capacity to permanently contain – led alone decisively defeat – armed opposition groups, even as their own abusive behaviour *vis-à-vis* local communities is likely to further nourish the kinds of grievances that lead to future armed group mobilisation. Predation on the part of FACA forces themselves is partly a function of poorly, irregularly paid soldiers being forced to 'live off the land,' which is itself indicative of the CAR state's precarious financial position.[14] Even in cases where civilian administrators have been installed in regional centres following the withdrawal of non-state armed groups, this presence remains fragile and tenuous; many have reportedly returned in relatively short order to Bangui, not least because they can only access their government salaries from the capital. The presence of CAR's national police, likewise, remains restricted to larger towns and cities. In short, as Ingasso et al. (2023) have noted, while the Wagner/FACA alliance has successfully pushed armed groups out of CAR's main population centres and its resource-rich territories, securing CAR's entire 620,000 square kilometres of land is another matter entirely. There are already signs, moreover, that Wagner's own priorities in CAR are shifting. According to one source interviewed by *Le Monde*, "their focus is now to contain armed groups while maintaining a sufficient level of instability to justify their presence. The main concern for Wagner now is economic predation" (cited in Grynszpan et al. 2023). While Wagner's presence in CAR has both enabled CAR's authoritarian turn and encouraged a hardline approach towards the armed opposition, it remains an open question whether this combination can deliver sustainable peace and stability to CAR's long-suffering civilian population. Certainly, the idea of CAR emerging as a 'domineering state' – à la its ally Rwanda – appears improbable, especially given the historic inability of the government to control either borders or territory beyond the national capital. Wagner's forces may have effectively stiffened the spine of CAR's own security forces while integrating themselves into Bangui's power structures, but beyond this Wagner's presence has done little to shore up the institutional foundations of the state.[15] Rather than short-term pain for long-term gain, then, it remains possible that absent a coherent clear/hold/develop strategy on the part of the government – which remains institutionally weak and chronically dependent on ongoing donor funding – the current military balance of power could represent just another phase in CAR's long-running, back-and-forth conflict between government and anti-government forces.

Despite such concerns – which are becoming more rather than less acute in CAR as a consequence of creeping state authoritarianism in recent years – there remains little space in contemporary UN peacekeeping/peacebuilding discourse for challenging the primacy of the state as the ultimate source of both legitimacy and security. State-centrism and respect for the primacy of state sovereignty lie at the very heart of the UN system, and the exit strategies of all contemporary peace operations are, implicitly or explicitly, premised on the progressive handover of responsibilities to an increasingly capable, responsible, rights-respecting state. The continued insistence on the 'improvability' – if not perfectibility – of even the most problematic states is especially evident with regard to SSR, which remains in principle the key element to enabling the state to fulfil its protection responsibilities. The latest iteration of the MINUSCA mandate, found in Security Council Resolution 2759 of November 2024, calls on the mission to provide CAR authorities with 'strategic and technical advice' on the implementation of a national SSR strategy and national defence plan, in close collaboration with a range of international partners. Indeed, despite SSR's poor track record – in CAR and elsewhere – and the particularities of CAR's political, security and geopolitical context, the basic SSR template for CAR has for years remained both unaltered and unchallenged. As Adedeji Ebo and colleagues (2020: 132) have observed, this model is grounded in a persistent belief that the so-called monopoly model of SSR – premised on consolidating in the hands of the state a monopoly on the legitimate use of force – can be achieved on the basis of

> … expanded work by the UN and international partners in further strengthening coordination, enhancing accountability and oversight, expanding security services beyond Bangui, developing a culture of inclusivity towards a security sector that serves all citizens – including through national dialogue – and bolstering the country's ability to respond to internal and external threats.

As a consequence of a shifting strategic balance of power on the ground and a rapidly changing geopolitical context, however, in CAR and elsewhere regimes in power have grown increasingly sceptical not only of conventional SSR formulas, but also of the simultaneously overbearing and underperforming narrative of liberal peacebuilding. As in neighbouring DRC, where the government has turned increasingly to regional allies willing to help impose peace, in CAR too the perceived failures of peacemaking appear to have convinced the government to abandon accommodationist strategies. While governments may continue to pay lip service to SSR and negotiated peace processes as a means of keeping donor funds flowing, in both CAR and DRC the first-order priority is not to reform the security services – certainly not in the sense of developing a culture of inclusivity and/or embedding security provision within the rule of law – but rather to unleash them. As Roland Paris has argued, this renewed enthusiasm for 'peace through victory' narratives is a consequence not only of the decidedly uneven track record of liberal peacebuilding throughout the post-cold war period, but of the growing assertiveness of both China and Russia in promoting 'strong state' solutions to the challenges of fragile and conflict-affected contexts. Especially in Africa, where the waning influence of France and the United States has created openings that their geopolitical rivals have been only too eager to exploit, what is emerging is an authoritarian model of peacebuilding, premised on "the idea of a domineering state that controls its society, suppresses dissent, and imposes its will" (Paris 2024: 18).

In thinking about the extension of state authority as a longer-term solution to the problems of civilian vulnerability, then, questioning linear narratives of progress also means grappling with difficult issues around what kind of state is being built. While it may in principle be possible to reconcile authoritarian and liberal models of state-building – with a hybrid state emerging that combines, however awkwardly, elements of both – in CAR all signs currently point to the authoritarian model as being in the ascendancy. There are also signs, moreover, that the Touadéra government – needing all the help that it can get wherever it can get it – can ill-afford to alienate either side of this emerging fault-line by casting its lot decisively with the other, so is playing the role of *équilibriste*.[16] This means engaging with MINUSCA on the elaboration of a national SSR strategy, working with the EUTM – which has shifted gears to focus on longer-term professional training for non-commissioned officers – in preparing the mid-level FACA leadership cadre of the future, and continuing to absorb operational guidance and training through its ongoing partnership with Wagner.[17] While it would be premature to predict the eventual outcome of such an ideologically heterodox state-building strategy, CAR's status as one of the world's most neglected conflicts – whose marginalisation has been furthered by the international preoccupation with wars in Gaza and Ukraine – bodes poorly for a concerted diplomatic push aimed at countering Russian influence and reversing the Touadéra government's authoritarian drift. For MINUSCA, therefore, on current trends the mission can only hope that efforts to extend state authority somehow manage to further marginalise armed groups to the point of irrelevance without at the same time fostering the emergence of a brutal yet brittle regime that pays little heed to the security and well-being of its own population.

Conclusion

A quarter-century has passed since the Security Council first formally included protection of civilians within the mandate of a UN peace support mission. Since then, almost every newly established mission has been similarly mandated, and PoC has emerged as one of the defining tasks of contemporary peacekeeping. There is little question that the work of UN peace operations – in unforgiving environments where there is increasingly no peace to keep – has saved and continues to save civilian lives. It is also the case, however, that the broader context in which peacekeepers operate has changed dramatically over the past 25 years, in ways that have increased PoC's degree of difficulty considerably. Downward pressure on peacekeeping budgets, increasingly difficult and intransigent national counterparts, world-shaking crises such as COVID and the Russian invasion of Ukraine, and the fragmentation of the liberal consensus around the means and ends of international intervention have combined to generate an existential crisis for the very institution of peacekeeping. Thus, while it may be premature to declare the end of the PoC era, it is worth asking whether 'peak' PoC may be behind us, and what this may entail for those who continue to be caught up in ongoing armed conflict.

Like its sister missions elsewhere in Sub-Saharan Africa, MINUSCA is struggling to come to terms with these new realities, all the while continuing to use the conventional peacekeeping tools at its disposal to do what it can to protect civilians and improve the odds of sustainable peace emerging in CAR. This chapter has diverged somewhat from the previous chapters' emphasis on mission-specific protection practices in order to focus on these wider contextual shifts, in large part because CAR has emerged in recent years as a key site of contestation between a beleaguered liberal peacebuilding model and an alternative vision that aims to build peace on an authoritarian foundation. Whether the latter represents a fully formed 'alternative paradigm of peacemaking' (Lewis 2022: 653) and/or a cynical manifestation of what Anne Applebaum (2024) has labelled *Autocracy Inc.*, the stakes are high not only for the future of international intervention in conflict-affected contexts but also for the citizens of CAR who are living through this contestation in real time.

For MINUSCA, there are sound reasons to believe that as the geopolitical ground has shifted beneath it, the mission has lost leverage over the behaviour of armed groups, has seen its influence with its governmental partners decline, and has watched as the taken-for-granted assumptions it has long championed about CAR's path to peace and stability have been increasingly sidelined. In the absence of a significant recalibration of its mandate and a re-consideration of the resources at its disposal – improbable in the current context as CAR, which has never enjoyed significant international attention or political will, slips ever further from the global spotlight – the paradox noted throughout this chapter seems likely to persist. Lives will continue to be saved by MINUSCA interventions, while the prospects for sustained improvements in human security for its long-suffering citizens recede ever further over the horizon.

Notes

1. A statue honouring deceased Wagner Group founder Yevgeny Prigozhin was also recently unveiled in front of Bangui's Russian House.
2. Author interview, Bangui, May 2022.
3. For further details on the peace agreement, see ICG (2019).
4. Author Interview, Bangui, June 2022.
5. Author interview, Bangui, November 2024.
6. Author interview, Bangui, May 2022.
7. Author interviews, Bangui, May-June 2022.
8. Author Interviews, Bangui, May–June 2022.
9. Author interview, Bangui, May 2022.
10. Author interview, Bangui, December 2024.
11. Author interview, Bouar, May 2022.
12. Author interview, Bouar, May 2022.
13. Anecdotally, at least, my own experience interviewing MINUSCA personnel in CAR was that officials much preferred to discuss day-to-day protection activities and responsibilities, and had a tendency to shrug their shoulders when asked about broader political dynamics, especially those at the state level, that affected civilian vulnerability.

14 Author interview, Bangui, November 2024.
15 The recent fall of Syria's Bashar al-Assad, whose regime was left to its fate by its distracted Russian allies after having been rescued by Russian firepower during the height of the Syrian civil war, is at least suggestive in this regard.
16 Author interview, Bangui, November 2024.
17 Author interview, Bangui, December 2024.

Works Cited

Adegoke, Y. (2023) 'Why Wagner is winning hearts in the Central African Republic', BBC World News (online), 10 December; Available at: https://www.bbc.com/news/world-africa-67625139

Applebaum, A. (2024) *Autocracy Inc.: The Dictators Who Want to Run the World* (Oxford: Signal Books).

Barron's (2024) 'C. African Republic Mulls Kremlin-like 'Foreign Agent' Bill', 25 October; Available at: https://www.barrons.com/news/c-african-republic-mulls-kremlin-like-foreign-agent-bill-bfc56e81

Bax, P. (2021) 'Russia's influence in the Central African Republic', International Crisis Group (ICG) Commentary, 3 December; Available at: https://www.crisisgroup.org/africa/central-africa/central-african-republic/russias-influence-central-african-republic

Bensimon, C. (2023) 'How Wagner strengthened its control in the Central African Republic, despite the war in Ukraine', *Le Monde* (English version), 29 June.

Burgis, T. (2015) *The Looting Machine: Warlords, Oligarchs, Corporations, Smugglers and the Theft of Africa's Wealth* (New York: PublicAffairs).

de Coning, C. (2020) 'The impact of COVID-19 on peace operations', International Peace Institute Global Observatory, 2 April; Available at: https://theglobalobservatory.org/2020/04/impact-covid-19-peace-operations/

Debout, B. (2024) 'In the Central African Republic, "They say their peacekeepers came to protect us, but they rape us"', *Le Monde* (English version), 16 October.

Di Razza, N. (2016) 'France's CAR departure creates uphill battle for UN', International Peace Institute (IPI) Global Observatory, 14 November; Available at: https://theglobalobservatory.org/2016/11/sangris-central-african-republic-france-peacekeeping/

Ebo, A. et al. (2020) 'UN support to SSR in peacekeeping contexts: A case study of the Central African Republic', in A. Ebo and H. Hanggi (eds.), *The United Nations and Security Sector Reform: Policy and Practice* (Munster: Lit Verlag), 113–135.

Freedom House (2024) 'Central African Republic'; Available online at: https://freedomhouse.org/country/central-african-republic/freedom-world/2024

Grynszpan, E. et al. (2023) 'Wagner Group's influence spreads across Africa even as war rages in Ukraine', *Le Monde* (English version), 1 February.

Howard, L. et al. (2020) *Assessing the Effectiveness of the United Nations Multidimensional Integrated Stabilization Mission in the Central African Republic/MINUSCA*. Effectiveness of Peace Operations Network (EPON) Report. Oslo: Norwegian Institute of International Affairs.

Human Rights Watch (2022) 'Central African Republic: Abuses by Russia-Linked Forces,' 3 May; Available at: https://www.hrw.org/news/2022/05/03/central-african-republic-abuses-russia-linked-forces

Ingasso, V. et al. (2023) 'Wagner is only one piece in Central African Republic's Messy Puzzle', *World Politics Review* (online), 31 January; Available at: https://www.worldpoliticsreview.com/central-african-republic-civil-war-politics-russia-touadera/

International Crisis Group (ICG) (2019) 'Making the Central African Republic's latest peace agreement stick', ICG Africa Report No. 277, 18 June; Available at: https://www.crisisgroup.org/africa/central-africa/central-african-republic/277-making-central-african-republics-latest-peace-agreement-stick

International Crisis Group (ICG) (2024) 'Bringing lasting peace to the Central African Republic', ICG Africa Commentary, 15 October; Available at: https://www.crisisgroup.org/africa/central-africa/central-african-republic/bringing-lasting-peace-central-african-republic

Labuda, P. (2020) 'With or against the State? Reconciling the protection of civilians and host-State Support in UN peacekeeping', International Peace Institute Report, May; Available at: https://www.ipinst.org/2020/05/reconciling-poc-and-host-state-support-in-un-peacekeeping

Le Cam, M. (2024) 'Putin builds on Progozhin's foundations in Africa', *Le Monde* (English version), 23 August.

Lewis, D. (2022) 'Contesting liberal peace: Russia's emerging model of conflict management', *International Affairs* 98(2): 653–673.

Lombard, L. (2016) *State of Rebellion: Violence and Intervention in the Central African Republic* (London: Zed Books and International African Institute).

Mailman School of Public Health (2023) 'Extreme mortality rate found in Central African Republic', Columbia University, 19 April; Available at: https://www.publichealth.columbia.edu/news/extreme-mortality-rate-found-central-african-republic

Obaji Jr., P. (2024) '"They turn out farms into rape centres": Russian mercenaries accused of abuse in Central African Republic', *The Guardian* (online), 23 July; Available at: https://www.theguardian.com/global-development/article/2024/jul/23/central-african-republic-women-girls-rape-sexual-violence-conflict-food-security-wagner-russian-mercenaries-un

Paris, R. (2024) 'The future of UN peace operations: Pragmatism, pluralism or statism?', *International Affairs* (online first): 1–20.

Salih, Z.M. and J. Burke (2023) 'Wagner mercenaries sustain losses in fight for Central African Republic gold', *The Guardian* (online), 2 February;Available at: https://www.theguardian.com/world/2023/feb/02/wagner-mercenaries-sustain-losses-in-fight-for-central-african-republic-gold

Schnieder, M. (2013) 'Responding to the crisis in the Central African Republic', Testimony to the US Senate Foreign relations committee, 17 December; Available at: https://www.crisisgroup.org/africa/central-africa/central-african-republic/responding-crisis-central-african-republic

Sorensen, G. (1992) 'Utopianism in peace research: The Gandhian heritage', *Journal of Peace Research* 29(2): 135–144.

The Sentry (2023) 'Architects of terror: The Wagner group's blueprint for state capture in the Central African Republic', June; Available at: https://thesentry.org/reports/architects-of-terror/

UN News (2021) 'UN sends Gabon peacekeepers home from Central African Republic, following abuse allegations', Press Release, 15 September; Available at: https://news.un.org/en/story/2021/09/1100032

United Nations (2023) 'A New Agenda for Peace', Our Common Agenda Policy Brief 9; July; Available at: https://dppa.un.org/en/a-new-agenda-for-peace

United Nations (2024) 'Independent strategic review of the United Nations Multidimensional Integrated Stabilization Mission in the Central Africa Republic, March-June 2024', S/2024/615; Available at: https://documents.un.org/doc/undoc/gen/n24/241/58/pdf/n2424158.pdf

United Nations High Commissioner for Refugees (UNHCR) (2024) 'Central African Republic Situation: 2025 situation overview', Undated; Available at: https://reporting.unhcr.org/operational/situations/central-african-republic-situation

Whalan, J. (2017) 'Dealing with disgrace: Addressing sexual exploitation and abuse in UN peacekeeping', New York: International Peace Institute; Available at: https://www.ipinst.org/wp-content/uploads/2017/08/IPI-Rpt-Dealing-with-Disgrace2.pdf

Zahar, M.-J. and D. Mechoulan (2017) 'Peace by Pieces? Local Mediation and Sustainable Peace in the Central African Republic', International Peace Institute Report, November; Available at: https://www.ipinst.org/wp-content/uploads/2017/11/1701_Peace-by-Pieces.pdf

7 Conclusion

PoC's Uneven Past and Uncertain Future

Peacekeepers protect civilians. This conclusion, as Lise Howard (2022) has noted, has been drawn independently by a diverse range of quantitative studies in recent years. Moreover, she suggests, the correlation between peacekeeper presence and civilian protection "is one of the most robust findings in the field of international relations." As noted in the introduction to this study, however, this finding is not as counter-intuitive as it may initially appear. Despite peacekeeping's bad press – in addition to the ongoing struggles of peace operations to contain violent conflict, peacekeepers make the news far more often for their own sins of omission (failing to prevent massacres) or commission (sexual exploitation and abuse) than for pre-empting the sins of others – it still should not be entirely surprising that large, multidimensional missions with explicit PoC mandates should be able to offer some protection to at least some vulnerable civilians at least some of the time. At a bare minimum, the presence of peacekeepers in conflict-affected contexts acts as sand in the gears of killing machines. One need only reflect on the brutal reality of contemporary humanitarian crises where peacekeepers are absent – Haiti, Gaza, Myanmar, Sudan – to appreciate the role peacekeepers play in moderating the most predatory and abusive inclinations of fighting forces. There is therefore both merit to, and data to support, the argument that the mere presence of international actors – and peace operations by their very nature are able to be more present in conflict zones than other actors – changes the calculus of conflict parties and shifts the border between acceptable and unacceptable behaviour in protective ways, and in a very literal sense saves lives (Mahoney 2006: 20). To the extent that missions are able to effectively leverage the multidimensional range of assets at their disposal for protective purposes – shifting from passive presence to active engagement – their actions can make the difference between life and death for thousands.

Peacekeepers also, of course, fail to protect civilians. From the 'too little, too late' responses to attacks on South Sudan's PoC sites, to the paralysis of peacekeepers in the face of abuses committed by Wagner mercenaries in the Central African Republic (CAR), to MONUSCO's inability to confront the scourge of conflict-related sexual violence in the eastern DRC, broader political and strategic realities and the make-up and disposition of peace operations – especially their uniformed elements – pose real limits on the protection capacities of peacekeepers. The inability or unwillingness to confront attacks and/or abuses against civilian

DOI: 10.4324/9781003291114-7

populations by host government forces or their allies, in particular, constitutes an important gap in the contemporary protection framework. Missions have also demonstrated consistent inconsistency with regard to protection responses; while some contingents have embraced the ethos of 'all necessary means,' the persistence among others of 'Chapter VI syndrome' (dos Santos Cruz et al. 2017) has fostered uncertainty and inertia at critical moments of crisis, with fatal consequences for imperilled civilians. Moreover, while missions in all three of the country contexts that have been the focus of this volume have demonstrated some ability to address the downstream consequences of ongoing violent conflict on civilian populations, developing important innovations along the way, it is also the case that in none of the three cases have peace operations managed to transform underlying drivers of violence or keep fragile peace processes on track. As noted in Chapter 5, too often this has placed peacekeepers in the role of under-resourced and overwhelmed fire-fighters, capable of making a difference here and there, but slowly being exhausted by the depth and breadth of violence in both its direct and structural manifestations. The actions of peacekeepers may save lives on a regular basis – sometimes through acts of genuine heroism and courage – but in contexts of unrelenting suffering and insecurity, one might forgive the absence of gratitude on the part of those Congolese, for example, who have come to view UN peacekeepers in eastern DRC as part of the problem rather than as part of the solution.

Reconciling these contradictory conclusions into an overall balance sheet of peacekeeper performance with regard to PoC implementation over the 25 years that protection mandates have been crucial components of peace operations is no easy task. While peacekeepers undoubtedly make a difference in the contexts where they are deployed, 'better than nothing' is neither an inspiring defence of the record of contemporary peacekeeping, nor a compelling argument for reversing declining peacekeeping budgets. Yet if the better question, as I've suggested in the introductory chapter, is whether peace operations reduce civilian insecurity as much as is realistically possible given the mandate and asset mix available to them, there remain substantial obstacles to providing a clear answer, let alone one that can be quantified with any degree of confidence. In the first place, studying how peacekeepers protect civilians remains an inherently difficult exercise. By definition, the very sites where protection practices unfold are both dangerous and difficult to access, and developing a comprehensive picture of state-level protection dynamics in states as diverse as the DRC or South Sudan – where the context can vary enormously from one province, or even one municipality, to the next – requires significant investments in time and resources. This is especially true in an era of mis/disinformation, where both official and informal sources of data are not only scarce but must be treated with appropriate levels of scepticism. Shrinking budgets, increased sensitivity to criticism and the corrosive effects of mis/disinformation have also generated a growing defensiveness within individual peace operations in recent years, along with a growing number of gatekeeping mechanisms that increasingly control – and limit – access to peacekeeping personnel, field offices and UN bases. At the same time, it remains the case that understanding what works in protection terms – from 'neutralising' spoiler groups to supporting state-level security sector reform – remains a deeply fraught exercise. As noted in Chapter 3, for example, while the projection of force may save lives in the immediate term by deterring an armed group from attacking a specific community, 'protection' in such a context is never a one-off event. Lives saved today may be lost tomorrow if an attack is merely deferred until peacekeepers move on to the next hotspot, just as lives saved in one locality may be lost in another if the presence of peacekeepers simply displaces violence elsewhere. At a more macro level, the long-term effects of UN peace operations forcefully inserting themselves into an armed conflict – whether fighting alongside government forces or deploying their stopping power against rebel groups – on the UN's more traditional 'good offices' and conflict mediation roles remain unclear (Karlsrud 2015). The challenges are even more profound with regard to unarmed, non-coercive forms of protection, where long causal chains – often extending over the course of years – and myriad intervening variables cloud the relationship between inputs and outcomes. It is exceedingly difficult, for example, to trace cause-and-effect relationships between specific human rights training for host-country security personnel and reductions in human rights violations by soldiers or police officers months or even years down the road.

Such considerations notwithstanding, it is still possible to draw broad conclusions from the UN's experiences with the implementation of PoC mandates. The most general, and perhaps the most obvious, is that over the past several decades UN peacekeeping has amassed an enormous amount of experience – much of it earned through painful trial-and-error – as one of the international community's few institutional vehicles through which human agency can be mobilised for protection purposes. While it may not always be immediately visible on the ground given the messy realities of contemporary conflict zones, a protection ethos is now woven into the very fabric of peacekeeping, while innovation and experimentation have generated both effective practices and a clearer understanding of the limitations of PoC as a field of activity (UN DPO 2024: 1). This legacy is worth bearing in mind in an era when the future of peacekeeping is being actively debated, and when experimentation with different forms of non-UN intervention is actively underway. While the African Union, for example, is increasingly seen as the future of peacekeeping on the African continent, and while it has generated PoC guidelines – relying heavily on UN precedents – for its own operations, AU missions still face a steep learning curve, and considerable capacity deficits, with regard to navigating the practical challenges of operationalising PoC mandates in the field. The experience of the AMISOM mission in Somalia – where civilian protection strategies rarely extended beyond military efforts to degrade the threat posed by al-Shabaab, while avoiding civilian harm in the process – is especially telling (Issa and Donais 2023). Haiti is also emerging as a cautionary tale in this regard, as the Kenyan-led Multinational Security Support (MSS) mission has foundered, under-supported and outgunned, since its initial deployment in June 2024, to the extent that Haiti's transitional authorities have belatedly requested that it be replaced by a full-fledged UN peace operation. While the future may indeed feature a wide range of intervention modalities, configurations and collaborations, at present the UN continues to hold unparalleled structural advantages – and a comparative wealth of institutional memory – with regard to putting protection mandates into actual practice in some of the world's most insecure environments.

In addition to hard-earned experience in challenging protection contexts, it also remains the case that the mix of hard- and soft-power assets available to multidimensional peace operations renders them uniquely configured as agents of protection. Despite downward budgetary pressures in recent years and a persistent gap between the responsibilities entrusted to missions and the resources allocated to them, peace operations remain – by virtue of the diplomatic, military, policing and civilian expertise at their disposal – key centres of gravity in conflict contexts, and key stabilising influences. While this study has distinguished, for heuristic purposes, coercive from non-coercive protection strategies, in practice the most effective forms of protection involve the creative integration of different elements of the peace operations toolkit. As noted in Chapter 5, for example, the development of a functional early warning and rapid response mechanism in the DRC was dependent not only on effective community engagement, and the patient work of facilitating the development of dozens of community alert networks, but also on the ability and willingness of MONUSCO's military contingents to respond to community-generated alerts in a timely and effective manner.

At the same time, as elaborated in Chapter 3, it is also indisputably the case that despite ongoing controversy – and inconsistency – around more robust, force-first forms of protection, the coercive dimension of UN peace operations offers intangible advantages that go well beyond their ability to intervene in acute crises where civilian lives are actively threatened, and that are impossible to capture in quantitative terms. While often taken for granted, the military elements of peace operations provide a protective umbrella within which not only other elements of the mission can function but which also enable – as demonstrated by the myriad non-governmental organisations that operated within South Sudan's PoC sites – a broader humanitarian presence in especially volatile areas where civilians are most in need of outside assistance. Among armed groups, a robust peacekeeping presence is also a crucial source of credibility; given the importance for protection purposes of engaging with a proliferating array of such groups, the military dimension of peace operations remains a crucial asset for opening and maintaining channels of communication.[1] A final intangible surrounds the deterrent effect of armed peacekeepers. Deterrence in protection contexts remains imperfectly understood, and is dependent at least as much on the motivation and rationale of the attackers as on the capacity of the defenders. In some circumstances the mere fact of international presence – whether in the form of armed peacekeepers or unarmed civilians – is sufficient to deter attacks on civilian targets, while in others deterrence requires not only a strong show of armed force but a demonstrated willingness to use it. Whatever else it might offer, an armed peacekeeping presence gives decision-makers the flexibility of tailoring a deterrence response to the specificities of a particular situation, and escalating if and as necessary, even if in practice this calibration/adjustment exercise has proven to be far from frictionless. While much of the foregoing may also seem self-evident, especially to those with experience in conflict-affected contexts, it is nevertheless worth reiterating the value-added of the military side of peace operations in light of the growing tendency towards light-footprint Special Political Missions (SPMs) as the UN's intervention tool of choice, and in the context of a creeping suspicion that the era of large, multidimensional peace operations may in fact be coming to an end (Boutellis and Novosseloff 2017: 3).

It is also clear, however, that Berdal's (2018) 'inescapable limits' continue to apply to UN peace operations with regard to their capacity to offer meaningful levels of protection to civilians trapped by conflict, and that some of these limits have become more, rather than less, intractable over time. Three decades on from the twin catastrophes of Rwanda and Srebrenica, the reverberations of which ultimately propelled UN peacekeeping into the PoC era, the ability of UN missions to physically protect civilians at imminent risk of bodily harm remains uneven at best. Ambivalence persists around the use of force by UN peacekeepers for protective purposes, with troop-contributing countries continuing to hold widely disparate views on this critical question. While some contingents have come under heavy criticism for their failure to respond to force with force in circumstances where civilians are directly threatened, in fairness use of force debates continue to sow division across the entire UN system, and at both tactical and strategic levels there are good reasons why peacekeepers and their commanders may be reluctant to engage militarily with conflict parties. These include not only the immediate considerations around inflicting and absorbing casualties – which in peacekeeping contexts should never be taken lightly – but also concerns around the UN becoming a party to the conflict and around compromising the UN's role as a potential neutral third party in future peace negotiations. Between the HIPPO Report's emphasis on the 'primacy of politics' and the Cruz Report's contention that 'the language of force' is the only effective means of communicating with hostile forces, there continues to be a wide and unbridged gulf on the appropriate role of force in peacekeeping contexts, even after 25 years of PoC practice. While the identity of peacekeepers matters in terms of coercive responses to proximate threats, so too does the identity of the perpetrators. As Patryk Labuda (2020) has demonstrated, peace operations cannot escape the difficult contradictions involved in confronting abuses perpetrated by host government security forces, and this tension has complicated protection efforts in all three case studies considered here; if peacekeepers still rarely use force for protection purposes, they almost never use force where those threatening civilians are in the employ of the host government. The introduction in recent years of 'other security personnel' – most notably Wagner mercenaries in CAR – has further complicated the use of force calculus on the part of peacekeepers. So too has the re-emergence of the Rwandan-backed M23 in eastern DRC, which has captured significant territory – killing thousands and displacing more than a million in the process – largely undeterred and unchallenged by a diminished MONUSCO presence (Townsend 2024). Ultimately, those on the receiving end of robust protection responses on the part of UN peacekeepers are far more likely to be smaller, less well-connected armed groups; notwithstanding the language of UN policy guidance, therefore, the source of the threat continues to matter a great deal in terms of the strategic calculations underpinning the response.

If UN peace operations continue to struggle with so-called Tier II responsibilities – and in particular those situations in which civilians find themselves under direct attack by fighting forces – they have also struggled with the longer-term structural protection tasks associated with Tier III of DPO's protection framework. Establishing a 'protective environment' over the longer term requires a progressive, if not always linear, transition between peacekeeping and peacebuilding, on the understanding that "the only sustainable form of protection and stability is a peace process that ends the violence" (de Coning 2023: 157). Invariably, it also means partnerships with host states, especially since the endgame of any PoC mandate involves a transition of responsibilities to host state security forces that are willing and able to offer meaningful levels of protection to their own citizens. Failures to progress along this peacekeeping-peacebuilding continuum have meant, inevitably, that protection demands inevitably outstrip protection resources over the long, and violent, tenures of contemporary peace operations. While the failures of peacebuilding in Africa and elsewhere cannot be laid solely at the UN's feet – the nature of conflict has changed in recent decades, while the standard model of liberal peacebuilding that has been applied, albeit unevenly, to conflict contexts since the end of the cold war has not kept up – peace operations may in fact be contributing to a stabilisation dilemma that undermines longer-term conflict resolution efforts. As Cedric de Coning (2023: 157–158) has argued, this stabilisation dilemma generates a number of perverse effects, from enabling authoritarianism by lending legitimacy, material resources and military support to incumbent elites with little interest in democracy or the rule of law, to perpetuating an unpeaceful status quo in ways that disincentivise conflict parties from making the difficult and risky compromises that peace negotiations require while enabling them to enmesh, and enrich, themselves ever further in domestic conflict economies.

While such dynamics have played out in unique ways across South Sudan, CAR and DRC, the common denominator across all three is that none has progressed along a trajectory that could be described, even at a stretch, as either liberal or democratic. While some approximation of 'good governance' – with those in power possessing at least some popular legitimacy and some capacity to deliver a core set of public goods, including security – might still be considered a basic requirement for sustainable peace, it is far from clear in any of these cases that years of external intervention have managed to foster even 'improved governance.' In the words of Adrian Johnson (2023: 167), "liberal assumptions about building impartial state institutions that deliver services to the citizenry are often at odds with the aggrandising interests and motivations of local elites." All three states, and their citizens, remain trapped in conditions of political unsettlement, characterised by persistent if shifting conflict and an inability to craft negotiated agreements of sufficient resilience to mark a definitive break between war and peace (Bell and Pospisil 2017: 581). At the risk of understatement, such conditions are hardly conducive to the kinds of structural reforms associated with state-building or to the emergence of strong domestic political forces advocating tolerance, reconciliation and democratic peacebuilding. States, and those in control of them, remain both difficult partners and active parties to the conflict, more interested in short-term strategic advantage (and regime survival) than in abstract ideals such as human rights, democratic accountability or the rule of law. In the absence of political will on the part of ruling elites to engage seriously with the state reform dimensions of peacebuilding, exercises such as SSR take on an increasingly formulaic and ceremonial character, with little hope or expectation of meaningful change. Increasingly, as in both DRC and CAR, it is the host state itself which has begun to tire of the unsettlement status quo, and has started to explore post-liberal alternatives – emphasising military victory rather than negotiated settlement – as a means of escaping the unsettlement trap. In the case of the DRC, where the latest M23 initiative has visited fresh horrors on the civilian population of the Kivus, and where the MONUSCO mandate was renewed for an additional year in late 2024 in light of a rapidly deteriorating security situation, the evidence thus far suggests that this shift in strategy has done little to convince long-suffering civilians that their dire security situation will improve anytime soon (Townsend 2024).

Throughout this study, the emphasis has been placed firmly on the practices of protection, or on what peacekeepers actually do in mission contexts in the name of protecting civilians, and what has come to represent 'competent practice' *vis-à-vis* PoC over the course of the past quarter century. Mandates also matter, of course, as do budgeting exercises, detailed headquarters-generated guidance and the dynamics of force-generation as they play out between the UN Secretariat and troop- and police-contributing countries. However, while these and other factors constitute the hand that missions are dealt with regard to particular PoC mandates in specific country contexts, the decisions made and actions initiated by missions and the field-based personnel who comprise them determine how that hand is played. In doing so, they have also over time defined the parameters of the possible in PoC terms, struck balances (however tenuous) in terms of the mix of coercive and non-coercive instruments (and combinations thereof) that comprise PoC, and navigated tensions between PoC and other mandated tasks. The most dramatic of these decisions have involved the use of (or failure to use) force in the context of imminent or unfolding atrocities against civilians, and peacekeeper performance in moments of acute crisis has done much to shape broader narratives and perceptions of the UN as a protection actor. Others, such as the decision to open the gates of UN bases to fleeing civilians at the beginning of South Sudan's civil war, shaped in crucial ways the manner in which protection was both understood and practiced for years to follow. Still others, including the establishment of community liaison assistants or the establishment of early warning systems, represent important innovations emerging from the field in response to the practical challenges of providing meaningful levels of protection in active war zones. In short, given the inherent ambiguities of PoC mandates and the invariable gaps between protection needs and protection resources, missions have been left to work through the practicalities of delivering on PoC mandates while also striving to establish defensible boundaries to the PoC enterprise, given that no mission can protect all vulnerable civilians all the time.

While field-level developments have been crucial to the evolution of PoC practice within contemporary peace operations, contextual factors – domestic and, increasingly, geopolitical – continue to impose real and unavoidable constraints on the exercise of peacekeeper agency in protection contexts. Missions develop PoC practices, in other words, but not in conditions of their own choosing. Indeed, just as PoC mandates have grown in importance within UN peace operations, the ability of these same operations to shape the conflict contexts in which they operate appears to be diminishing. Increasingly, peace operations represent one actor among many in conflict contexts, and their influence has declined in recent years both as a function of the changing nature of conflict and as a consequence of the declining moral authority of the liberal peacebuilding project that peacekeepers represent. As the CAR case demonstrates, tectonic geopolitical shifts are currently underway that will dramatically shape the possibilities of peacekeeping well into the future. In all likelihood, therefore, the evolution of PoC will be determined less by lessons-learned exercises leading to incremental and evidence-based improvements to field-level practices, and more by broader trends – now underway – pertaining to the very shape of global security governance and the role of UN peace operations therein.

PoC's Uncertain Future

If it is true that peacekeeping is always 'a product of its time' (Dunton et al. 2023: 215), then the current era of UN peace operations is likely to be remembered as one of turbulence, uncertainty and discontinuity. While UN member states adopted the Sustainable Development Goals in 2015 as a "shared blueprint for peace and prosperity" – grounded in commitments to equality, inclusion, partnerships, peace and justice, and a belief in the will and capacity of states to prioritise the well-being and dignity of their own citizens (Donais 2023: 233) – a short decade later the SDGs now read as a defiant manifesto of a fading liberal international order. From the rise of the BRICS group of developing countries[2] to the ongoing global crisis of democracy and civic space to the erosion of, and contestation around, the liberal norms and principles that have underpinned global security governance over the past several decades, the post-cold war international order is undergoing a period of rapid, possibly epochal change. As Ivan Krastev (2025) has noted, the pace of change at such historical moments can be dizzying: "what only yesterday was considered unthinkable seems self-evident today." While others have suggested that the current multilateral system is likely to persist, even if diminished and weakened (Lehne 2023), in the here and now growing dissensus around 'shared blueprints' carries serious consequences for collective action, whether around climate change, global trade or international conflict management. While the UN itself has been a casualty of these shifting tides – buffeted by budget cuts and sidelined in the world's most contentious conflict zones – it is also the case, as Caroline Dunton and colleagues (2023: 215) have noted, that "shifting power dynamics and the advent of a multipolar world order have profound financial, political, ideological, and operational implications for UN peacekeeping."

While few serious observers are predicting the end of peacekeeping as a key instrument in the international security system – or the end of PoC mandates as key features of peace operations – from the perspective of early 2025 some trends with regard to the future of peacekeeping are slowly coming into focus. First, in an era in which armed conflicts are on the rise, it is telling that it has now been more than a decade since the UN launched its last large-scale mission (MINUSCA in 2014). While the absence of new missions is partly a function of escalating tensions within the UN Security Council, especially among the permanent five members, it is also in part a function of a crisis of confidence in the ability of peace operations to successfully shepherd conflict-affected societies towards sustainable peace, with the big three African missions serving as key exhibits for those reluctant to drag the UN into additional peacekeeping quagmires. Thus, pressures to contract and retrench remain strong – since 2015, the UN peacekeeping budget has been reduced by a quarter, while civilian staff have been cut by a third (Karlsrud 2023: 261) – while the UN is making increased use of SPMs and UN country teams as alternative means of engaging with conflict-affected states. Declining ambitions and expectations for UN peace operations are also reflected in the scholarly literature on peacekeeping, which has of late emphasised the merits of 'pragmatism.' Acknowledging the hubris embedded in the belief that peace operations can be instrumental in transforming conflict-affected states into peaceful liberal democracies, the pragmatic turn eschews specific end-goals for peace operations in favour of continuous experimentation and a willingness to pursue peace – at whatever level – guided by local context rather than by liberal norms. In other words, as Cedric de Coning (2020: 844) has argued, pragmatism – or what he terms 'adaptive peace' – means that peacekeepers (as well as other international actors in conflict-affected spaces) need to redefine themselves as facilitators rather than social engineers and accept that "it is not possible to resolve a conflict or to build peace on behalf of a society from the outside." All these trends portend a future in which UN peace operations are fewer in number, less ambitious in scope, and mostly shorn of their multidimensionality. While PoC is still likely to feature prominently in such missions, it seems improbable that better protection outcomes can be delivered with less presence, while the ability of missions to mix and match different components of a multidimensional toolkit to fit the specific protection context is also likely to be much reduced. At the same time, it remains to be seen how much moral and political weight the PoC agenda will continue to carry if – as the pragmatic turn seems to suggest – it is practically disengaged from the wider normative project of human rights and rule of law promotion that has been part-and-parcel of liberal peacebuilding since the end of the cold war. One possible outcome of the pragmatic turn in peacekeeping, as Dunton et al. (2023: 228) have suggested, is a shift in emphasis from PoC as something that peacekeepers actually 'do' to PoC 'reimagined' in ways that place more normative pressure on host states to uphold their own protection responsibilities.

A second key trend with potentially profound implications for PoC mandates is that the UN's shrinking peacekeeping footprint may be gradually being replaced by an entirely new architecture constructed around the concept of 'partnership peacekeeping.' Africa in general – and Somalia in particular – has emerged as a key testing ground for the viability of the broader concept, with the UN having provided of late a form of 'back office' support for frontline peace operations led by the African Union. A major step forward on this front came in 2023, when the UN Security Council adopted Resolution 2719, which opened the door to allowing AU-led (but

Security Council-authorised) peace operations to access assessed UN peacekeeping contributions as a means of sustainable financing. Such developments are consistent not only with longstanding calls for the development of 'African solutions to African problems,' but also with the Secretary General's calls – in his 'New Agenda for Peace' (UN 2023: 26) – for greater UN support for a 'new generation' of enforcement missions led by African partners. While it remains to be seen what the implications of a fully articulated partnership peacekeeping model will be for the future of PoC mandates, it is clear – as noted above – that the AU's own doctrine and practice with regard to the protection of civilians remains nascent, particularly in light of the UN's own comparatively well-institutionalised set of policies and practices. Of greater concern for PoC, perhaps, is the emerging convergence of views among key African states, China and (to a lesser extent) Russia around the means and ends of future peace operations. As Katharina Coleman and Brian Job (2021) have observed, Africa and China in particular appear to be coalescing around a vision of peacekeeping that downplays its liberal dimensions – especially the centrality of human rights promotion – while emphasising stabilisation and the primacy of host-state sovereignty. While not necessarily inconsistent with commitments to protecting civilians – it was Rwanda, after all, that spearheaded the so-called Kigali Principles, which exhorted troop-contributing countries to commit to robust PoC in peacekeeping contexts – the state-centrism embedded within this vision does suggest that PoC will emerge as a byproduct of successful stabilisation policies, rather than be a core priority in its own right. As Roland Paris (2024: 18) has suggested, a more critical take on these same trends suggests the emergence of a distinct model of authoritarian peacebuilding, with robust stabilisation efforts exacting a heavy toll on civilians while also generating a repressive state that stifles dissent and individual liberties in the name of stability. While far from the model of partnership peacekeeping envisioned by UN and AU bureaucrats, the evolving partnership between Wagner mercenaries and the CAR government appears to be edging ever closer towards this authoritarian paradigm, which in its more extreme manifestations would appear to drain the PoC concept of any meaningful content.

As these wider trends play out on the international stage, therefore, it appears that the PoC agenda may itself be destined to undergo its own period of political unsettlement, characterised by persistent contestation around PoC's core premises and an uphill struggle to further institutionalise the protection practices that have evolved over the past 25 years. While the normative commitment to PoC appears to be well-entrenched across the relevant parts of the UN system, the more fundamental reconsideration of both the means and ends of peacekeeping that is currently underway may further undermine the fragile consensus around 'people-centred' peacekeeping that PoC represents. While the UN's diminishing peacekeeping footprint and the emergence of the partnership peacekeeping paradigm pose new questions about the institutional configurations that will take on PoC mandates in the future, the erosion of the liberal foundations of contemporary peacekeeping is also reigniting old questions about the relative importance of state security vs. human security in conflict-affected contexts. While civilian suffering in war zones is likely to remain a constant of global politics in the years and decades to come, so too – it seems – is ongoing contestation and discord around international responsibilities for alleviating such suffering, and around the most effective mechanisms and instruments for doing so.

Notes

1 Author interview, New York, March 2024.
2 While the original BRICS members were Brazil, Russia, India, China and South Africa, in 2024 the forum was expanded to include Egypt, Ethiopia, Iran and the United Arab Emirates.

Works Cited

Bell, C. and J. Pospisil (2017) 'Navigating inclusion in transitions from conflict: The formalised political *un*settlement', *Journal of International Development* 29: 576–593.

Berdal, M. (2018) 'The State of UN peacekeeping: Lessons from Congo', *The Journal of Strategic Studies* 41(5): 721–750.

Boutellis, A. and A. Novosseloff (2017) 'Road to a better UN? Peace operations and the reform agenda', International Peace Institute report, November; Available at: https://www.ipinst.org/wp-content/uploads/2017/11/1711_Road-to-a-Better-UN2.pdf

Coleman, K. and B. Job (2021) 'How Africa and China may shape UN peacekeeping beyond the liberal international order', *International Affairs* 95(5): 1451–1468.

de Coning, C. (2020) 'Adaptive peace operations: Navigating the complexity of influencing societal change without causing harm', *International Peacekeeping* 27(5): 836–858.

de Coning, C. (2023) 'How not to do UN peacekeeping: Avoid the stabilization dilemma with principled and adaptive mandating and leadership', *Global Governance* 29: 152–167.

Donais, T. (2023) 'Conclusion: Goal 16 and the uncertain future of peace', in T. Donais, A. Edgar and K. Van Houten (eds.), *Sustainable Development Goal 16 and the Global Governance of Violence: Critical Reflections on the Uncertain Future of Peace* (London/New York: Routledge), 233–244.

dos Santos Cruz, C.A. et al. (2017) 'Improving security of United Nations peacekeepers: We need to change the way we are doing business', 19 December; Available at: https://peacekeeping.un.org/sites/default/files/improving_security_of_united_nations_peacekeepers_report.pdf

Dunton, C. et al. (2023) 'Pragmatic peacekeeping in a multipolar era: Liberal norms, practices, and the future of UN peace operations', *Journal of Intervention and Statebuilding* 17(3): 215–234.

Howard, L. (2022) 'UN peacekeeping in Africa is working better than you might think', *The Conversation*, 27 May; Available at: https://theconversation.com/un-peacekeeping-in-africa-is-working-better-than-you-might-think-183748

Issa, A. and T. Donais (2023) 'The United Nations, African Union, and protection of civilians in Africa: Analyzing inter-institutional approaches to protection', paper presented to the 2023 Meetings of the International Studies Association, Montreal (unpublished).

Johnson, A. (2023) 'Tough lessons for UN peacekeeping operations', *Survival* 65(5): 161–176.

Karlsrud, J. (2015) 'The UN at war: Examining the consequences of peace-enforcement mandates for the UN peacekeeping operations in the CAR, the DRC and Mali', *Third World Quarterly* 36(1): 40–54.

Karlsrud, J. (2023) '"Pragmatic Peacekeeping" in practice: Exit liberal peacekeeping, enter UN support missions?', *Journal of Intervention and Statebuilding* 17(3): 258–272.

Krastev, I. (2025) 'Why liberals struggle to cope with epochal change', *The Atlantic* (online), 3 January; Available at: https://www.theatlantic.com/international/archive/2025/01/liberals-wrong-about-1989/681165/

Labuda, P. (2020) 'With or against the State? Reconciling the protection of civilians and host-state support in UN peacekeeping', International Peace Institute report, May; Available at: https://www.ipinst.org/2020/05/reconciling-poc-and-host-state-support-in-un-peacekeeping

Lehne, S. (2023) 'After Russia's war against Ukraine: What kind of world order?', Carnegie Endowment for International Peace, 28 February; Available at: https://carnegieendowment.org/research/2023/02/after-russias-war-against-ukraine-what-kind-of-world-order?lang=en&center=europe

Mahoney, L. (2006) 'Proactive presence: Field strategies for civilian protection', Centre for Humanitarian Dialogue; Available at: https://hdcentre.org/insights/proactive-presence-field-strategies-for-civilian-protection/

Paris, Roland (2024) 'The future of UN peace operations: Pragmatism, pluralism or statism?', *International Affairs* 100(5): 2153–2172.

Townsend, M. (2024) 'Children executed and women raped in front of their families as M23 militia unleashes fresh terror on DRC', *The Guardian*, 21 December; Available at: https://www.theguardian.com/global-development/2024/dec/21/children-executed-and-women-raped-in-front-of-their-families-as-m23-militia-unleashes-fresh-terror-on-drc

United Nations (UN) (2023) 'Our common agenda policy brief 9: A new agenda for peace', July; Available at: https://www.un.org/sites/un2.un.org/files/our-common-agenda-policy-brief-new-agenda-for-peace-en.pdf

United Nations Department of Peacekeeping Operations (UN DPO) (2024) '25 years of protecting civilians through UN peacekeeping: Taking stock and looking forward', Reflection Paper 24 October; Available at: https://cepsi-cipss.ca/announcements-annonces/25-years-of-protecting-civilians-through-un-peacekeeping-taking-stock-and-looking-forward

Index

Action for Peacekeeping (A4P) initiative 27–28, 38; *see also* initiatives
ADF *see* Allied Democratic Forces (ADF)
African conflicts, 21st-century 49
African missions 11, 36, 114, 139; *see also* missions
Africa's World War 91; *see also* wars
Agreement for Peace and Reconciliation in the Central African Republic (APPR) 15, 114
agreements: Agreement for Peace and Reconciliation in the Central African Republic 15, 114; Global and Inclusive Agreement (2002) 91, 92; Revitalised Agreement on the Resolution of the Conflict in South Sudan 2, 78, 81, 82; Status of Forces Agreements 72, 75
Allied Democratic Forces (ADF) 105
'alternative paradigm of peacemaking' 127
AMISOM mission in Somalia 133; *see also* missions
Andersen, L. R. 26
Annan, K. 10
anti-MINUSCA sentiment 113
anti-MONUSCO protests in Goma 89
anti-rebel campaign 117
A4P initiative *see* Action for Peacekeeping (A4P) initiative
Applebaum, A. 127
APPR *see* Agreement for Peace and Reconciliation in the Central African Republic (APPR)
armed actors: kaleidoscopic range of 53; non-state armed actors 54, 96
armed conflicts 11, 13, 24, 34, 48, 49, 52, 57, 61, 69, 89, 92, 112, 126, 133, 138
armed peacekeepers 51, 62, 63, 85, 99, 134
Aru Act of Commitment 104
Autesserre, S. 39
authoritarian peacebuilding, distinct model of 125, 126, 140
Autocracy Inc. 127
Avungura clan of the Azande tribe 82

back-to-basics movement 11
Baines, E. 18, 55, 56
Bangui's Renaissance Palace 123
Beadle, A. 64
Belgian colonialism 91
Bellamy, A. 40
Bell, C. 58
Berdal, M. 33, 70, 85, 106, 135
big four peace operations, on African continent 10
Bonwick, A. 18, 55
Bosnian Serb Army 10, 15, 53
bottom-up peacebuilding 80, 120
Bourgeois, H. 29
Boutellis, A. 11, 57
Bozizé, F. 114
Brahimi Report (2000) 10, 25, 29, 38, 47
BRICS group of developing countries 138
budget-driven 'projection' strategy 99
Burgis, T. 116
Buskie, A. 97

Cammaert, P. 32
CANs *see* community alert networks (CANs)
capital-based elites 57
Captier, C. 13
CAR *see* Central African Republic (CAR)
Carpenter, C. 15
Carstensen, N. 55
Carver, F. 95
Center for Civilians in Conflict (CIVIC) 99
Central African Republic (CAR) 4, 35, 56, 58, 75, 112; authoritarian turn 124;

authorities with 'strategic and technical advice' 125; bilateral military presence in 115; bottom-up peacebuilding in 120; broader security environment in 120; case of 121, 138; cause of peace in 117; civic space in 116; conflict context in 121; current context as 122, 127; economic situation 121; latest peace process 114; MINUSCA's performance in 113, 117; national police 124; path to peace and stability 127; peace/protection context in 114–117; political elites 123; political environment in 118; security forces 124; shifting conflict landscape 114; SRSG in 120; support for bottom-up peacebuilding in 120; sustainable peace emerging in 127; Wagner mercenaries in 131, 135, 140
'Chapter VI syndrome' 27, 132
Chenoweth, E. 49
Chinese peacekeepers 33; *see also* UN peacekeepers
Christian just war tradition 12
'Christmas tree mandate,' in MONUSCO 11, 33–34, 102
CIVIC *see* Center for Civilians in Conflict (CIVIC)
Civil Affairs Division 46, 79
civilian-centric 'detectors' 96
'civilians': insecurity 5; nature of 15–19; protection strategies 4, 105, 106; security 102; self-protection strategies 18
CLAs *see* community liaison assistants (CLAs)
Club Med 1
CNDP rebellion 92, 93
Coalition of Patriots for Change (CPC) 114, 115
Cockayne, J. 24
CODECO 104
coercive counter-violence 3; *see also* violence
coercive protection strategies 3, 5, 19, 25, 60, 64, 86, 91, 99, 121, 134, 137; *see also* strategies
Coleman, K. 140
colonial-era mission civilisatrice 51
communities: CANs 48, 90, 95–98; community-centric PoC 96; community-engaged PoC 96, 97; community-engaged protection 56; community-engaged system 108; community-level detectors 48; community liaison assistants 48, 90, 95, 96; core community engagement tools 96; Dinka and Nuer 79; East African 103; effective community engagement 57; humanitarian 14, 62, 76; international 133; Southern African Development Community 103
community engagement tools 96
'competent practice' vis-à-vis PoC 137
Comprehensive Planning and Performance Assessment System (CPAS) 105
conflict resolution processes 6, 11, 34, 36, 37, 52, 54, 61, 69, 70, 91, 136
Coning, C. de 136, 139
contemporary conflicts 12; African 68; dynamics 100; management 113
contemporary Congolese politics 92
contemporary crisis of peacekeeping 103–104
contexts: conflict context in CAR 121; DRC 99, 100, 123; enforcement context 15; humanitarian context protection 13; organised social contexts 7; peace/protection context in CAR 114–117; PoC 9, 43, 64; 'the protected,' in conflict contexts 55; UN peacekeeping 3–5, 9, 13
conventional SSR formulas 125
Corbett, J. 55
Cormack, Z. 69
Cornut, J. 7
countermobilisation process 92
CPAS *see* Comprehensive Planning and Performance Assessment System (CPAS)
CPC *see* Coalition of Patriots for Change (CPC)
Cruz Report 27, 31, 41, 49, 53, 62, 135

Day, A. 75, 84, 93, 101
Declaration of Shared Commitments 27
'de-confliction' efforts 123
de facto governing authorities 93
'default militarism' 48
'default pacifism' 61
'defensive PoC' strategies 29, 108; *see also* strategies
Democratic Republic of the Congo (DRC) 2, 4, 10, 11, 19, 75, 103, 107; Armed Forces 35, 58, 96; authorities 58; CAR and 125; case of 35, 58, 101, 137; civilians 89–91, 98, 101, 104–105; conflict 91–94; conflict-related sexual violence in 131; context 99, 100, 123;

domestic security forces 97; government and citizens 89; international actors in 93; militarised peacekeeping in 33; MONUSCO operation in 33; particular conflict complex 90; peacekeepers 89, 90, 94, 132; protecting without peacebuilding in 99–104; protection practices in 91; security forces 89, 94; soldiers 101; South Sudan and 57
Department of Peacekeeping Operations (DPKO) 15
Department of Peace Operations (DPO) 27–28; *Policy on the Protection of Civilians in United Nations Peacekeeping* 28
Department of Political and Peacebuilding Affairs (DPPA) 28
detectors: civilian-centric detectors 96; community-level detectors 48
deterrent effect, of armed peacekeepers 134
'developmental violence' 24, 122, 124; *see also* violence
Dinka and Nuer communities 79; *see also* communities
disarmament, demobilization and reintegration (DDR) 54, 57, 59
domestic security forces 60, 97–100; *see also* security forces
Dong, J. N. 78
Dorn, W. 23, 105
DPKO *see* Department of Peacekeeping Operations (DPKO)
DPO *see* Department of Peace Operations (DPO)
DPPA *see* Department of Political and Peacebuilding Affairs (DPPA)
DRC *see* Democratic Republic of the Congo (DRC)
Dunton, C. 138, 139
Duursma, A. 100

early warning and rapid response (EWRR) 95, 96, 98, 99
East African Community 103; *see also* communities
Ebo, A. 125
Effectiveness of Peace Operations Network (EPON) 51, 52, 72, 105, 117, 118
effectors: military-centric effectors 96; mission-level effectors 48
Einsiedel, S. von 51–52
elite-level peacemaking 84; *see also* UN peacekeeping
elite-level power dynamics 81
enforcement context 15; *see also* contexts
ethno-military system of governance 84
European Union Training Mission (EUTM) 120, 126; *see also* missions
EWRR *see* early warning and rapid response (EWRR)

FACA 112, 115, 116, 118–120, 124
FARDC 58, 98, 101, 103
FDLR 102
Ferguson, K. 97
FIB *see* Force Intervention Brigade (FIB)
First Congo War 100; *see also* wars
Foley, C. 46
Foot, R. 59
force-first stabilisation agenda 102
Force Intervention Brigade (FIB) 2, 24, 90, 102–103
Fourth Geneva Convention (1949) 17
FPRC 115
French-led Operation Sangaris 122
Fund for Peace's Fragile States Index 83
Futuyo, A. 82

General Assembly's Special Committee on Peacekeeping Operations 37
geopolitical factors 6
Giffen, A. 28
Gilder, A. 40, 42
Gilmore, J. 48
Global and Inclusive Agreement (2002) 91, 92; *see also* agreements
Global Protection Cluster 13
global security governance 138
'good enough' protection 3
Gorur, A. 55
governance: ethno-military system of 84; global security 138; Tier III (importance of addressing security governance) 101
Gowan, R. 6, 11, 37, 100
Grotius, H. 17
Guterres, A. 27

Hagemann, A. 71, 72
Haiti 23, 24, 38, 61, 62, 131, 133
Haysom, N. 84
heterodox state-building strategy 126; *see also* strategies
High-Level Independent Panel on Peace Operations (HIPPO) Report 4, 10, 26, 27, 34, 38, 47, 61, 95, 96, 135

hit-and-run tactics of rebel groups 116; *see also* rebel group
hourglass model of intervention 49
Howard, L. 131
Howes, D. E. 49
HRDDP *see* Human Rights Due Diligence Policy (HRDDP)
HRL *see* human rights law (HRL)
Hultman, L. 51
Human Development Report (1998) 12
humanitarian/humanitarianism 7; actors 113; agencies 12, 14; community 14, 62, 76; Humanitarian Policy Group 14; organisations 13; protection 13; space 53
Human Rights Due Diligence Policy (HRDDP) 35, 98, 101, 102
human rights law (HRL) 29; *see also* laws
Human Rights Watch 33, 116
Hunt, C. 40
Hutu-dominated rebel group 102; *see also* rebel group
'hybrid' protection strategies 64; *see also* strategies
hyper-robust peacekeeping 23; *see also* UN peacekeeping

IASC *see* Inter-Agency Standing Committee (IASC)
ICISS *see* International Commission on Intervention and State Sovereignty (ICISS)
ICRC Commentary 17
IDPs *see* internally displaced persons (IDPs)
IGAD *see* Intergovernmental Authority on Development (IGAD)
IHL *see* international humanitarian law (IHL)
Ingasso, V. 122, 124
initiatives: A4P initiative 27–28, 38; local initiatives for peace 120; local peacebuilding 78, 79; UN-facilitated social cohesion 120
institutionalised kleptocracy 93
Inter-Agency Standing Committee (IASC) 13
Intergovernmental Authority on Development (IGAD) 36
internally displaced persons (IDPs) 68, 71, 73, 74, 80, 106
international: actors, in conflict-affected contexts 52; agency 4, 55; community 133; diplomats and peacekeepers 94; NGOs 50; peace and security architecture 31; politics 7; relations scholarship and policy 3; relations theory, 'practice turn' in 7; security forum 15
International Commission on Intervention and State Sovereignty (ICISS) 14
International Committee of the Red Cross 14, 53
International Criminal Court 4, 13
International Crisis Group 69, 84, 117
international humanitarian law (IHL) 4, 12–14, 16, 53, 94, 120; *see also* laws
interventions: Force Intervention Brigade 2, 24, 90, 102–103; hourglass model of 49; International Commission on Intervention and State Sovereignty 14; NATO 10, 14; Swiss army knife of international conflict 60
'irregularisation,' of fighting forces and modalities 12
Israeli Defence Force 12

Jackson, R. 3, 48, 61
Janjaweed militias in Darfur 53
Job, B. 140
Johnson, A. 136
Johnson, H. 75
Juba 43, 70, 75, 76, 81
Juba-based elites 78, 80

Kabila, J. 93, 102, 103
Kaldor, M. 11
Karlsrud, J. 36, 103
Kenyan-led Multinational Security Support (MSS) mission 133; *see also* missions
Kigali Principles on the Protection of Civilians (2015) 26–27, 140
Kiir, S. 75, 84
Kilroy, W. 71, 72, 76
Kinsella, H. 17
Kinshasa-based elites 92
Kiwanja massacre (2008) 32, 33, 95
Kjeksrud, S. 47, 62–64, 106
Koopman, S. 50, 51
Krastev, I. 138
Krause, J. 81

Labuda, P. 29, 122, 135
laws: human rights law 29; international humanitarian law 4, 12–14, 16, 53, 94, 120; rule of law 34, 58, 59, 73, 92, 94, 103, 117, 125, 136, 139; settled international law 16

'learning by doing' process 6, 83
'leave no trace' principle 119; *see also* principles
Lederach, J. P. 79
Le Monde 124
Levine, D. 18
Levine-Spound, D. 95
Lewis, D. 113
liberal internationalism 4, 103
liberal peacebuilding 125; paradigm 34; standard model of 136
Lie, J. H. S. 6
Lipsky, M. 71
local initiatives for peace 120; *see also* initiatives
local-level: alert networks 56; conflict in Sudan 78; peacebuilding 78; peace dialogues 79
local peacebuilding initiatives 78, 79; *see also* initiatives
local protection committees (LPCs) 90, 95–97, 99
'local turn,' in field of peacebuilding 54
Lombard, L. 116
LPCs *see* local protection committees (LPCs)
Luanda Joint Roadmap of September 2021 115

Machar, R. 74, 82
Mahoney, L. 50, 53
Mali mission 6, 62; *see also* missions
Mechoulan, D. 54, 120, 121
Mednick, S. 2
Metcalfe-Hough, V. 13
'middle-out' peacebuilding 79
mid-level FACA leadership 126
military-centric 'effectors' 96
Millar, M. 73, 75, 85
Miller, W. 50–51
'minimum legal obligations' 42
M23 movement 35–36, 89, 137
MINUSCA *see* United Nations Multidimensional Integrated Stabilization Mission in the Central African Republic (MINUSCA)
MINUSMA *see* United Nations Multidimensional Integrated Stabilization Mission in Mali (MINUSMA)
MINUSTAH *see* United Nations Stabilization Mission in Haiti (MINUSTAH)
missions 2, 95; African missions 11, 36, 114, 139; AMISOM mission in Somalia 133; European Union Training Mission 120, 126; Kenyan-led MSS mission 133; large African missions 114; Mali 6, 62; MINUSTAH 62; mission-centric PoC 113; and mission-hosting states 72; mission-level effectors 48; MSS 61; peace support 126; with PoC 83; special political missions 47, 135, 139; UNAMSIL mission, in Sierra Leone 10; UNPROFOR mission in Bosnia 9; 'whole of mission integrated approach' 80, 83
mobilisation/countermobilisation process 92
modus vivendi 73, 75, 82
monopoly model: of security provision 57; of SSR 125
MONUC *see* United Nations Organization Mission in the Democratic Republic of the Congo (MONUC)
MONUSCO *see* United Nations Organization Stabilization Mission in the Democratic Republic of the Congo (MONUSCO)
Morillon, P. 10
Multinational Security Support (MSS) mission 61; *see also* missions

Nando, J. 82
national and international NGOs 78
national-level political dynamics 81
NATO intervention in Libya 14; *see also* interventions
Netanyahu, B. 4
'New Agenda for Peace' 47, 123, 140
Nkunda, L. 92
non-coercive protection 46–48, 60–64; mechanisms 40; presence/accompaniment 50–60; strategies 3, 4, 19, 46, 63, 134; unarmed protection toolkit 48–50
non-governmental organizations (NGOs) 13, 50, 77, 78 non-state armed actors 54, 96
non-state security actors 35, 122
non-UN security partnerships 107
norm and practice, interplay of 6–9
Novosseloff, A. 11

Ondieki, J. 74
organised social contexts 7; *see also* contexts

Paddon, E. P. 18, 55, 56, 90, 102, 105
Paris, R. 125, 140
'partnership peacekeeping' 11, 108, 139, 140; *see also* UN peacekeeping
Peace Brigades International and Nonviolent Peaceforce 50
peacebuilding processes: authoritarian 125, 126, 140; bottom-up 80, 120; liberal *see* liberal peacebuilding; local-level 78; 'local turn' in 18, 54; 'middle-out' 79; post-conflict 63; short-term protection *vs*. long-term 34–38; subnational 77–83
peaceforce 23, 41, 50, 61
peace/protection context, in CAR 114–117
Peace, Security and Cooperation Framework (PSCF) 36, 103
'peace through victory' narratives 125
Pendle, N. 69
'people-centred' peacekeeping 18, 95, 140
'people-centred' protection strategies 56; *see also* strategies
Permanent Representative of India 41
PoC *see* protection of civilians (PoC)
Pospisal, J. 58, 78
post-cold war international order 138
post-conflict peacebuilding 63; *see also* peacebuilding processes
post facto retributive justice 13
post-independence civil war 67; *see also* wars
post-MONUSCO period 90, 96
practice theory 7
'practice turn,' in international relations theory 7
'pragmatism' 139
presence-centric protection strategies 99; *see also* strategies
Prighozin, Y. 119
'primacy of politics' 34
principal flaw in the 'developmental violence' 124; *see also* violences
principles: bedrock UN peacekeeping principles 26; of civilian immunity 15; Kigali Principles on the Protection of Civilians (2015) 26–27, 140; 'leave no trace' principle 119; of liberal peacebuilding 103; PoC 5; of robust peacekeeping 90; traditional peacekeeping principle of 'consent of the parties' 12, 61, 107; of UCP 63; UN peacekeeping 27
protecting civilians and state authority, in CAR 112–114, 117–121, 126–128; peace/protection context 114–117; PoC *vs*. 121–126
protection: debates *see* robust protection debates; meanings of 12–14; practices 2, 3, 6, 9, 18, 47, 56, 69, 83, 91, 113, 127, 132, 140; through subnational peacebuilding 77–83
'protection-from' model of PoC 18
protection of civilians (PoC) 1–10, 13–19, 23–43, 46–48, 50–52, 54–57, 60–64, 67–86, 90, 91, 94–102, 104–108, 112, 113, 118–123, 126, 131–141; case of 8; commitments 28; context of 9, 43, 64; debate 3; discourse 17; doctrine and practice 48; evolution of 9–12, 138; *vs*. extension of state authority 121–126; goals of 121; guidelines 133; language 5; limitations of 133; mandates 42; missions with 83; in peacekeeping contexts 7, 8, 26–27, 61, 68; in peace operation contexts 7; PoC-focused engagement 55; PoC-mandated mission 85; policies 9, 31, 40, 46; 'practical meanings' of 69; practices of 6, 7, 19, 25, 94–99; principles 5; project 3; 'protection-from' model of 18; research 55; responsibilities 38; robust forms of 46; R2P and 15; sites 1, 2, 68, 70–78; in South Sudan 71; spectrum 34; strategies 54, 55, 120; and WPS agendas 16
protection-oriented engagement 54
protection-peacebuilding continuum 113
PSCF *see* Peace, Security and Cooperation Framework (PSCF)
Putin, V. 4

quick reaction force (QRF) 73, 74

radical Islamist 11
Ramsbotham, O. 31, 49
Rapid Support Forces in Sudan 53
R-ARCSS *see* Revitalised Agreement on the Resolution of the Conflict in South Sudan (R-ARCSS)
RCD 92
realist international relations theory 63
rebel group: hit-and-run tactics of 116; Hutu-dominated rebel group 102
'recruiting sergeants' for armed groups 116
responsibility to protect (R2P) 9, 16, 46, 57, 101, 103; doctrine 4, 25; notion of

13; and PoC 15; UN peacekeeping and 14
'restoration' model, of security provision 57
Revitalised Agreement on the Resolution of the Conflict in South Sudan (R-ARCSS) 2, 78, 81, 82
ripple effect 81, 105
Roberts, A. 12
'robustification,' of peacekeeping 26
robust PoC: activities 119; in peacekeeping contexts 140
robust protection 23–25, 48, 104–107; discord and doctrine 25–30; in the DRC 90; mandates *vs*. resources 38–40; risk tolerance and cost-benefit analysis 31–34; short-term protection *vs*. long-term peacebuilding 34–38
robust/robustness 95; military engagement 85; NATO interventions 10; peacekeeping 5, 14, 23, 33, 37, 40, 41, 61, 90, 106, 134; PoC *see* robust PoC; protection *see* robust protection; security assistance 58; UN defence 40
R2P *see* responsibility to protect (R2P)
Rugwabiza, V. 120
rule of law 34, 58, 59, 73, 92, 94, 103, 117, 125, 136, 139; *see also* laws
rule of the gun 93
Russia: and Central African forces 122; invasion of Ukraine 126; legislation 116; Wagner Group 35, 58, 112, 115, 118, 119
Russo, J. 33, 34
Rwandan genocide (1994) 91
Ryan, K. 71, 72, 76

'safe areas' across Bosnia 10
Santos Cruz, C. dos 23
Schindler, O. 68
SEA *see* sexual exploitation and abuse (SEA)
Secretary-General's 2023 'New Agenda for Peace' 47, 107, 123, 140
Security Council Resolution 1325, 25th anniversary of 15
security forces: CAR 124; DRC domestic security forces 60, 97–100; militarily government 73; South Sudan 73; support to non-UN security forces 35
security sector reform (SSR) 57–58, 101, 137; in conflict-affected contexts 60; monopoly model of 125; programming 59
Sedra, M. 59
Seko, M. S. 91, 93
The Sentry (investigative group) 117, 119
settled international law 16; *see also* laws
sexual exploitation and abuse (SEA) 4, 11, 112, 119, 120
Shearer, D. 2, 70, 85
Sherman, J. 27
short-term protection *vs*. long-term peacebuilding 34–38
Slim, H. 12, 16
Smith, R. 64
SOFA *see* Status of Forces Agreements (SOFA)
Sorensen, G. 24
Southern African Development Community 103
South Sudan: authorities 1; civilian protection in 83; civil war 81, 137; complex conflict context 85; complex system of patronage 81; conflict actors in 70; context 68; displacement crisis 67; and DRC 57; first Transitional Government of National Unity 74; fragility 83; irreversible peace in 85; National Police Service 73; peace implementation process 79, 85; PoC sites 50, 71, 131, 134; population 81; resource-poor periphery 79; security forces 2, 73; sustainable peace in 69
special political missions (SPMs) 47, 135, 139; *see also* missions
Special Representatives of the UN Secretary General (SRSGs) 6, 9, 23, 32, 120
Spink, L. 80
SPLA *see* Sudan People's Liberation Army (SPLA)
SPLM *see* Sudan People's Liberation Movement (SPLM)
SPLM-IO 82
SPMs *see* special political missions (SPMs)
Srebrenica massacre (1995), 30th anniversary of 15, 17
SRSGs *see* Special Representatives of the UN Secretary General (SRSGs)
SSR *see* security sector reform (SSR)
'standard' international treatment for civil wars 8, 100
Staples, K. 48
state-centric fabric of the UN system 57
state-centrism 124

Status of Forces Agreements (SOFA) 72, 75; *see also* agreements
Stearns, J. 92, 94, 106
Stedman, S. J. 37, 100
Stephan, M. J. 49
strategies: 'civilian' protection 4, 105, 106; 'civilian' self-protection 18; coercive protection 3, 5, 19, 25, 60, 64, 86, 91, 99, 121, 134, 137; 'defensive PoC' 29, 108; heterodox state-building strategy 126; 'hybrid' protection 64; non-coercive protection 3, 4, 19, 46, 63, 134; 'people-centred' protection 56; PoC 54, 55, 120; presence-centric protection 99
subnational peacebuilding 77–83; *see also* peacebuilding processes
Sudanese Armed Forces 53
Sudan People's Liberation Army (SPLA) 73, 74
Sudan People's Liberation Movement (SPLM) 78
Sustainable Development Goals (2015) 138
sustainable PoC strategy 55, 57; *see also* strategies
Syrian conflict 11

Tambura crisis 82
Tanguay, E. 38
Tardy, T. 14, 31, 38
Thiong, D. A. 82
tiered action matrix (Tier I): conflict parties and conflict-affected communities 28; dialogue and engagement 48; protection activities 77; of UN peacekeeping's PoC policy 52
tiered action matrix (Tier II): priority of immediate physical protection 101; provision of physical protection 28, 48; responsibilities 135
tiered action matrix (Tier III): of DPO's protection framework 136; priority of addressing the security governance 101; protective environment 28
Touadéra, F.-A. 115
traditional peacekeeping principle, of 'consent of the parties' 12, 61, 107
'train-and-equip' type of security sector reform 59
Transitional Government of National Unity 84
troop- and financial-contributing countries (TCCs) 26, 32
Tshisekedi, F. 89
Tull, D. 35

UCP *see* unarmed civilian peacekeeping (UCP)
Ukraine conflict 120
UN *see* United Nations (UN)
UNAMA *see* United Nations Assistance Mission in Afghanistan (UNAMA)
UNAMID *see* United Nations-African Union Mission in Darfur (UNAMID)
UNAMSIL mission, in Sierra Leone 10
unarmed civilian peacekeeping (UCP) 50
unarmed civilian protection 53
unarmed protection toolkit 48–50
uniformed peacekeepers 33
UNITAMS *see* United Nations Integrated Transition Assistance Mission in Sudan (UNITAMS)
United Nations (UN): accompaniment 101; actions in Srebrenica 10; agencies 13, 36, 77; 'Agenda for Protection'(2024) 108; bases and facilities 29, 32; bedrock peacekeeping principles 26; broader peace and security architecture 27; Capstone Doctrine 37; Commission on Human Rights in South Sudan 2; in conflict-affected contexts 103; context of peace operations 24; core *raison d'être* in theatre 91; Development Programme 12; diplomatic influence 37; doctrine 37; 'does not wage war' 26; dual nature 31; Emergency Peace Service 31; facilities 72; figures 96; flag 10; forces 32, 38; hitherto-unsystematic approach to protection 95; human rights 58; Independent Special Investigation 74; and international actors, in DRC 93; interventions in conflict-affected contexts 46; intervention tool of choice 135; large African missions 114; long-standing presence in the DRC 108; member states 3, 6; MINUSTAH mission 62; and mission-hosting states 72; missions 16, 25, 39, 57, 67, 94, 97, 100, 135; myriad protection failures in DRC 90; and NGOs 77; obligations to civilian populations 9; peace and security agenda 31, 47; peace committees 61, 120; peacekeepers *see* UN peacekeepers; peacekeeping *see* UN peacekeeping; peace operations 2, 3, 5, 25, 30, 31, 35, 38, 47, 49, 51, 53, 55, 60, 62–64, 67, 68, 99, 106, 112, 126, 133–135, 138, 139; PoC policy 122; police 1;

policies 32, 101; political and diplomatic heft 6; protection *see* UN protection; *raison d'être* in conflict environments 26; representatives 77; Secretariat 3, 9, 24, 73; Secretary General 19; Security Council *see* UN Security Council; sensitivity on protection issues 105; signature contribution to non-violent management 49; soldiers 1; structural and operational limitations 91; support to non-UN security forces 35; system 3, 9–12, 29–30, 32, 43, 123, 125; traditional comfort zone of mediation 52; UN-commissioned independent strategic review of MONUSCO 94; UN-facilitated social cohesion initiatives 120; UN-level narratives 59; vehicles and office containers 72; vision for peace 112; well-established third-party role 36
United Nations-African Union Mission in Darfur (UNAMID) 52
United Nations Assistance Mission in Afghanistan (UNAMA) 47
United Nations Integrated Transition Assistance Mission in Sudan (UNITAMS) 47
United Nations Mission in South Sudan (UNMISS) 4, 5, 10, 54; accomplishments 76; bases 74; Civil Affairs Division 46; conservative posture adopted by 73; detention practices 72; establishment of 81; evolution of 85; experience 2, 68; influence on internal political processes 70; leadership 85; mandate extension of 5, 73; military response 74; with multi-pronged approach 80; officials 68; opinion survey commissioned by 83; peacekeeping 1; preliminary incident report 42; protecting civilians and building peace 83; protection mandate/story 69; reconnaissance drones 75; reputation of 85; Security Council 58; soldiers 73; and South Sudanese government 2; troops 80; UN Secretary General on 77
United Nations Multidimensional Integrated Stabilization Mission in Mali (MINUSMA) 10, 11, 35, 52, 62, 76
United Nations Multidimensional Integrated Stabilization Mission in the Central African Republic (MINUSCA) 4, 10, 39, 54, 113, 139; comprehensive independent assessment of 117; extension of state authority 122; military components 118; and national SSR strategy 126; operational capacity 119; PoC strategy 120, 121; protection efforts 121; protection-peacebuilding continuum 113; robust military capacities and extensive civilian resources 113–114; supporting peace and protecting civilians 118
United Nations Organization Mission in the Democratic Republic of the Congo (MONUC) 90, 93–95, 102, 104, 105
United Nations Organization Stabilization Mission in the Democratic Republic of the Congo (MONUSCO) 2, 4, 10, 11, 33–35, 37, 39, 48, 57, 58, 64, 69, 90, 107–108, 121–123, 131, 135, 137; evaluating robust protection 104–107; exit strategy 89; Force Intervention Brigade 123; military contingents 134; PoC practice 94–99; protecting without peacebuilding, in DRC 99–104
United Nations Stabilization Mission in Haiti (MINUSTAH): robust approach 23; war on armed gangs 24
UNMISS *see* United Nations Mission in South Sudan (UNMISS)
UNMISS-Office of the High Commissioner on Human Rights report 82
UN peacekeepers 3–4, 7, 9, 13, 19, 24, 25, 28, 30, 40, 57, 59, 60, 100, 112, 122, 135; actions of 5; armed peacekeepers 51, 62, 63, 85, 99, 134; Chinese peacekeepers 33; day-to-day work of 34; DRC 89, 90, 94, 132; front-line peacekeepers 40; 'key priority task' for 94; *sine qua non* of 14–15
UN peacekeeping 6, 7, 10–11, 14, 16, 18, 35, 51, 53, 60, 108, 123, 126, 133, 135, 138; budget 139; chronic mandate-resource gap 39; contexts 3–5, 9, 13; doctrine 37; ecosystem 9; foundational pillars 8; instruments 41; militarisation of 26; principles 27
UNPROFOR mission in Bosnia 9
UN Security Council 46, 47, 73, 94, 107, 108, 119, 126; debate in 2014 39, 41; discord 100; mandate 47; reform 84; Resolutions 5, 27, 41, 57, 125
UPC 115
US Defence Intelligence Agency 11

US-led war on terror 31
US Treasury Department 82

Verweijen, J. 92
violence: coercive counter-violence 3; conflict-related sexual violence in DRC 131; 'developmental violence' 24, 122, 124; principal flaw in 'developmental violence' 124; *victims* of (primarily sexual) violence 18

Wagner Group, in CAR 58, 113, 115, 118, 119, 123, 124
Walikale incident (2010) 95
Walter, B. 11
wars: Africa's World War 91; Christian just war tradition 12; First Congo War 100; post-cold war international order 138; post-independence civil war 67; South Sudan civil war 81, 137; 'standard' international treatment for civil wars 8, 100; US-led war on terror 31; war-induced population movements 80
Weberian definitions of the state 57
'white knight' protection narratives 3, 17
'white soldiers,' in vicinity of Bouar 117
'whole of mission integrated approach' 80, 83; *see also* missions
Williams, P. 55, 99
Women, Peace and Security agenda 15, 16
Woodhouse, T. 31
Wunlit Peace and Reconciliation Conference (1999) 79

Zahar, M.-J. 54, 120, 121

FSC
www.fsc.org
MIX
Papier | Fördert
gute Waldnutzung
FSC® C083411

Kolibri 360 GmbH
Ferdinand-Jühlke-Straße 7
99095 Erfurt, Deutschland
produktsicherheit@kolibri360.de